# The Railroads of U.S. Sugar: History Through the Miles

### Barton Jennings

The Railroads of U.S. Sugar: History Through the Miles
Copyright © 2022 by Barton Jennings

All rights reserved. This book may not be duplicated or transmitted in any way, or stored in an information retrieval system, without the express written consent of the publisher, except in the form of brief excerpts or quotations for the purpose of review. Making copies of this book, or any portion, for any purpose other than your own, is a violation of United States copyright laws.

Publisher's Cataloging-in-Publication Data
Jennings, Barton

The Railroads of U.S. Sugar: History Through the Miles
410p.; 21cm.
ISBN: 978-1-7327888-7-9

Library of Congress Control Number: 2022934307

Front cover photo by Barton Jennings
Back cover photo by Sarah Jennings
All interior photos by Barton Jennings unless otherwise noted.

Please send comments or corrections to sarah@techscribes.com

TechScribes, Inc.
PO Box 2199
Alma, AR 72921
www.techscribes.com

Printed in the United States of America

# Dedication

To the "sweet" people of U.S. Sugar and its railroads...

## Other books by Barton Jennings

### History Through the Miles

*Arkansas & Missouri Railroad: History Through the Miles*
*Alaska Railroad: History Through the Miles*
*Iowa Interstate Railroad: History Through the Miles*
*Everett Railroad: History Through the Miles*
*Tennessee Central Railway: History Through the Miles*
*Whitewater Valley Railroad: History Through the Miles*
*Oregon's Joseph Branch: History Through the Miles*
*Missouri & North Arkansas Railroad: History Through the Miles*
*Hennepin Canal Parkway: History Through the Miles*
*Idaho's Payette River Railroads: History Through the Miles*
*Delta Heritage Trail (Missouri Pacific's Wynne Subdivision): History Through the Miles*
*The Choctaw Route: History Through the Miles*

### Textbook

*The Basics of Transportation: Policies, Practices and Pricing – An Applied Perspective*

## Contents

Acknowledgments .................................................................. 7
Creating a Route Guide for the Railroads of U.S. Sugar .... 9
Safety Around the Operations of U.S. Sugar ..................... 13
United States Sugar Corporation .......................................... 15
Sugarcane ................................................................................. 29
Charles Stewart Mott and U.S. Sugar ................................... 37
Welcome to Clewiston ............................................................ 41
Maps .......................................................................................... 51
The Railroads of the U.S. Sugar Corporation .................... 61
The Locomotives of U.S. Sugar ............................................. 87
The Basics of Seeing the Railroads of U.S. Sugar ............. 115
<u>Route Guide for the Railroads of the South Central Florida Express (SCFE)</u> ....................................................................... 121
SCFE Sebring Subdivision ................................................... 123
SCFE Sebring Subdivision Route Guide ........................... 135
SCFE Sebring and Fort Pierce Subdivisions .................... 217
SCFE Sebring and Fort Pierce Route Guide .................... 225
SCFE Okeelanta Lead ........................................................... 317
SCFE Okeelanta Lead Route Guide ................................... 319
<u>Route Guide for the U.S. Sugar Corporation Railroad (USSC)</u> .................................................................................... 333
USSC Clewiston Mainline Division Route Guide ........... 341
USSC Bolles Lead Route Guide .......................................... 385
USSC Prewitt Lead Route Guide ........................................ 389
USSC Martinez Lead Route Guide ..................................... 391
USSC Flaghole Mainline Division Route Guide ............. 393
USSC Citrus Lead Route Guide .......................................... 401
Changes at U.S. Sugar ........................................................... 405
About the Author .................................................................. 409

*The Railroads of U.S. Sugar: History Through the Miles*

## Acknowledgments

The railroads of the U.S. Sugar Corporation have long been an attraction for rail enthusiasts. This comes from a combination of interesting equipment and operations, a peak of activity during the winter tourism season, and the unique nature of the railroads. Nowhere else in the United States can similar railroading be found. Nowhere else in the United States does an agricultural company use railroads to move their crops from the field to the processing facilities. This has led to several articles being published in railroad trade and hobby magazines, adding further interest in the railroads of U.S. Sugar.

These route descriptions were first written for the author's use while exploring the various rail lines on the south side of Lake Okeechobee. Interest in the railroad came about from years of conducting regulatory training for the railroad industry, which many of the maintenance-of-way employees of both the South Central Florida Express and the U.S. Sugar private lines have attended. This has led to conversations with many of the managers of the railroads and the sugar company, providing behind-the-scenes information about the daily rail operations. Additionally, information from internal railroad records, government and public records, railroad workers, and conversations with old and new friends have added to this guide.

A big thanks must go out to the employees and management of the United States Sugar Corporation and its railroads who assisted with the writing and reviewing of this book, and who have always opened doors for my visits. Thanks also go out to those at FMW Solutions who shared information about their work with U.S. Sugar steam locomotive #148. My wife also deserves thanks for her patience with the writing of this book, even though sitting on a canal levee on a warm winter day, listening to the wind rustle the nearby sugarcane and watching the many birds and alligators, is one of her most favorite Florida activities.

# Creating a Route Guide for the Railroads of U.S. Sugar

For years, almost 300 miles of track have quietly been operating in what some describe as a no-man's land south of Lake Okeechobee, and between the busy Florida cities of Palm Beach to the east and Fort Myers to the west. This book is designed to provide a guide to the U.S. Sugar Corporation operations with those miles of railroad. The tracks were initially built by several early organizations, dating back to the 1920s, but many are modern and have been built over the past decade. Few of the original structures still exist, but an amazing amount of the railroad's history can still be found. No book can be a complete history of the United States Sugar Corporation and its railroads, but this book is designed to provide a great deal of information for those who like to ask "where are we and what once happened here?" To do this, the guide includes information about the company, current as well as former station locations, historic towns, and major stream crossings along the various rail lines. While this book provides great detail about the sugar company and railroad, more information is available elsewhere. For additional information, check out the Facebook pages of U.S. Sugar and their Engine No. 148.

When writing a book like this, there is always the question about how much detail to provide. One reader told me that in a previous book, if someone tied a mule to a she-shed along the line, I reported it. While that is not quite the goal, there is an effort to explain the history of each community along the line, what shippers were located there, and what facilities the railroad had and still has. Obviously, all of these changed over the one hundred years of the railroad's history, so the challenge is how much information to report. In writing this book, I attempted to include information about the first few years of the railroad's existence, the peak of a community's activity, and what is there today.

Two major railroads (Atlantic Coast Line and the Florida East Coast) built the mainline of the South Central Florida Express and historically used north-south as their line's description, although in some areas it curves greatly from these directions. A complication is that with the lines connected, the north and south descriptions of the original railroads conflict with each other. Nevertheless, the route description will use these north-south railroad directions, but will often include the real directions when describing certain features along the various routes.

Other features of the various lines will also be described in railroad terms. For example, the tracks were often described by their car-lengths. These car-lengths varied over the years, but were generally around 45 feet per car. Therefore, a track listed as being 20 cars in length could hold about 900 feet of train.

An important help in following the railroad and knowing what was at various locations are the many maps available on the internet. County road maps, topographic (topo) maps, and many other maps from various eras can be found. Comparing these older maps with newer maps can often make finding the railroad easier. One map site that I found very helpful while following the railroad is TopoZone (www.topozone.com), whose maps clearly show the railroad. The U.S. Geological Survey has also been very active in making their Historical Topographic Map Collection available through TopoView. Both are recommended.

The fast changes at the company have also impacted this book. Several times it was thought that the book was ready for publishing, but another major change would take place. This could be a new diesel or steam locomotive, a new rail

*Creating a Route Guide*

line, the acquisition of a turntable, or the reconstruction of part of the railroad. Change will certainly continue, so please forgive anything that gets missed as the book goes to the publisher.

A final issue deals with all of the names and abbreviations that were used to represent the railroad over its one-hundred-plus years. To simplify the issue, the name of the railroad will generally be accompanied by the year. However, information about the South Central Florida Express and the U.S. Sugar cane line operations will generally use the modern names, even when another railroad originally built the line. Additionally, an ampersand (&) will be used in railroad company names to make them easier to identify. Especially with companies like the Moore Haven & Clewiston Railroad, mixing the railroad name and the cities that it served can get very confusing. Therefore, even if the firm did not use or always use an ampersand, one will be used in this book. Although the reporting marks of South Central Florida Express are actually SCXF, the more commonly seen SCFE will often be used. Likewise, USSC will be used for the United States Sugar Corporation instead of its USCX/USSX reporting marks. Please forgive these simplifications.

It is hoped that you enjoy your adventure with the U.S. Sugar Corporation and its railroads, and that this book is of assistance in some way – *The Railroads of U.S. Sugar: History Through the Miles*.

## Sources of Information

A large number of resources were used in writing this book. Some date from today while others go all the way back to the original construction of the various rail lines. The author has been fortunate enough to know some of the employees who worked for the railroad over the past few decades. Many of the employees and managers of U.S. Sugar and its railroads have also contributed their time by answering questions and providing documents about the rail operations. Additionally, I have had the pleasure to get to know several people who have researched the railroad. These all deserve a thanks for their help.

A number of documents were also used in writing this book. It is amazing what can be found on the internet these days. Copies of the *Official Guide*, the annual reports of various state railroad and corporation commissions, Interstate Commerce Commission reports, and other such government and industry documents are great resources. Related sources such as local histories published by the Goodspeed Publishing Company, Sanborn Insurance Maps, the State Library and Archives of Florida, and others were a great aid. Newspapers and trade magazines also reported heavily on the construction and operations of the various railroads that became the South Central Florida Express. Finally, the author has a house with several rooms full of books, timetables and other documents about this and other railroads – important research items from a time long before today's internet. Many of these sources will be cited in the book, especially when there are conflicts between various sources.

## Safety Around the Operations of U.S. Sugar

While the railroads of the United States Sugar Corporation have long been an attraction, and the employees and managers have generally been friendly to the visitors, it is still an industrial operation. Because of this, the employees are focused on their jobs and not on entertaining visitors.

The first rule of spending time around the railroads of U.S. Sugar is safety. This is farming country, and no matter what road you are on, farm equipment is probably there also. Much of this equipment is huge, much larger than your family car, so be careful. Also, don't trespass into the cane fields or down cane roads. These roads can be very busy with vehicles moving cane, or heading to the next field to cut. The fields are generally burned before the sugar cane is harvested. Fires can quickly consume a field, and the resulting smoke can make it difficult to see.

Flame and smoke can be one of the most dramatic parts of the sugarcane harvest, but it can also be one of the most dangerous. Please stay out of these areas and watch them from a safe distance.

The next issue is train speed. The tracks are well maintained (many of the track maintenance employees have been through courses that the author teaches on the subject) and trains often operate about 40 miles per hour. Few trains can actually be chased, with the trains to Sebring (U.S. Highway 27) and Fort Pierce (U.S. Highway 441 and Florida Highway 709) being the easiest to follow for a day's entertainment. Most photographers figure out where the action is and then choose a favorite location, knowing that trains will come by frequently.

The managers and employees of the United States Sugar Corporation and its railroads welcome visitors to the area, but not on their private property. This is not a theme park, it is a large farm and processing facility. Please treat it as such and watch the action, but don't get in the way and possibly ruin the opportunity for others. Should you have an emergency, Clewiston has all of the basic necessities such as the Hendry Regional Medical Center, a number of gas stations and auto dealerships that can make car repairs, several major discount stores, plus hotels and restaurants. Belle Glade, Lake Placid, Sebring, and Fort Pierce have similar facilities.

Enjoy your visit and return home safe and sound.

# United States Sugar Corporation

The U.S. Sugar Corporation has long been THE industry in the Clewiston area, supporting local jobs, charity groups, and the economy, while playing a major role in the sugar industry across the United States. However, U.S. Sugar was not the first sugar company at Clewiston, and it did not found the community. Its roots do date back to the founding of the city, though, and the beginning of the sugar industry on the south side of Lake Okeechobee. To understand the company's history, a review of the Southern Sugar Company is provided.

This sign on a crane in North Shop at Clewiston says it all: "U.S. Sugar – We Raise Cane."

## Southern Sugar Company

Clewiston was created by John J. O'Brien, his wife Marian Horwitz O'Brien, both of Philadelphia, and banker Alonzo Clewis of Tampa. The O'Briens had earlier developed Moore Haven, Florida, and then the Moore Haven & Clewiston Railroad. Their plans included developing the area for traditional farming, something that started as soon as the town opened and the railroad was completed. However, things changed in 1922 when the Clewiston Development Company was formed and the Clewiston Bank was established, under the control of the O'Briens, Alonzo Clewis, Alfred H. Wagg, D. F. Dunkle and Bert Winters. Wagg, Dunkle and Winters soon controlled the organization. A few years later, a group of investors from Kansas City and St. Louis who had already purchased 70,000 acres west and south of Clewiston bought into the Clewiston Development Company.

By 1924, Bror G. Dahlberg, president of the Celotex Corporation of Chicago, began to invest in the Clewiston Development Company. The original investors soon were gone and Dahlberg controlled much of the area. According to the report of a series of hearings by the House of Representatives' Select Committee Investigating National Defense Migration (May 7- 8, 1942), Dahlberg bought 47,000 acres in the Everglades in 1925. He continued to buy land in Palm Beach, Glades, Hendry, and Martin Counties until he owned or controlled some 160,000 acres.

Dahlberg had an amazing history. He was born in Sweden in 1881, the son of an artist, and he immigrated to the United States with his family as a child. After his father died, he supported the family by raising and lowering a freight elevator with a rope at age thirteen. He worked as a chief rate clerk for the Northern Pacific Railroad, and then went into business for himself collecting railroad claims. He later went to work for the M&O Paper Company where he served as vice president and general manager. In 1921, he founded the Celotex Company, which converted waste bagasse (processed cane with little commercial use) into a tough, fibrous building material (wallboard) with several immediate construction uses. His first plant was in Marerro, Louisiana, then the center of the United States sugar industry. However, there wasn't enough bagasse for his needs, so he began searching for other sources of the fiber.

Initially, research on sugar production was focused on Louisiana and Cuba. But by the 1920s, there were several diseases moving through the existing fields and Florida was being looked at as a potential new source of sugarcane production. The difference in soil required new cane varieties, cultivation practices, and fertilizers. Nevertheless, Dahlberg and a few other investors formed the Southern Sugar Company, chartered in December, 1925, with a capitalization of $11,000,000. With the creation of the firm, Dahlberg focused not only on bagasse, but the production of sugar. His firm drained fields, established a reliable source of electricity and fresh water for Clewiston, built housing and a hotel (with many of the buildings using celotex products), and started construction of the sugar mill, which opened on January 19, 1929.

Southern Sugar Company tried to be ready for the opening of the mill, and began planting sugarcane during the winter of 1927-28. Soon, 11,000 acres were planted and expansion continued. Starting in late 1928, the cane was processed at a mill at Canal Point, but two cane processing units opened at Clewiston a year later. Unlike many sugar mill operations at the time, the Southern Sugar Company was designed to use machinery for many of the tasks involved. The company purchased 144 crawler tractors, 408 cane wagons, 13 cultivators and 4 railroad locomotives. The 1929 auditor's report bragged that "Most of the work on the Southern Sugar Co. plantations is done by efficient machines. No horses or mules are used." In August 1930, fourteen new cane harvesting machines were also bought in response to labor shortages during the 1929-1930 harvest.

There are a number of equipment displays outside the Clewiston Museum. One of these is this old sugarcane wagon, which features crawler tracks to help move across the muck in the area.

Dahlberg's ventures seemed to be followed as much in his birthplace of Sweden as in the United States. The Swedish newspaper *Svenska Tribunen-Nyheter* had an article entitled "Bror Dahlberg Heads the Country's Largest Sugar Manufacturing Company" in their January 15, 1930, issue. It stated that "Last week it was reported that the Southern Sugar Company, which maintains headquarters in Chicago, had started production from last year's crop at the firm's large plants in Clewiston, Florida, which now consume 4,000 tons of raw material daily, as compared to 1,500 tons the previous season. The head of the company is our well-known countryman, Bror Dahlberg, who several years ago attracted much attention in industrial circles by his invention of Celotex, a building material, which is produced from corn stalks....He organized the Southern Sugar Company in order to extract the sugar from the cornstalks. The Company now owns large areas of land in Florida, and sugar manufacturing plants which already are the largest

## U.S. Sugar Corporation

of their kind in the country, and which will be further expanded. Dahlberg has just announced that during the next few years his company's sugar production will amount to 450,000 tons annually."

However, the odds seemed to have been against Dahlberg. There was flooding from the hurricanes of 1926 and 1928, the powerhouse was not always reliable, and labor was an issue. Additionally, using the machinery from the defunct Pennsylvania Sugar Company Miami mill and the former Florida Sugar Company Canal Point mill created problems as some modernization was required. The Miami mill that Dahlberg bought started as a sugar mill in San Benito, Texas, so this was the third mill that used the machinery. In 1919, the Pennsylvania Sugar Company started planting sugarcane along the Miami Canal in Pennsuco, not too far from what today is Hialeah. The Texas sugarcane mill had been bought and relocated to near Miami. Pennsylvania Sugar grew its sugarcane on farms west of Hialeah. However, there was inadequate water control and the shallow peat soil was deficient in minerals. The soil was also loose and shifting, making it unable to hold the roots of the cane. Because of this, there was not enough sugarcane to make the operation a paying concern and the mill only operated for two harvest seasons. It was sold in 1927 to the Southern Sugar Company and it took two years to move the parts and rebuild it with the Canal Point Mill.

The Canal Point Mill started when the founders of the Palm Beach Farms Company, a land development company that created the cities of Lake Worth and Greenacres, got into the sugar business. Owners Frederick Edward Bryant, Harold J. Bryant, William Greenwood, and G. T. Anderson formed the Florida Sugar and Food Products Company, based at Canal Point, Florida. The firm acquired about 800 acres of land and began building the first commercial sugar house in the Everglades by 1921, with the first production of sugar in 1923.

Florida Sugar had a number of issues. First, because the area at that time had neither railroad nor highway facilities, building materials and supplies had to be moved by flat-bottom barges operating on the Palm Beach Canal. The mill only had a capacity of 800 tons of cane per day, and transportation was again an issue to move out the sugar and move in the fuels to operate the mill. The firm was quickly reorganized as the Florida Sugar Company, producing brown sugar and black-strap molasses. As difficulties mounted, the Canal Point Mill was acquired by Southern Sugar in 1925.

The Southern Sugar Company sugar mill finally opened at Clewiston in 1929, just in time for the Great Depression. On June 30, 1930, the company entered receivership. In 1931, a number of the creditors and large stockholders asked the management firm of Bitting, Inc., to investigate the possibility of reorganizing the sugar company. On April 28, 1931, the United States Sugar Corporation was formed to take over Southern Sugar.

However, things were much more complex as a subsidiary, the United States Sugar Corporation of New York, was created to be the owner of the Clewiston Company. The Clewiston Company then owned the Clewiston Telephone Company, the Glades Power & Light Company, the Clewiston Hotels Company, and the Glades Water Company. In 1937, the United States Sugar Corporation of New York was dissolved, and the Clewiston Company became the Clewiston Realty & Development Company. U.S. Sugar received 3.4 percent of the 400,000 shares of common stock of Clewiston Realty, with the rest distributed as dividends among holders of corporation common stock. For a number of years, there was also the Glades Land Corporation. This company held the liens and encumbrances on lands inherited from the Southern Sugar Company. As clear title was obtained on the land, ownership was transferred to the United States Sugar Corporation.

For those wanting more details about the start of the Florida sugar industry, *The Florida Historical Quarterly* (Summer 1998) has an article entitled "The Beginnings of Big Sugar in Florida, 1920-1945" by John A. Heitmann.

## United States Sugar Corporation

As the 1930-31 sugar harvest was being completed, the Southern Sugar Company was sold and reorganized as the United States Sugar Corporation on April 28, 1931. The negotiations for the sale were reportedly complex as Dahlberg and his partners had lost a great deal of money with the venture and looked to preserve anything they could. Additionally, a number of different related businesses were also included in the deal. One of the operations that came with the mill were 21 miles of railroad and the equipment used to move the cane.

With the sale, Charles Stewart Mott, vice president of General Motors, took control of the Southern Sugar Company and restructured it as the United States Sugar Corporation. General Motors Corporation was one of the largest stockholders in the new company, and several of the directors of the new sugar corporation were General Motors stockholders and officers. Mott became chairman of the board, a position that he held until 1934.

At the time of its creation, the United States Sugar Corporation was the primary player in the Florida sugar industry, accounting for more than 95 percent of Florida's total sugar production. At the time of a 1942 House of Representatives hearing, about 90 percent of the cane processed was grown by U.S. Sugar and was known as administration cane. The rest of the sugarcane came from 28 independent growers, operating almost like a cooperative. The growers were paid a price determined by the sucrose content of the cane they supplied and the current market price for raw sugar. Additionally, there was a "cooperative participation supplement" which paid the independent growers a share in the profits of the sugar house. The growers also received help from U.S. Sugar on improved methods of cultivation and varieties of cane.

This aerial view of the Clewiston Sugar House dates from before World War II. The mill and the surrounding Clewiston area are today much more developed. *Aerial view of the United States Sugar Company mill.* 1930 (circa). State Archives of Florida, Florida Memory. https://www.floridamemory.com/items/show/141813.

To make the sugar mill profitable, further investments were necessary, much of which came from Mott himself. Mott also hired Clarence Bitting to change operations at the mill. Biting was an accountant who had previously managed a large Mississippi cotton plantation, and he supported efforts to make the production of sugar more efficient. To do so, he invested in new equipment, funded scientific research and engineering efforts, and partnered with local farmers and the mill's labor source to keep the mill going during the Depression. Production at the mill was increased to 7000 tons a day thanks to the engineering work of J. B. Scharnberg, who had designed many of the modern sugar mills in Cuba. Scharnberg was a German-born engineer and inventor who lived at Clewiston from 1931 until his death in 1940. The home in which he lived in was placed on the National Register of Historic Places in 1999. At the time of Scharnberg's death, the sugar house of U.S. Sugar was recognized as the largest and most efficient single tandem sugar mill in the world.

This Florida Memory photo shows the Clewiston Sugar House in 1946, plus many of the tracks in the adjacent mill rail yard. *U.S. Sugar Corp. mill in Clewiston, Florida.* 1946. State Archives of Florida, Florida Memory. https://www.floridamemory.com/items/show/255916.

The use of modern machinery started by Southern Sugar Company was continued by U. S. Sugar, as shown in this photo from early 1939. This Caterpillar crawler is pulling six wagons of freshly cut sugarcane, heading towards a railroad cane loading facility. Wolcott, Marion Post, photographer. *Harvesting sugarcane*, United States Sugar Corporation, Clewiston, Florida. 1939. [Feb.?] Photograph. Retrieved from the Library of Congress, https://www.loc.gov/item/2017754372/.

New varieties of sugarcane were introduced to south Florida to increase production and fight cane disease, drainage was improved, and transportation continued to be modernized by building more track and acquiring larger steam locomotives from the Florida East Coast and other railroads. Bitting also played a role in creating the Florida Cooperative Sugar Association in 1939. This association created rules and regulations about sugar quality and provided educational workshops for area farmers. It also represented many of the area's independent sugar farmers, giving them access to the sugarcane market. This diversified the sources of sugarcane for area producers, providing a reliable source of cane for mills at stable prices for the growers. By 1941, U.S. Sugar was profitable.

Despite the use of machinery, harvesting sugarcane was still heavily dependent upon manual labor during the first half of the twentieth century. This photo from 1939 shows workers bundling and loading cut sugarcane into a field wagon, soon to be pulled to a nearby railroad line. Wolcott, Marion Post, photographer. Untitled photo, possibly related to: *Cut sugarcane being carried to the trucks for USSC United States Sugar Corporation. Clewiston, Florida.* Clewiston, Florida, Hendry County, Jan. 1939. Photograph. Retrieved from the Library of Congress, https://www.loc.gov/item/2017800277/.

## Today's U.S. Sugar

As with most companies today, the United States Sugar Corporation has built itself around being as efficient as possible, minimizing waste and using every part of the sugarcane. The sugarcane is first crushed and ground to obtain the sugar out of the fluids in the stalk. On a daily basis, U.S. Sugar can grind up to 42,000 tons of sugarcane, all delivered by rail. Once processed, the remains of the sugarcane stalk, known as bagasse, is used to generate electricity. It is estimated that a ton of bagasse produces the same amount of energy as 50 gallons of fuel oil. The process and equipment used by U.S. Sugar to make electricity from bagasse earned the company the Energy Institute's prestigious Environment Award in 2006 for setting a new standard in emission control performance.

The annual production of the company is about 800,000 tons of refined sugar. It is packaged in almost all sizes of containers, from 2-pound bags for the grocery store to 200,000 pounds shipped by railcars for food processing companies. Approximately three-quarters of the sugar is used for commercial food production, such as making bread, canning fruits and vegetables, beverages, cereals and other food products. The rest is packaged in large industrial bags for local bakeries and companies, or smaller bags for retail sale to consumers.

Locomotive 204 is shown switching the sugar mill at Clewiston. The mill produces many tons of sugar each year, and the covered hoppers are being used to ship this sugar to market.

## U.S. Sugar Corporation

Sugarcane farming is the 2nd largest farming activity in Florida. U.S. Sugar routinely plants fresh sugarcane to reduce disease and increase the production of sugar. The firm employees nearly 12,500 workers and has a yearly economic impact of more than $3.2 billion on Florida. In addition, U.S. Sugar Corporation has diversified into other crops, including corn and citrus.

U.S. Sugar advertises its sweet corn as "Fresh from Florida" and produces half of Florida's sweet corn crop. The company boasts that it produces more than 175,000 ears of sweet corn a year. Other vegetables such as green beans, several varieties of lettuces, peanuts, squash and watermelons are grown on U.S. Sugar land leased to independent farmers. This allows a change in crops to enrich the soil naturally and to prevent sugarcane disease from spreading.

U.S. Sugar also owns **Southern Gardens Citrus**. The company produces up to 90 million gallons of Florida orange juice annually, making the company one of the largest suppliers of pure Florida orange juice.

Southern Gardens Citrus, which has a facility west of Clewiston, is a part of the U.S. Sugar Corporation.

Southern Gardens Citrus packages the juice for several customers, including national brands and private store labels. The oranges come from both the orange groves of Southern Gardens Citrus and from independent growers. It is not unusual to see trucks of oranges driving next to trains of sugarcane through the fields of U.S. Sugar.

U.S. Sugar is owned by four major groups. These include the Charles Stewart Mott Foundation, the Mott Children's Health Center, the employees, and the company's pension fund. The company supports the local community many ways, including the Laces of Love shoe drive, Habitat for Humanity of Lee and Hendry Counties, summer reading programs, student scholarships and internship programs, and the donation of agricultural equipment to school mechanics programs.

The #148 steam locomotive restoration program is a part of the effort to benefit the local community. Operating special passenger trips with the steam locomotive will attract tourists to the area from around the world, filling hotel rooms and local restaurants. Other area attractions will also benefit from the increase in tourism in Clewiston and the area along the railroads of U.S. Sugar.

# Sugarcane

A major question by many visitors to a sugarcane farm is what is sugarcane, also often spelled sugar cane. Technically, sugarcane (Saccharum officinarum) is a perennial grass of the family Poaceae. Each stalk is made up of more than 70 percent water, and the rest is sugar and fiber. The grass can grow to 10 to 20 feet high or even more, and is primarily used for the production of sugar, molasses, and rum. In some countries, sugarcane is grown for the production of ethyl alcohol (ethanol), cattle feed, and the source of materials for grass huts. Sugarcane was originally cultivated by natives of Southern Pacific islands, with most modern sugarcane dating back to Java. However, the grass quickly spread around the world, with Muslim and Arab traders introducing sugar from South Asia as far west as the Mediterranean by the 8th century. The crop was so popular that by the 10th century, reportedly no village in Mesopotamia (today's Iraq, Kuwait, eastern Syria, and southeastern Turkey) failed to grow sugarcane. The Spanish and Portuguese brought the product to the Western Hemisphere, starting large plantations across their colonies.

The sugarcane of today little resembles the sugarcane of even a century ago, although it can still interbreed with its wild relatives. Centuries of disease and insects have created the need for the new varieties that are used today. However, most sugarcane is still grown in subtropical and tropical areas. Within the United States, it is grown in Florida, Louisiana, Texas and Hawaii, with Florida and Louisiana producing more than 95 percent of the total. The United States is the tenth largest producer of sugarcane in the world, behind such countries as Brazil, India, China, and Thailand.

Brazil, the largest producer in the world, grows 30 times as much as the United States. Much of its production is for biofuels.

Sugarcane like this can be seen throughout the Clewiston area.

The Lake Okeechobee area is today the heart of the United States sugar industry. Four counties – Glades, Hendry, Martin and Palm Beach – are the key to this Florida activity. In 1960, approximately 55,000 acres were used to grow sugarcane. In 1961, the United States placed an embargo on sugar from Cuba after Fidel Castro seized the private holdings of the sugar companies across that country. Today, there are approximately 400,000 acres of sugarcane in these four counties. Three primary producers operate four sugar mills in the area. Florida Crystals Corporation operates the Okeelanta and Osceola Sugar Mills (at South Bay and Pahokee), Sugarcane Growers Cooperative of Florida operates the Glades Sugar House at Belle Glade, and U.S. Sugar Corporation operates the Clewiston Sugar Mill.

Sugarcane is propagated using two different methods. The first is known as ratooning. This is where the cane is cut when it is mature, but the bottom of the stalk and the roots are left to allow the plant to grow back. This is often done several times, but the plant does not grow back as well and produces less sugar. This ratoon or stubble crop is also more susceptible to disease and pests. Eventually, the plant must be plowed out and replaced.

The second way to grow sugarcane is by the planting of cuttings. Known as seed cane or cane sets, these are small sections of immature cane that are planted in rows, much like new trees. This planting process happens between September and January. This work, which can plant 4000 to 10,000 sets per acre, is done by mechanical planters which also fertilize during the planting. It generally takes several years before the new cane is ready to cut. This explains the pattern of fallow fields, freshly planted fields, and mature fields that you can see in the Clewiston area.

Cool temperatures (below 68 °F) and dry weather force the sugarcane to mature. Therefore, harvesting of the sugarcane takes place between late September and late April. The harvesting is done following the burning of a field. The burning removes leaves and other debris that would choke the soil, causing disease. The cane is then cut using mechanical sugarcane harvesters, supported by a number of tractors and wagons to haul off the cut cane. The equipment often works in teams, allowing a field to be cut quickly since the cane stops producing sugar when burned. With both the planting and harvesting happening in winter, U.S. Sugar is the busiest during this time.

This photo shows sugar cane being cut near Clewiston. Note the harvesting machine loading cane into trailers being hauled by a large tractor. Also note all of the egrets and other birds who have learned that lots of bugs, snakes and other meals will be stirred up by the machinery.

Sugarcane is one of the most environmentally friendly crops grown. The cutting and replacement of varieties allows the plant to require minimal fertilizer and pesticides. By removing the full plant during harvesting, the production of runoff is also reduced. According to a number of studies, the water leaving the sugarcane fields is actually cleaner than that entering the fields. In some places where any farming would impact the water flow into the Everglades, land has been set aside. For example, in October 2010, U.S. Sugar sold 26,800 acres of land to the South Florida Water Management District for the River of Grass initiative to help restore the Everglades. Currently, almost 100 percent of the Everglades meets water quality standards set by the federal Everglades Forever Act thanks in part to these efforts.

## The Growers of Sugarcane

The growers of Florida sugarcane have been many, but few have remained for long. The United States Department of Agriculture was looking at South Florida by 1892, working on how to covert the largely uninhabitable area into farmland. By 1910, sugarcane growers from Louisiana were considering the area for possible new fields. However, the soils were very different and new varieties of cane, and methods to grow it, were required. One of the earliest attempts was the Malabar Sugar Company, which by 1919 was advertising land on which to grow sugarcane.

During the early 1920s, the **Pennsylvania Sugar Company** (Pennsuco) built a mill from parts of a Texas operation, and grew sugarcane on 75,000 acres adjacent to the Miami Canal and west of Hialeah. Pennsuco was actually a Philadelphia-based sugar refiner, and the company planned to use machines in its harvesting. However, the firm used Louisiana cane which was unfit for the loose peat soils of the Everglades. By the late 1920s, the mill was closed and vegetables were being grown where sugarcane had previously been planted.

About the same time, the **Florida Sugar & Food Products Company**, located at Canal Point, began to produce sugar commercially in 1923. While the sugarcane grew well and the mill processed as much as 800 tons of cane per day, the lack of good transportation prevented the operation from being successful. By the late 1920s, the operation was taken over by the **Southern Sugar Company**, which later became the **United States Sugar Corporation**. The depression of the 1930s, and then World War II, was hard on the industry and no major new operations started up. However, in 1938 about one hundred farmers in the Belle Glade-Pahokee area pledged over 12,000 acres to the production of sugarcane to support building a sugar house as part of the creation of the **Florida Cooperative Sugar Association**. Still, after World War II, the United States Sugar Corporation accounted for more than 95 percent of Florida's total sugar production.

In 1946, the **Okeelanta Growers and Processors Cooperative** bought the machinery of the old Playa Grande Sugar Mill in Vieques, Puerto Rico. The equipment was moved to South Bay and was in operation for the 1947 season. However, the company was almost immediately in trouble and was foreclosed on in 1949. In 1952, the sugarcane plantation and mill were sold to **Okeelanta Sugar Refinery, Inc.** In 1964, the operation was sold to South Puerto Rico Sugar Company, which was acquired by Gulf+Western in 1967. The refinery and 90,000 acres of sugarcane was sold to the Okeelanta Corporation in 1984, whose owners also control the Osceola Farms sugar mill in Belle Glade. It now operates as a subsidiary of Florida Crystals Corporation.

The Cuban revolution and the nationalization of the Cuban sugar industry in the late 1950s can be given the credit, or the blame, for a boom in sugar production in South Florida. Loss of access to Cuban sugar and mills gave an opportunity to U.S. sugar producers. During the late 1950s, only 55,000 acres of sugarcane were being grown in Florida, and about 150,000 tons of raw sugar were being produced at U.S. Sugar, Okeelanta Sugar Mill, and Fellsmere Sugar Producers Association (created in 1937 and located in Central Florida near Vero Beach). Within three years of the change in government in Cuba there were 140,000 acres of sugarcane and the mills were producing approximately 400,000 tons of raw sugar. A large number of new sugarcane associations and mills were created, or at least planned.

At Belle Glade, the **Sugarcane Growers Cooperative of Florida** was established in 1960 as a cooperation of 45 members who owned approximately 70,000 acres of sugarcane. This led to the construction of the Glades Sugar House which began grinding in 1962. On February 27, 1961, **South Florida Sugar Company, Incorporated** was created by the owners of a large Puerto Rican mill and refinery. They moved their mill from Puerto Rico to Florida, but it was sold to the Talisman Sugar Corporation by the end of the 1964 harvest season.

Later in 1961, the **Florida Sugar Corporation** was established. This company was created by the Chairman of the Cuban American Sugar Corporation at Belle Glade, using a mill brought from Louisiana. The organization was acquired by the Talisman Sugar Company and shut down in 1971. The **Talisman Sugar Company** was established in 1962 by a number of Cuban expatriates with the backing of Henry Ford II. The South Bay firm soon struggled and only survived due to additional support from American politicians and businessmen. The firm acquired a few other sugar companies before being acquired by The St. Joe Company in 1972. In 1999, the operation was shut down and sold to the United States government as part of the Everglades Restoration Project.

In 1963, another farmers cooperative mill was established at Belle Glade by the **Atlantic Sugar Association**. This firm was backed by Allis-Chalmers and the Columbia Bank for Cooperatives, and in 2005 it became part of the Okeelanta Corporation. Beyond this, there have also been some independent farms that produce sugarcane and sell their harvests to the various mills, often under long-term contracts. While few of these firms still exist, all these combined efforts have led to there being 400,000 acres of sugarcane in South Florida, producing about 1.4 million metric tons of sugar annually.

*The Railroads of U.S. Sugar: History Through the Miles*

# Charles Stewart Mott and U.S. Sugar

An important part of the history of the U.S. Sugar Corporation is Charles Stewart Mott and his Foundation. The Mott Foundation dates back to 1926 when it was created for the benefit of Flint, Michigan, the base of many of the operations of General Motors. Initially, it was a means of providing small donations to Flint charities, but in 1935 it expanded when Charles Stewart Mott teamed with Flint educator Frank Manley to create community schools. This Depression-era effort provided more than just local education, it also provided needed community services such as medical care and meals. This project led to an international focus, providing "positive change in the areas of education, civil society and the environment."

## Charles Stewart Mott

Charles Stewart Mott was in a unique position to start and fund the Foundation. Born in Newark, New Jersey, Mott grew up working in the Mott Beverage Company, owned by his family, and earned a mechanical engineering degree at the Stevens Institute of Technology. He also studied in Europe during the 1890s, learning about Zymotechnology (the science of fermentation) in Copenhagen, Denmark, and the chemistry of fermentation in Munich, Germany.

He took over the management of the Weston-Mott Company of Utica, New York, after his father died. The company had manufactured wire wheels since 1884, and became an early supplier to the automobile manufacturing industry. In 1906, the Weston-Mott Company moved to Flint, Michigan, gaining contracts from many of the companies in the car assembly industry. In 1908, when the General Motors Corporation (GM) was created, Mott sold 49 percent of his company to GM in exchange for GM stock. Five years later, GM acquired the rest of Weston-Mott and Charles Stewart Mott began to serve on the GM board of directors, something he did for sixty years (1913-1973).

Mott's efforts soon made him one of the largest holders of GM stock, and his other investments made him very wealthy. He headed up several GM divisions and helped to start additional companies that were later bought by GM. During the 1910s, he served three terms as Flint's mayor, leading efforts to build a modern sewer system and pave the city's streets. During the Depression of the 1930s, he looked for other opportunities and became involved with the sugar industry of south Florida. This interest in sugar dated back to his years of studying fermentation in Europe, and he became involved with the Southern Sugar Corporation in Clewiston, Florida. At the time the company was in financial trouble, and to protect his investment, and those by GM and other business partners, Charles Stewart Mott bought out the sugar company on April 29, 1931, and created the United States Sugar Corporation.

Mott immediately began to invest in the company, modernizing both its manufacturing and farming techniques. New types of sugarcane were introduced, drainage improvements were made, and heavy equipment was added to the fields. By 1941, the sugar company was turning a profit and processing 1500 tons of sugarcane per day. U.S. Sugar continued to expand, especially with the leadership of his son, Charles Stewart Harding Mott, who diversified the family's holdings by acquiring cattle and citrus, and purchasing the winter vegetables company South Bay Growers.

Charles Stewart Mott died in 1973, leaving control of his holdings and his foundation in the hands of family members, who continued to expand their agricultural and charity efforts in multiple fields. In 1994, U.S. Sugar started a $100 million citrus facility using the name Southern Gardens Citrus. The facility was considered to be one of the most efficient and environmentally-sensitive juice facilities in the world, and was almost immediately expanded to meet the demands of the market. Also in the 1990s, U.S. Sugar closed their Bryant mill and consolidated all production at Clewiston. This allowed the company to invest in a state-of-the-art sugar refinery. Meanwhile, the Mott Foundation increased its endowment and the services that it funded.

## The Foundation

The Charles Stewart Mott Foundation has been managed by four members of the Mott family during its more than 90 years of existence. These include Charles Stewart Mott; Charles Stewart Harding Mott, his son; William S. White, C. S. Harding Mott's son-in-law; and Ridgway H. White, the great-grandson of Charles Stewart Mott. Started with a $320,000 endowment, the Foundation now has assets approaching $3 billion. Working in numerous places around the world, the Foundation has awarded grants totaling more than $3 billion to organizations in 62 countries. In fact, grants have been given to local organizations on every continent except Antarctica.

Today, the United States Sugar Corporation is still part of the Mott Foundation, as well as the Mott Children's Health Center of Flint, Michigan. The Mott Children's Health Center was started in 1939 by funding from the Mott Foundation, with the goal of serving "borderline medically indigent children of Genesee County" in Michigan. Its mission is still to improve health outcomes for at-risk children in Genesee County. The hospital has continued the public health outreach programs started by Mott and others in 1935.

Proceeds from the ownership of U.S. Sugar supports the efforts of the Mott Foundation as well as the Mott Children's Health Center. These efforts then benefit communities around the United States and the world. For example, in Florida, the Mott Foundation has funded afterschool programs coordinated by the Children's Services Council of Florida and provided numerous scholarships for both children and adults.

## Welcome to Clewiston

Clewiston is a community in the south Lake Okeechobee area created by land developers as part of the real estate boom of the 1910s and 1920s. Before the arrival of the Spanish in the 1600s, the area was never a permanent community, just a fishing camp used by various Native American tribes. Tribes and troops passed through the area during the three Seminole Wars (1817-18, 1835-42, 1855-58), but no permanent encampments or military forts were ever built here. However, Lake Okeechobee was a regular route of travel and the area was known for this reason. The Civil War affected areas around the Everglades, but again not the location of today's Clewiston.

The Clewiston area consists of what many described as muck. Muck is a mineral-rich dark soil, consisting of half-decomposed organic matter. The large amount of organic matter makes the soil hard to work, and it has very poor aeration and drainage. Muck is very hard to get dry once it is wet, and much of the South Florida area was often under several inches of water. However, when the land was drained and developed, much of the land was dried, and then it became difficult to again become wet. In addition to the organic mud, the soil includes sand that has been washed in from millions of years of storms. There are also deposits of limestone, and limestone has washed into some soils in the area. The result of this unique soil was that many normal farming techniques would not work, and the key for farmers was to find plants that were adapted to growing in the soil, much like the marsh plants that grew in the band between Lake Okeechobee to the north and the Everglades to the south.

The first full-time settlers were a number of Japanese farmers who arrived in 1915 and began to farm the area. They had been attracted by the promise of rich land and the ability to grow crops year-round. The Japanese produced beautiful vegetables in the fertile lakeside soil, but getting them to market was a challenge. With the availability of land and the suspected profits from developing the territory, developers were soon attracted to the location, some of the last undeveloped land in South Florida. This led John J. O'Brien and Marian Horwitz O'Brien of Philadelphia, and Alonzo Clewis of Tampa, to acquire land in the area. In 1920, they commissioned a town plan, originally known as Sand Point but later named Clewiston after Alonzo Clewis. With no access except for the lake, the plan also included a rail line to the nearby Atlantic Coast Line Railroad at Moore Haven, Florida.

John J. and his wife Marian Horwitz O'Brien had earlier developed the town of Moore Haven. They used the financial backing of Clewis, who was the president of the Exchange National Bank at Tampa, to not only plat Clewiston and build the railroad, but also to develop local industry. All of these efforts were helped when the first passenger train operated between Moore Haven and Clewiston on Labor Day in 1921. The Clewiston Development Company was soon created to attract industry, a bank was started, and a post office was established in Clewiston on February 24, 1922. Soon farms began to produce products and ship them out on the railroad, with as many as twenty cars a day being reported. Some of the early crops and products included celery, pineapples, bananas, poultry, oranges, watermelon, tomatoes, corn, peas, and grapes.

Later in 1922, the town took a big step forward when Bror G. Dahlberg, president of the Celotex Corporation of Chicago, began to invest in the Clewiston Development Company. The effort was to enter the sugar industry, something Dahlberg and a few associates did in 1924 when they created the Southern Sugar Company and bought up most of the existing sugarcane companies in the region. To expand the business, efforts were begun to drain nearby land so more crops could be grown. The company established a reliable source of electricity and fresh water for Clewiston. They also built the area's first hotel, the original Clewiston Inn (burned in 1937), out of celotex products from Dahlberg's original company. Clewiston was officially incorporated in 1925.

The first sugar mill – Southern Sugar – opened in Clewiston in 1929, using machinery from the defunct Pennsylvania Sugar Company Miami mill. However, the timing of the development was bad as the mill opened just before the Great Depression of the 1930s hit, and the Southern Sugar Company went into receivership in 1930. New money entered the company a year later when Charles Stewart Mott, former president of the Weston-Mott Company and a member of the board of directors of General Motors, took over the company to protect the investment of GM in the sugar industry. With the acquisition, the company became the United States Sugar Corporation. With the investment by Mott and General Motors, there was a need for housing for visiting executives. A new Clewiston Inn was opened in 1938, designed to host company executives and visiting dignitaries. Today, the inn is still open and is listed as a National Historic Site.

The sugar mill at Clewiston was initially used to produce raw sugar, sugar that was shipped elsewhere for refining. One of the common sights at the time were railroad cars of the raw sugar from the Clewiston mill, and later the Bryant mill, being shipped north to Savannah, Georgia, to be refined at the Dixie Crystals Refinery. Eventually a full mill was added to the Clewiston operation and sugar could be refined and packaged locally.

This is the entrance to the Clewiston Inn. Built in 1938, it is still open and is now listed as a National Historic Site.

Other industries such as citrus, vegetables and cattle also developed in the area. For a number of years, a few packing and processing facilities were here to handle the local vegetable and fruit crops. For example, Premier Melon Company of Schoolcraft, Michigan, handled much of their Florida watermelon crop at Clewiston. At first, these melons moved in special railroad boxcars, but later the railroad built a ramp at Clewiston so that they could be shipped in TOFC (trailer-on-flat-car) service. However, most of this business was actually located at nearby Belle Glade.

Even with these other businesses, much of Clewiston was still essentially a company town. For example, the Harlem neighborhood, originally known as Townsite and located just west of the sugar mill, "was a settlement established by the transient blacks that worked in the U.S. Sugar Corporation fields," according to the *WPA Florida* guidebook. The community was enlarged in the 1970s, and according to some sources, "has more Cuban ancestry people living in it than nearly any neighborhood in America." Many of these residents had fled the Cuban revolution of the late 1950s and got involved with the growing sugar industry, jobs that they had experience with. This population explains the Cuban restaurants that can be found around Clewiston.

This is one of several signs that welcome visitors to the Harlem community, located west of the Clewiston Sugar Mill.

However, the mill, the jobs, and the city almost went away in 2008 when Florida Governor Charlie Crist announced that the State of Florida had arranged to buy for $1.75 billion the company's 187,000 acres, including the refinery and citrus production facilities in Clewiston, as an effort to enlarge the Florida Everglades. The plan was controversial, often looked upon as an urban versus rural battle. There were also studies that predicted different results from the effort. Because of these issues, the plans have been greatly altered and the mill and sugarcane still flourish.

*The Railroads of U.S. Sugar: History Through the Miles*

Besides being the base of the USSC railroads, Clewiston is also the headquarters of the sugar company itself. Downtown across the street from the city park is a series of buildings that house the offices of many of the company's managers.

The City of Clewiston also still serves as a business and commercial center for a several county area. Known as "America's Sweetest Town" with a population of about 7500, Clewiston is also a center of sport fishing, particularly for largemouth bass, in Lake Okeechobee, the country's second-largest natural freshwater lake (behind Lake Michigan) contained entirely within the contiguous 48 states. Recreation, including hiking the lake's dike and many nearby trails through the Everglades, also attracts visitors to the town.

For those interested in the area's history, check out the Ah-Tah-Thi-Ki Museum and the Clewiston Museum. The Ah-Tah-Thi-Ki Museum, named for a Seminole term that means "a place to learn, a place to remember" is located on the nearby Big Cypress Seminole Indian Reservation. The Clewiston Museum is located in downtown Clewiston, near Civic Park.

Signs like this welcome visitors to Clewiston, "America's Sweetest Town."

Much of the machinery on display outside the Clewiston Museum looks more like art than something used to process sugarcane.

## The Railroad at Clewiston

For many years, Clewiston was an important center for the Atlantic Coast Line's operations in the area. Clewiston was identified as a register station for trains, and the station also housed bulletin books and a standard clock for train crews to review. The Atlantic Coast Line had an interesting station at Clewiston. It featured a covered patio on all sides of the two-story building, with a passenger station and freight house on the ground floor and agent housing on the second floor. By the 1990s, the station was a boarded-up complex. The west end of the complex still showed some of the heritage of the building, including the porch columns and roof line. However, the structure was torn down by 1996.

This photo shows the classic Clewiston train station, operated by the Atlantic Coast Line Railroad. It was torn down by 1996. *Atlantic Coast Line Railroad Depot - Clewiston*. Everglades (Fla.). State Archives of Florida, Florida Memory. https://www.floridamemory.com/items/show/1841.

The offices and locomotive shops of the South Central Florida Express were historically south of downtown Clewiston, where the railroad station once stood. Aztec Avenue is located just north of the mainline through town, while the shops and offices are to the south at the South W. C. Owen Avenue grade crossing. Known as the North Shops, they historically featured two through tracks and conducted most of the maintenance on the locomotive fleet. Several buildings in the complex also house the track and bridge maintenance forces of the railroad. A siding to the south of the mainline is often used to build the mainline trains. The area can be very busy and is clearly marked as private, but photo locations are available from Aztec Avenue to the north, and Basilan Crescent to the south.

With the restoration of steam locomotive #148, there are plans to convert the Clewiston shop, often known as the "North Shop," into the steam and passenger car shop. With this, all diesel work would be moved to the "South Shop" at the Clewiston Mill Yard. This complex is much less visible and has no public access. However, it has all of the facilities needed to maintain the U.S. Sugar Company (USSC) locomotive fleet.

This sign marks the North Shop, located just south of downtown Clewiston. This is where the steam locomotive program is currently based.

Just west of North Shop is the SCFE office where mainline train crews are based.

Signs like this can be found around the shops area, generally outside the new fencing that has recently been installed around the North Shops area.

# Maps

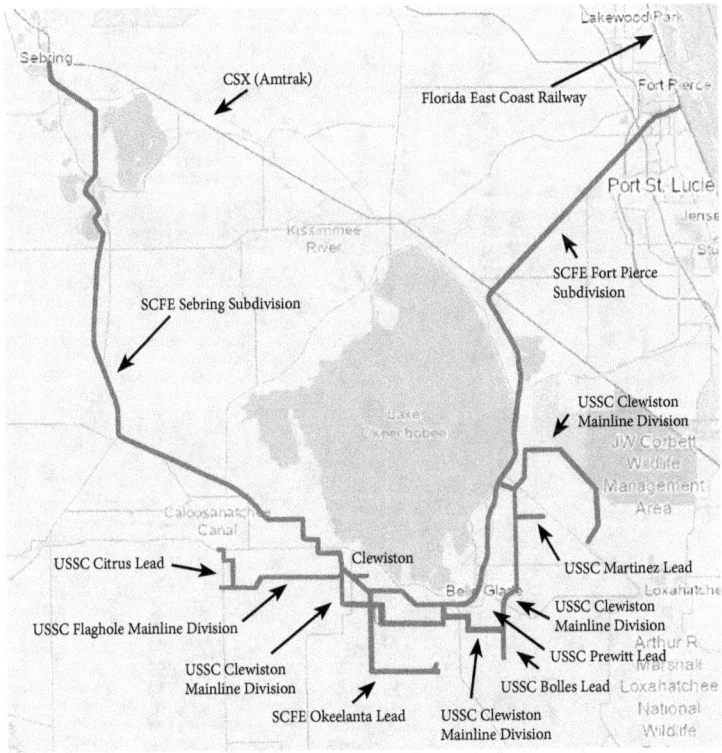

All maps in this chapter are based on USGS' US Topo series of topographical maps, with enhancements by Kaitlyn Vogt and Sarah Jennings.

*The Railroads of U.S. Sugar: History Through the Miles*

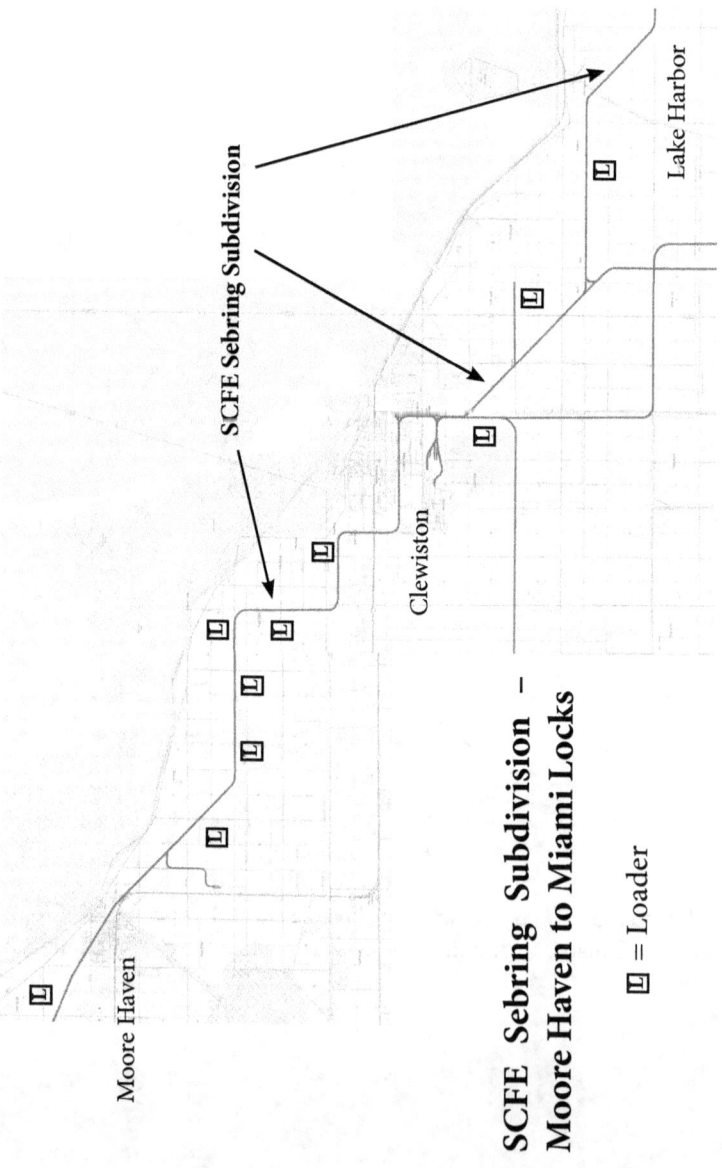

# Maps

# SCFE Sebring and Fort Pierce Subdivisions – Clewiston to Port Mayaca

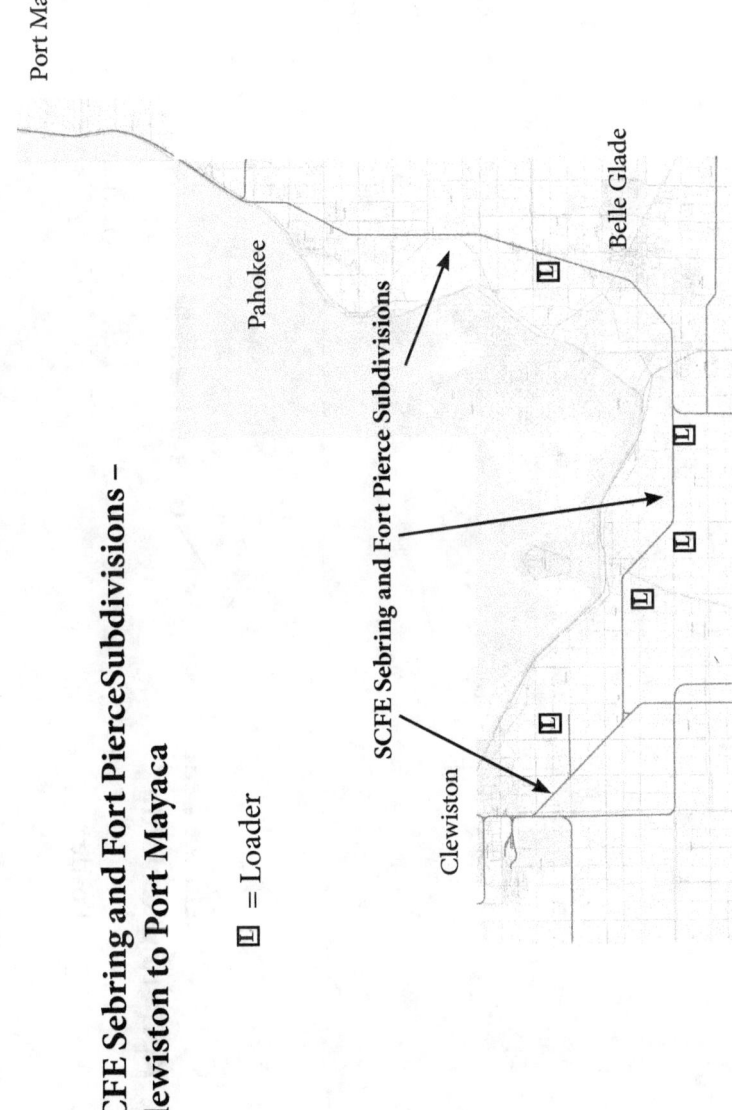

*The Railroads of U.S. Sugar: History Through the Miles*

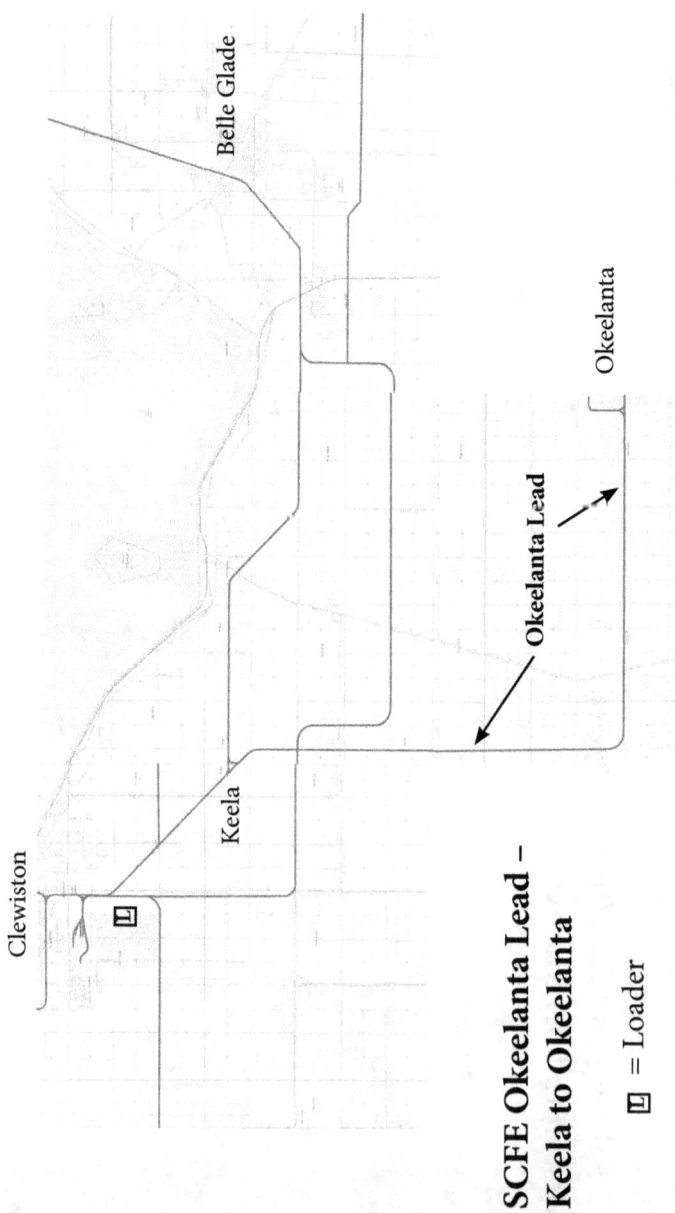

**SCFE Okeelanta Lead – Keela to Okeelanta**

L = Loader

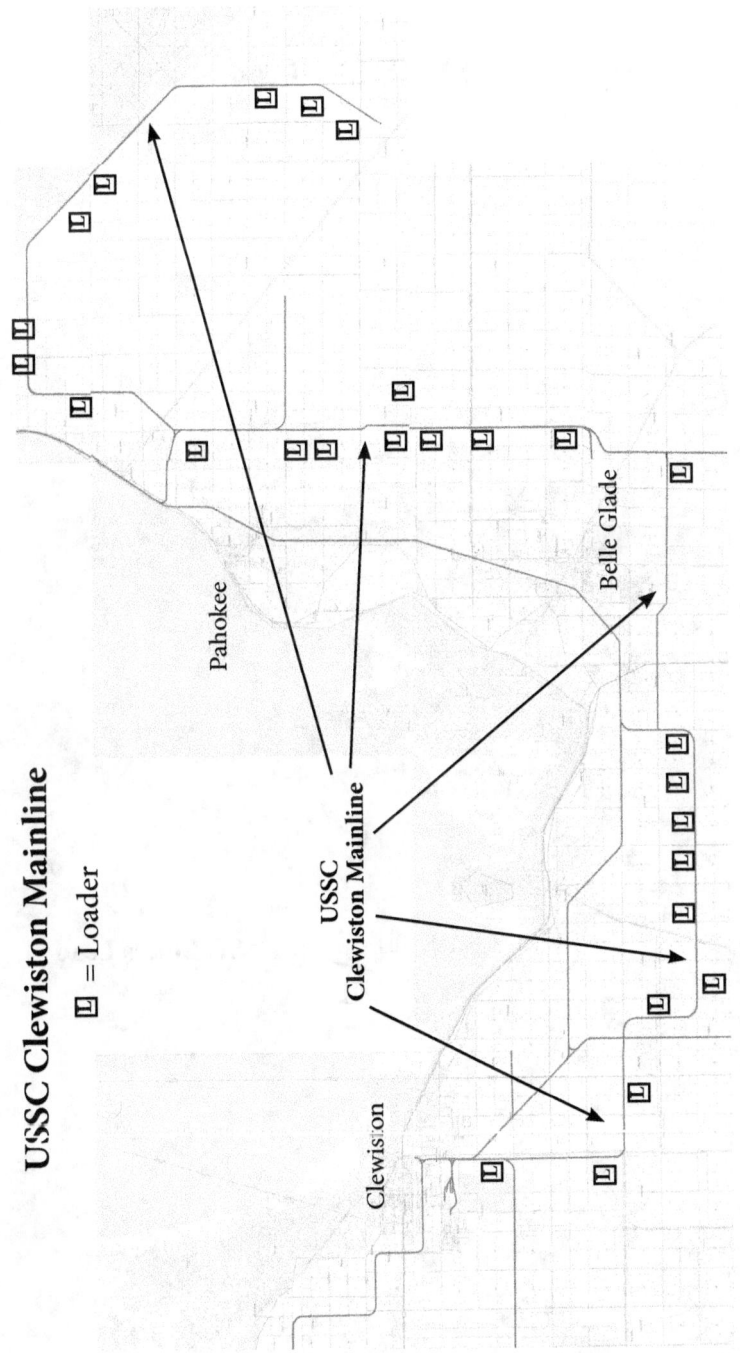

## USSC Bolles Lead

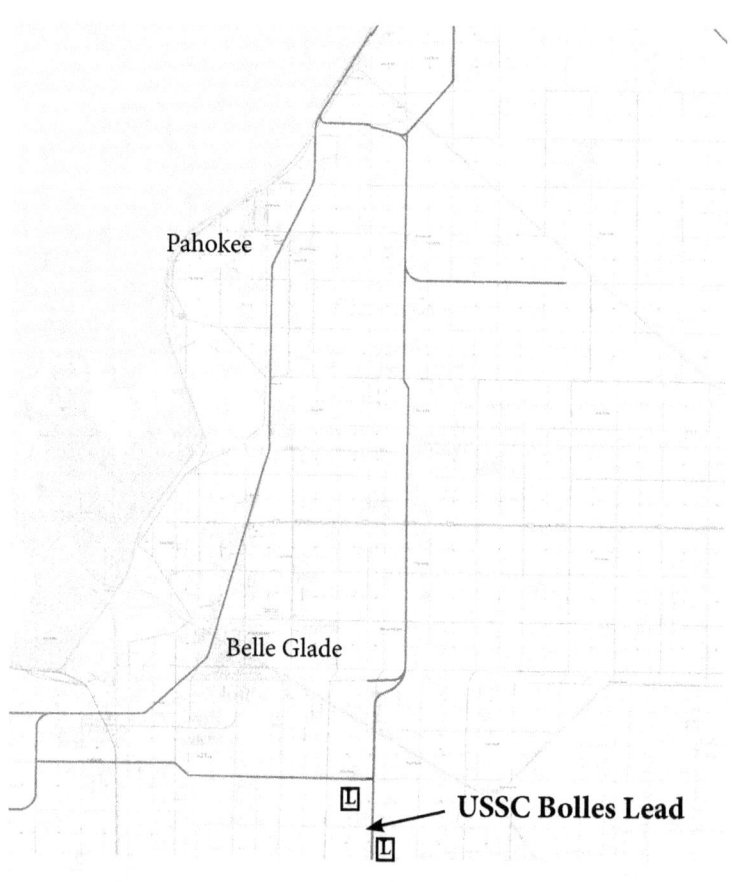

🅛 = Loader

## USSC Prewitt Lead

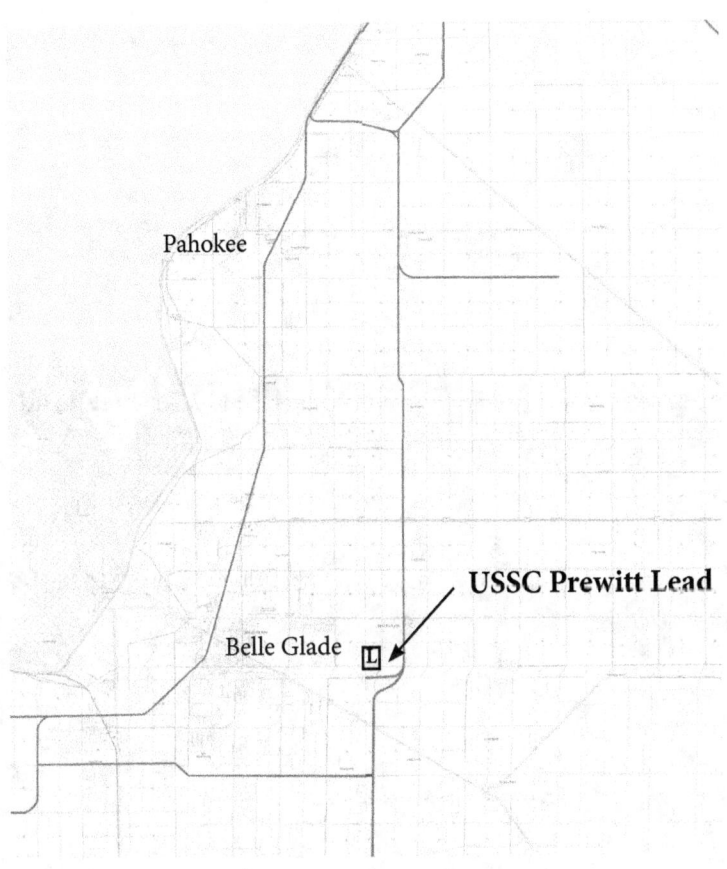

☐ = Loader

## USSC Martinez Lead

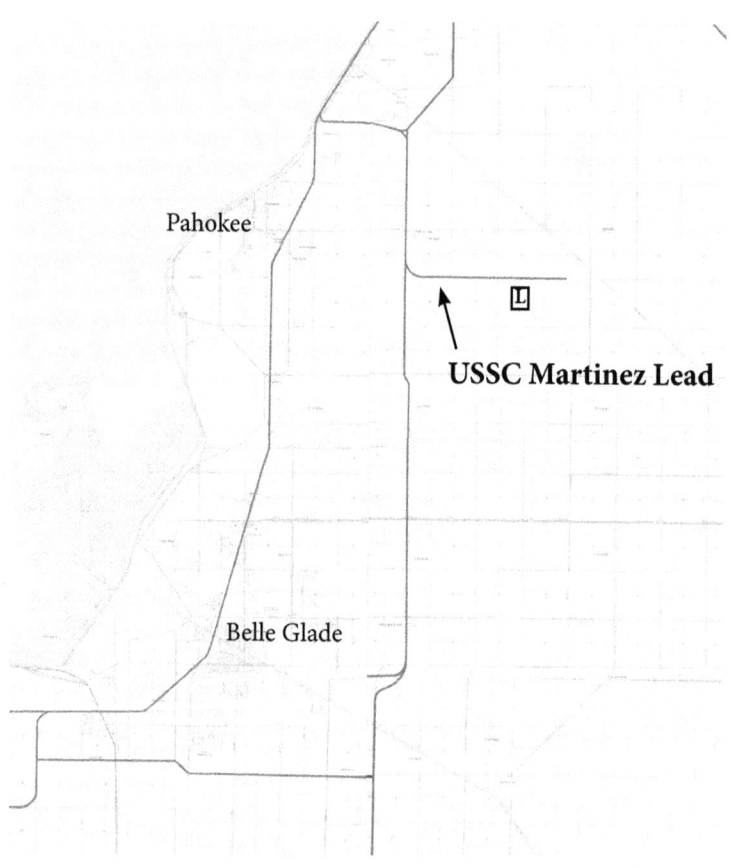

🅛 = Loader

## USSC Flaghole Mainline Division

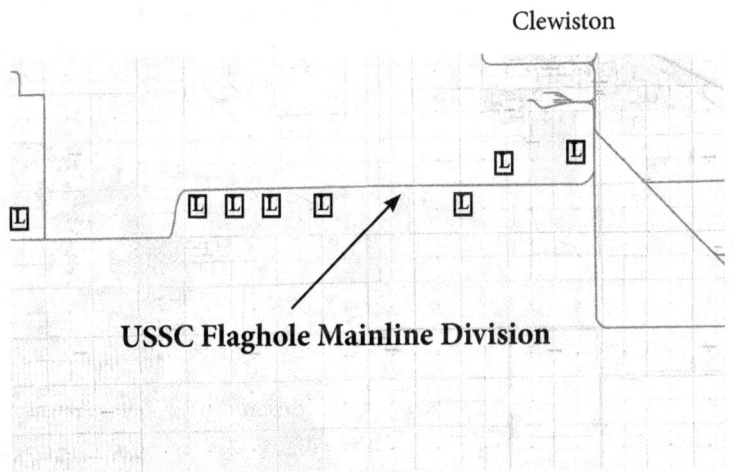

🄻 = Loader

## USSC Citrus Lead

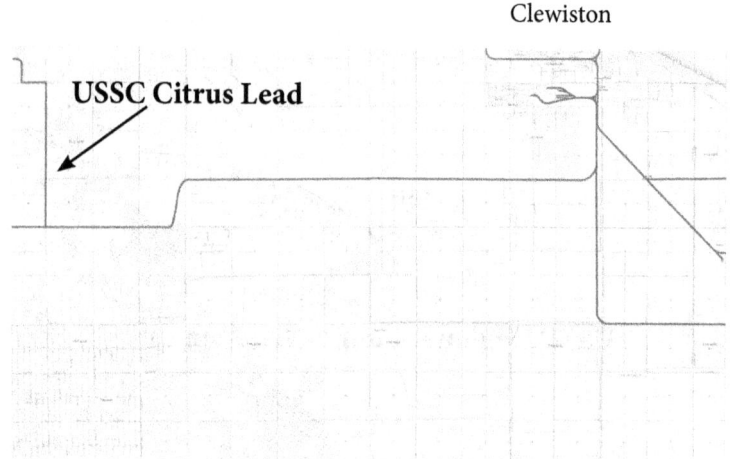

# The Railroads of the U.S. Sugar Corporation

The railroads of the United States Sugar Corporation (USSC) confuse many people, as they are really two different operations. The South Central Florida Express is a common carrier railroad operating the Sebring to Clewiston to Fort Pierce route, along with the branch to Okeelanta, all in Florida. The second rail operation is the private industrial railroad, known by the Federal Railroad Administration as "not part of the general railroad system of transportation." This private operation has two basic clusters – at Clewiston and at Bryant, again both in Florida. The company also operates more than a dozen locomotives shared by the two operations. This book will cover both systems with a detailed mile-by-mile route guide and history.

## Early Years of the U.S. Sugar Railroads

Like many companies, the day-to-day operations of U.S. Sugar were seldom thoroughly documented. This is especially true for the rail operations as they simply supported the production of sugar and molasses, but some information does exist. For example, on April 28, 1931, when the Southern Sugar Company became the United States Sugar Corporation, 21 miles of railroad and the equipment used to move the cane were part of the transfer. One of these steam locomotives was former Florida East Coast #98, a Pacific-type (4-6-2) built by Alco-Schenectady in 1911. It was acquired by Southern Sugar in February 1931.

In this Farm Security Administration photo by Marion Post Walcott, steam locomotive #98 hauls sugar cane to the mill at Clewiston in February 1939. Wolcott, Marion Post, photographer. *USSC United States Sugar Corporation hauls sugarcane from the fields to its mill by their own railroad system. Clewiston, Florida.* Clewiston, Florida, Hendry County, Feb. 1939. Retrieved from the Library of Congress, https://www.loc.gov/item/2017800319/.

One of the best histories of the early railroad days comes from a hearing of the National Railroad Adjustment Board that involved a protest by the locomotive firemen and enginemen, plus the railroad trainmen, against the Florida East Coast Railway. On March 25, 1939, the general chairmen of several unions contacted the FEC General Superintendent about the trackage rights that the United States Sugar Corporation, earlier the Southern Sugar Company, had to operate over the railroad. The unions were protesting the large and regular volumes of trains that were being operated by the sugar company. The protest went to the National Railroad Adjustment Board, and the research into the case provides a treasure trove of facts about the early years of operations.

The hearing reported that on August 21, 1929, "a trackage right agreement was made between the Southern Sugar Company to operate their trains over the tracks of the Florida East Coast Railway with their own crews and trains; started to operate about January 1st, 1930." The trackage rights over the FEC's Okeechobee Branch remained after the company was reorganized as the United States Sugar Corporation. The trackage rights contract allowed the sugar company to operate its own cane trains, using its own crews and locomotives, although some other documents mentioned an FEC pilot who worked with each USSC engine crew. The USSC trains could operate from the cane fields to the mill, actually located on the Atlantic Coast Line (ACL) tracks at Clewiston, reached over ACL tracks from Lake Harbor. In return, the sugar company was to ship the finished products via the Florida East Coast Railway (FEC).

Specifically, the sugar company operated daily during the harvest season "between Canal Point, MP. 172.8, and Lake Harbor, MP 194.0, or a distance of 21.2 miles." Specific information about the train movements was also provided. "Between Canal Point and Lake Harbor, United States Sugar Corporation sets out and picks up cars loaded with cane and any other material of the United States Sugar Corporation, at the following side tracks indicated on the Florida East Coast time table; Runyon MP. 180.7; Dahlberg MP. 186.1; side tracks United States Sugar Corporation MP. 192.2 and MP 192.7."

One issue that led the unions to protest the agreement was that at the Canal Point facility, Florida East Coast Railway crews switched the old sugar plant during the off-season, while sugar crews switched it during the sugarcane harvest. Initially on June 30, 1941, the union protests were denied. However, an appeal a year later led the National Railroad Adjustment Board to order both the Florida East Coast and the Atlantic Coast Line to end the trackage rights used by U.S. Sugar.

In 1948, the Interstate Commerce Commission (ICC) reviewed the movement of the raw sugar from the Clewiston mill to the refinery at Port Wentworth, Georgia, located about ten miles northwest of Savannah. For the 1947-48 season, the company shipped 686 carloads of sugar in bags, and 696 carloads in bulk, just below the annual average of 85,000 tons. About 35 percent of the sugar moved from Clewiston that year went via the Atlantic Coast Line Railroad to "Central Junction, Ga., about 5 miles west of Savannah, thence Savannah & Atlanta Railway Company to Port Wentworth." The rest of the sugar (65 percent) went east on the ACL to Lake Harbor, where the Florida East Coast took it to Jacksonville, Florida. There, the ACL again handled the sugar to the Savannah & Atlanta Railway. The distance of the two routes were almost identical – 470 and 490 miles respectively.

These shipment percentages were supported by the article "Transporting Everglades Cane," found in the September 2, 1950, issue of *Railway Age*. The article stated that during the sugarcane harvest season, the ACL operated five cane trains daily while the FEC operated three daily trains, with the trains interchanged at Lake Harbor, using the 110-car capacity interchange track. The coordination between the two railroads required a great deal of staff, and it was made even more complicated by the agreement that the amount of cane harvested on each railroad determined the amount of raw sugar that they moved. An FEC trainmaster at Belle Glade handled their moves, while the ACL had a general agent and a transportation/traffic officer at Clewiston. One task of the ACL was to provide all of the boxcars for sugar loading for the move to Port Wentworth.

As reported at the time, it typically required the use of three sets of crews and three different locomotives on the most basic moves. All cane moves started at a loading facility somewhere on the ACL, the FEC, or on the network of sugar company lines at Canal Point. At the time, there were six cane hoists on the ACL between Clewiston and Moore Haven, and three more between Clewiston and Lake Harbor. On the FEC, there were six cane hoists between Lake Harbor and Canal Point. Finally, there were "eight hoists on the Canal Point plantation of the sugar company, this plantation having several miles of sugar company tracks connecting with the FEC at Canal Point."

The most complicated move was probably the cane from the Canal Point facilities. This sugarcane move required four different crews and locomotives just to make the 30-mile haul from Canal Point to Clewiston. U.S. Sugar moved the cane to an FEC siding at Canal Point, and then FEC locomotives and crews handled the trains from there to Lake Harbor. At Lake Harbor, ACL crews and locomotives took over for the Lake Harbor to Clewiston move. Finally, U.S. Sugar crews and locomotives were used to spot the cane at the mill at Clewiston. This complexity was part of the reason for the construction of the Bryant sugar mill near Canal Point.

A 1951 report by the Interstate Commerce Commission stated that United States Sugar Corporation "uses its own railroad equipment to bring loaded cars from several loading points on its private tracks, about 12 miles east and south of Canal Point to the interchange track at that station. The Florida East Coast then consolidated the cane cars into trains "averaging 52 to 53 cars" and hauled them to Lake Harbor. There, the ACL moved the cars to Clewiston, where U.S. Sugar had about 16 miles of its own track to support the mill.

During the 1950-1951 sugarcane season, 37% of the sugarcane came from loaders on the Atlantic Coast Line, while 63% came from facilities on the Florida East Coast. On the ACL, 8801 carloads of sugarcane came from the loading points northwest of Clewiston (Sugarton, Liberty Point, Benbow No. 2 and No. 3, and Gramlin). This required 299 trains, with an average of 29.4 cars per train. The Florida East Coast used 490 trains to move 29,646 carloads of cane (an average of 60.5 cars) to Lake Harbor. There, the ACL combined the FEC loads with the 8652 carloads of cane from loaders to the southeast of Clewiston (Ritta, Bare Beach, and Watson). A total of 657 ACL trains operated to the east of Clewiston, hauling an average of 58.3 loads. While cane loading moved around each year, the following shows what happened during the harvest season of 1950-1951.

### Atlantic Coast Line Sugarcane Loading Points

|  |  |  |
|---|---|---|
| Gramlin | Mile 937.4 | 1928 carloads |
| Benbow No. 2 | Mile 938.8 | 1626 carloads |
| Benbow No. 3 | Mile 939.8 | 727 carloads |
| Liberty Point | Mile 941.0 | 2314 carloads |
| Sugarton | Mile 944.9 | 2206 carloads |
| Ritta | Mile 951.5 | 5593 carloads |
| Bare Beach | Mile 951.8 | 1741 carloads |
| Watson | Mile 956.6 | 1318 carloads |

### Florida East Coast Sugarcane Loading Points

|  |  |  |
|---|---|---|
| Canal Point | Mile 50.3 | 14,196 carloads |
| Runyon | Mile 57.6 | 3755 carloads |
| Dahlberg | Mile 63.0 | 3154 carloads |
| South Shore | Mile 65.8 | 4699 carloads |
| Miami Locks No. 2 | Mile 69.2 | 2192 carloads |
| Miami Locks No. 1 | Mile 69.8 | 1650 carloads |

The purpose of several of the ICC hearings were protests by the sugar company that the costs they were paying for the rail movement of sugarcane by the Atlantic Coast Line and Florida East Coast were too great. One example cited was that the "train crews of the East Coast consist of five men each who are on duty between Lake Harbor and Canal Point an average 4.5 to 5 hours daily. Under existing working arrangements, however, the crews must be paid for 8 hours plus an additional allowance of 1 hour at Lake Harbor." At the time, the Atlantic Coast Line had "three steam locomotives, three cabooses, and four train crews, with an additional relief engine when repairs and inspection are necessary." The Florida East Coast used "two diesel engines, three enginemen, two firemen, two conductors, and four trainmen."

Another point was made that the sugar company had large investments in their own cane tracks and equipment, thus reducing the costs to the Florida East Coast and Atlantic Coast Line railroads. A final argument was that the outbound shipments were apportioned between the two railroads "in proportion to the products of cane originating on their respective lines," so the railroads made their profits on that part of the business. Nevertheless, the ICC stated that intrastate rates for moving sugarcane were justified and should be based upon the valid costs involved.

The various rulings by the Interstate Commerce Commission and the National Railroad Adjustment Board forced U.S. Sugar to use the services of the Atlantic Coast Line and Florida East Coast railroads. This encouraged the company to build their own lines out of the Clewiston mill, and to build a new mill near Canal Point. It would be decades before the train operations were again simplified.

## South Central Florida Express

The South Central Florida Express (commonly SCFE, or its reporting marks SCXF) operates out of its headquarters in Clewiston, Florida, east to Fort Pierce and west to Sebring, both also in Florida. This gives the railroad and its customers direct access to the Florida East Coast and CSX railroads, multiple routes to the national market to the north. The railroad serves more than two dozen shippers, but most of its business comes from its owner – U.S. Sugar. Besides the raw and refined sugar, and the related molasses, the railroad also hauls products such as fertilizers, pulpwood, and farm equipment. A few other items that can be seen moving on the railroad include plastic pellets, lumber, and livestock feed. With work on the Herbert Hoover Dike around Lake Okeechobee over the past decade, the railroad has also been delivering stone to several locations along the line.

This sign at Clewiston marks the base of operations for the South Central Florida Express.

*Railroads of U.S. Sugar*

The tracks west of Lake Harbor, those once part of the Atlantic Coast Line (ACL), are owned by the company, bought by U.S. Sugar on September 17, 1994. These tracks were built by the Atlantic Coast Line and the Moore Haven & Clewiston Railway in the 1910s and 1920s as part of a plan to develop the south Florida wetlands for both farming and tourism. The ACL directly connected this area to the markets of the Northeast through connections in Richmond, Virginia. The Brandywine Valley Railroad Company acquired the lines from CSX on June 2, 1990, creating the South Central Florida Railroad (reporting marks SCFE). The Lake Harbor (milepost AVD 957.99) to Sebring (milepost AVC 875.00) line, as well as the Okeelanta Branch at Keela (milepost AVF 953.69 to AVF 970.50), were then acquired from the Brandywine Valley Railroad Company in 1994.

The tracks east of Lake Harbor to Fort Pierce are operated via trackage rights. Initially, the SCFE acquired local trackage rights from the Florida East Coast Railway (FEC) between Milepost K-49.8, at Canal Point, and the end of the line near milepost K-70.4, at Lake Harbor. This transaction was consummated on October 24, 1994, and allowed the SCFE to reach Bryant from the former ACL tracks that the company had acquired. According to a 1998 Surface Transportation Board report, the Florida East Coast Railway later granted "overhead trackage rights between milepost K-0.0 near Ft. Pierce, FL, and milepost K-15.0, and local trackage rights between milepost K-15.0 and milepost K-70.4, at or near Lake Harbor, FL, to South Central Florida Express, Inc." The effective date was March 2, 1998, although it was reopened later in 1998 to review some of the labor issues involved. This means that the SCFE essentially has leased the FEC line between Lake Harbor and Cana, the term used on a 1999 FEC Track Chart.

In addition to the trackage rights, there are other agreements between the Florida East Coast and the South Central Florida Express. As reported by the FEC, a Car Haulage Agreement is in effect between Fort Pierce and Jacksonville to handle railcars "for SCFE between Fort Pierce and Jacksonville for interchange with CSXT or NS."

The *Florida East Coast Industries 2006 Annual Report* stated that "On March 2, 1998, FECR entered into a Trackage Agreement with SCFE providing for, among other things, the operation and maintenance by SCFE of 56 miles of branch mainline owned by FECR extending from Fort Pierce, west to Lake Harbor. On November 25, 2005, FECR notified SCFE that the Trackage Agreement would terminate on January 1, 2025 after the required notice period." This essentially extended the trackage rights with a new twenty-year agreement.

The ownership of the railroad by its largest customer quickly reaped rewards for the company. According to several sources, "traffic on the railroad has increased from 41,000 to more than 73,000 annual carloads between 1994 and 2003." New customers and changes at the Clewiston Mill have only added to these numbers.

## U.S. Sugar Private Railroad

A large private railroad is used to move most of the sugarcane. This is the original railroad system of U.S. Sugar, with some parts dating back to the original Southern Sugar Company. When the U.S. Sugar Company was organized, it inherited a small rail system that reached into the nearby sugarcane fields at Canal Point. With the expansion of sugar production, the company needed a way to transport sugarcane from about 187,000 acres of fields to its sugar mill. Roads weren't good and trucks had very limited capacity, so rail was the logical solution. During the 1920s and 1930s, the use of large private railroads was a known practice, already being used by logging companies, quarries and coal mines, steel mills, and Hawaiian sugar plantations. Therefore, it was the chosen solution and the company eventually installed about 120 miles of rail across its fields for its internal rail line.

The second part of the solution was power. While several companies manufactured steam locomotives, and small diesel locomotives were becoming available, the market was full of used but reliable mainline steam locomotives. These were often relatively modern and produced more power than needed, but they were much less expensive than buying anything new. Therefore, U.S. Sugar became an expert at buying and maintaining used steam locomotives.

Today, cane trains still operate over the 120 miles of rail lines owned by U.S. Sugar that simply serve the various sugarcane loaders in the fields, and a number of farm maintenance facilities. U.S. Sugar is reportedly the only sugarcane farming company in the continental United States that still transports all of its cane to a sugar factory by railroad, eliminating large volumes of truck traffic. This practice also reduces the amount of fossil fuel consumption and emissions.

The private rail network has been the key to moving the sugarcane to the mill since the start of sugar production in 1929. Most sugar plantations at the time used rail to move the cane, and this was especially true in south Florida where few roads existed. Railroads could be built cheaper and haul more cane, and it could connect directly with the two railroads that served the area. These early lines, however, have little to do with today's lines except for the routes. These lines are now maintained to the same standards as the SCFE, generally with large rail sitting on good ties. The locomotives and cane cars also are capable of operating on either system.

There are four major collections of these private trackage lines: east and west of the Clewiston mill, and north and south of the former Bryant sugar mill north of Belle Glade. To move the cane, there are about 800 specially designed rail cars that hold up to 40 tons of sugarcane, or about one acre's worth of cane. During the harvest season, 1000 or more railroad cars can move each day on a dozen or more trains. Because of these volumes, the railroad has recently been investing in more modern cane cars rebuilt from older freight equipment.

While the steam locomotives used by U.S. Sugar were secondhand, that doesn't mean they were in bad condition. The company had their own shop and expert machinists, and the crews took pride in what they operated. In early 1939, steam locomotive #98 is ready for another day of work along the sugar company's railroad. It was originally built as Florida East Coast #98 by Alco-Schenectady (American Locomotive Company) in 1911, and was sold to the Southern Sugar Company in February 1931. Wolcott, Marion Post, photographer. *USSC United States Sugar Corporation hauls sugarcane from the fields to its mill by their own railroad system. Clewiston, Florida.* Clewiston, Hendry County, Florida, Feb. 1939. Photograph. https://www.loc.gov/item/2017800326/.

*Railroads of U.S. Sugar*

A loaded cane train heads west across the bridge over the Miami Canal. Note that all three of these cars are different from each other. Also note the bridge design with a deck plate girder span over the center of the stream, with wooden pile trestles off each end.

U.S. Sugar owns about 800 cane cars, and no two seem to be the same. USSC #783 has solid sides that open on one side, a common sugarcane car design.

USSC #205 is part of a series of cars that have open sides. All cars open on one side which means the cars must face the proper direction to be unloaded at the Clewiston mill.

The heritage of many of the cane cars can be clearly seen by their markings. USSC #1019 still shows its CSX markings.

One thing that can be confusing is that the sugarcane cars are generally marked USSC, while the company's actual reporting marks are USCX, although some sources also show USSX.

Recently acquired ballast car #900335 shows off its USCX reporting marks in April 2021. Cars like this were acquired as part of a program to improve track maintenance practices across the system, leading to safer and more reliable operations.

## Today's Freight Trains

The freight train operations on the various U.S. Sugar Corporation (USSC) lines varies greatly by the season. During the summer months – late April to early September, the only regular trains operating are the Fort Pierce Turn (FPT), the Sebring Turn (SBT), and the Local out of Clewiston. The Fort Pierce Turn operates weekdays east out of Clewiston over the former Florida East Coast route to Fort Pierce, Florida. The Sebring Turn is generally called an hour after the Fort Pierce Turn on weekdays, and interchanges with CSX using the former Atlantic Coast Line route west of Clewiston. The SCFE Local serves shippers between Moore Haven and Belle Glade, as well as the Okeelanta Sugar Mill and the Southern Gardens Citrus plant. All of these trains operate on the mainline and industry tracks of the South Central Florida Express. A number of special work trains can also be seen during this time on any route as major track projects are completed.

It doesn't matter what train is being operated, the locomotive pulling it will feature this United States Sugar Corporation lettering.

During winter – late September to early April – the number of trains greatly increases to handle the sugarcane moves. Besides the three freight trains that run all year long, the SCFE adds approximately four Bryant Turn trains each day to move loaded cane cars from Bryant to Clewiston, and then empty cane cars back. There are also nearly a half-dozen cane trains that operate to and from the various cane loading facilities. Additionally, there are several utility trains that switch cars in and out of the sugar mill and handle other jobs as needed. On the sugar lines, traffic is also heavy. There are generally two Clewiston Road Jobs and two Bryant Road Jobs. An Industrial Job handles switching the yard and building trains at the Clewiston Mill, while a Dump Job unloads the cane cars at the mill. Work trains can also be found at any time on any line.

These trains operate both day and night to keep the sugarcane moving. Their routes are based upon where the sugarcane is being cut and where empty cars are needed for the next day. Summer sees fewer moves, but trains can still be found on the private sugar lines as they move fertilizer and support track and bridge work.

## The Sugar Express

A very recent addition to the railroads of U.S. Sugar is the Sugar Express, a component of the company with plans for public steam excursions using steam locomotive #148, and possibly other steam and diesel locomotives over the years. Planning for these excursions has been taking place for years, with different equipment and proposals evaluated by company leadership. In particular, U.S. Sugar CEO Robert H. Buker, Jr., has pushed for the creation of this branch of the company as a public relations and education tool.

This emblem is used by the Sugar Express to promote its operations.

Steam locomotives #148 (former Florida East Coast 4-6-2) and #1504 (former Atlantic Coast Line 4-6-2) were acquired for restoration, along with a number of passenger cars. FMW Solutions was hired to assist with the steam locomotive restoration projects. Taking an additional step forward, in 2021 a full-time operations manager was hired for the Sugar Express to oversee the department's day-to-day operations and maintenance, and to facilitate the outreach programs.

Steam locomotive #148 crosses a canal bridge on the north side of Rogers Road on the Okeelanta Line.

Initially, the train was operated to mark the start and end of the annual sugar harvest, and for fundraising events for various projects of U.S. Sugar like Toys for Tots. However, after the acquisition of three passenger cars from the United Railroad Historical Society of New Jersey, the ability to operate public trips led to the first public train ride being offered in December 2021. This trip sold out almost immediately, and other events were made available, such as a special photo train for *Trains Magazine*, and a private train operation for the American Association of Private Railroad Car Owners. It should be noted that due to the regulations of the Federal Railroad Administration, passenger train trips of the Sugar Express will take place only on the lines of the South Central Florida Express and not on the private sugar cane lines of U.S. Sugar.

Even the freight cars used by The Sugar Express are designed to promote the passenger train, U.S. Sugar, and the farmers that depend upon the company for a living. This boxcar carries the message "American Farmers Feeding American Families."

## Passenger Cars of the Sugar Express

In August 2021, U.S. Sugar acquired three high capacity railroad passenger coaches from the United Railroad Historical Society of New Jersey (URHS). URHS owns a number of historic pieces of rail equipment and decided to sell pieces of duplicate equipment to raise funds for the restoration of other rail cars. As stated by both organizations, the sale of the equipment benefitted both groups. According to the president of the URHS: "When we listed the three coaches for sale, we knew that we wanted them to go to a good home. We are thrilled that the Sugar Express will be providing a secure future for these cars." The Sugar Express Operations Manager was quoted as saying: "We are excited about acquiring these high capacity coaches for use with our new operation, and they will be an excellent addition to our heritage fleet."

The three coaches acquired by the Sugar Express all date from the 1950s. Two of them, cars #326 and #327 have identical histories. Both were built in 1950 by Pullman-Standard for the *Empire Builder* passenger train of Great Northern Railway (#1139 and #1127), and then were sold to the Central Railroad of New Jersey in the early 1970s. Their new owner converted them into high-capacity commuter coaches (#129 and #119), which became the property of New Jersey Transit when it took over operations of commuter trains in New Jersey (#5326 and #5327).

Coach #333 was built for Union Pacific in 1953 by American Car & Foundry as leg-rest coach #5471. It was sold to Great Northern Railway (#1002) and then the Central Railroad of New Jersey in the early 1970s. Like the other two coaches, it was rebuilt into a high-capacity commuter coach (#123), which later became New Jersey Transit #5333. These and other passenger cars were transferred to the URHS in the early 1990s.

The Sugar Express has created their "Lake" class for coaches. Coach #1002 has been named *Lake Okeechobee*, while the other coaches have not been names as of yet. All other cars will be part of the "Community" series and will be named for communities along the railroad.

*Railroads of U.S. Sugar*

The Sugar Express has rebuilt its passenger cars, and this photo shows coach #333 – *Lake Okeechobee* – being rebuilt in the shops at Clewiston.

In 2021, the Sugar Express also acquired a 48-seat dining/lounge car, originally built by Budd Company for Pennsylvania Railroad as a 1 Drawing Room, 29-seat parlor car. Budd built 16 of these cars in 1952 for use on New York-Washington D.C. trains like the *Senator* and various *Congressionals*. This car was named "William Penn" and was later converted into a lounge car (#7137 named "Anthony Wayne"). The car was later owned by Penn Central, Amtrak (#3322), and the Heart of Dixie Railroad Museum before coming to Clewiston, Florida. The car is now named *Palmdale*.

The *Palmdale* is a former Pennsylvania Railroad dining car and features 48 seats.

A business car has also been on the property for several years. This car was painted as Pennsylvania Railroad #7507 and named *Martin W. Clement*. This car dates from 1928 when it was built by the railroad's Altoona shops. The car was originally named *Philadelphia* and was assigned to the railroad's Vice President of Operations, and Vice President of Personnel, who at the time was Martin W. Clement. After the car was upgraded with ice-activated air-conditioning, it was renamed *Pennsylvania* and assigned to the Chairman of the Board of Directors of the railroad. In 1952, the car gained its third name – *Baltimore* – and was assigned to the Vice President of Operations. More modernization of the car took place in 1952 and it was renamed Quaker City in 1954. The car continued to be modernized until it became the property of Penn Central on February 1, 1968. It was retired on August 4, 1969, and has been owned by several individuals before arriving at Clewiston. During this time it was renamed *Martin W. Clement*, who was an early user of the car and later the 11th president of the Pennsylvania Railroad.

Besides these cars, a few other passenger cars have been on the property of U.S. Sugar for several years. One of these is baggage car #3674, originally built by ACF (American Car & Foundry Company) in 1955 for the Atchison, Topeka & Santa Fe. The car was originally a baggage-express-messenger car and was used on the *Super Chief* and similar trains. The car was sold to Amtrak when it took over providing passenger service across the country. In 2018, it became the property of the Fort Wayne Railroad Historical Society, and then the Nashville Steam Preservation Society. It has been leased to the Sugar Express and serves as an open door car for viewing the countryside. It carries the name *Miami Locks*.

Included on the passenger trains of The Sugar Express is often a baggage car like *Miami Locks*, shown here at the shops in Clewiston.

## Sugar Express and CHOX

In the railroad industry, companies use reporting marks to identify their equipment. Just as the South Central Florida Express and the U.S. Sugar private rail operations have their own reporting marks, the Sugar Express now also has its own to identify their equipment. This is CHOX, with the "X" indicating that the equipment is owned by a non-commercial railroad company.

The CHOX reporting mark is actually a very creative solution to the need for this identification. A molecule of sucrose, or sugar, contains 12 carbon atoms, 22 hydrogen atoms and 11 oxygen atoms. The molecular formula is thus written as $C_{12}H_{22}O_{11}$. Taking the atomic symbols of the three types of elements – carbon, hydrogen and oxygen – and adding the X creates the CHOX reporting marks for the Sugar Express.

## Dispatching Trains

The railroads of U.S. Sugar can be very busy, so rules and practices have been created to maximize the safety of the rail operations. Traveling around the railroad, it is easy to see one of these practices – the use of blocks. Large signs exist at the end of all blocks to remind the train crews of the end of these territories.

So what is a block? Basically, the railroad has been broken up into a series of sections or territories known as a block. Each block has a specific name that is used to identify the territory, using the name of a nearby community or landmark. This practice is generally known as Direct Traffic Control (DTC). Using the DTC system, the railroad has train dispatchers who will authorize a train to occupy one or more specific blocks, using either written or verbal orders. Generally, only one train will be allowed within a single block, thus keeping the trains away from each other.

The limits of the blocks are shown in the various route guides. Note that some are long, like the Fort Pierce Block which stretches from Milepost K49.0 to Milepost K15.5. This block is long because generally only one train a day (Fort Pierce Turn) uses this part of the railroad. However, other blocks are relatively short. For example, the Lake Harbor Block is little more than three miles long (K70.9 to K67.5). This block is short because of the number of cane loading facilities in the area and the need for train movements to its west around Clewiston, and to the east around South Bay.

Another train dispatching system used on the railroad is yard limits. In these areas, multiple trains can operate on the same track, but they must be prepared to stop within half the range of vision. This means if the train crew can see far ahead, they can go a bit faster. However, if there are curves, vegetation along the right-of-way, or other items that could shorten the visibility, the trains must go slower. Additionally, the railroad also assigns a maximum speed even when visibility is good. For example, in the Clewiston area, this maximum speed is 20 miles per hour.

Just like on any railroad, the purpose of the DTC and yard limit systems is to ensure the safety of the operations of the many daily trains that operate on the railroads of U.S. Sugar.

*The Railroads of U.S. Sugar: History Through the Miles*

# The Locomotives of U.S. Sugar

Since the South Central Florida Express was created, it has been powered by modern diesel locomotives. However, the history of the sugarcane rail lines dates back to the days of steam locomotives, and that history has been returned with the acquisition and restoration of steam locomotive #148, a locomotive that used to work the fields for U.S. Sugar.

Early reports indicate that the Southern Sugar Company tried a wide variety of devices to move cane cars. An early unique solution was taking a Fordson tractor and mounting rail wheels on it, a solution that was soon found to be insufficient. A small Davenport gasoline locomotive was also tried, but it too had insufficient power to do the task of switching full trains of sugarcane. A small saddle tank steam locomotive was acquired from a contractor, but it was also soon replaced. The next move was to acquire larger locomotives that could be used on the mainlines and mill tracks. All of these came from other railroads, primarily nearby Florida East Coast and the Atlantic Coast Line. As diesel locomotives were acquired, they came from sources across the country, including railroads like Illinois Central, Union Pacific, and Boston & Maine. Like the steam locomotives, most were rebuilt to extend their lives and to modernize their operations.

## Steam Locomotives

Few if any of the steam locomotives used by Southern Sugar/U.S. Sugar were bought new. Essentially all were acquired secondhand from other railroads and used equipment dealers. Most of these steam locomotives went from mainline service on large railroads to wandering the sugarcane lines south of Lake Okeechobee. The sales which extended the life of these steam locomotives attracted attention from rail enthusiasts from across the country, making U.S. Sugar a popular South Florida rail enthusiast attraction.

Both before and after World War II, railroads were adopting diesel locomotives and replacing their more expensive steam locomotives. This left many inexpensive steamers available to U.S. Sugar. While diesel locomotives were cheaper to operate, U.S. Sugar was using the locomotives for relatively short hauls and only for the six-month cane harvest. The company had its own shop that could rebuild mill parts and the steam locomotives, so little investment was needed. Basically, when a steam locomotive failed, another could be bought and put in its place for only a few dollars. This practice lasted until the 1950s when the supply of steam locomotives began to end, and secondhand diesel locomotives started to become available.

The following steam locomotive roster and history was compiled from many sources and covers the locomotives used by U.S. Sugar. Each steam locomotive is identified by its number, wheel arrangement, builder information, and history. Note that U.S. Sugar never had its own numbering system, instead using the former owner's locomotive number. A few of the first locomotives used during the construction of Southern Sugar are not included. Additional information on these is welcomed.

**65**     **4-6-2**     This steam locomotive was built as Florida East Coast #65 by Alco-Schenectady (American Locomotive Company) in 1907. Built with construction number 44605, #65 was the first 4-6-2 steam locomotive built for the FEC, and the first of the 31 locomotives in the FEC Class 65, all Pacific-type steam locomotives. While most of this class were later superheated to provide more power, #65 never received this modernization. In 1930, #65 was sold to the Bond-Booker Lumber Company, but a lack of payments led to it being returned to the FEC. After the 1935 Labor Day Hurricane and the collapse of the Florida land boom, the FEC sold off many of their smaller and older locomotives. #65 was sold in 1938 to the United States Sugar Corporation where it remained #65. It was later scrapped after being retired for a final time.

98     4-6-2   This steam locomotive was built as Florida East Coast #98 by Alco-Schenectady (American Locomotive Company) in 1911. Built with construction number 50143, #98 was part of the FEC Class 151 superheated Pacific steam locomotives used to move fast trains across the railroad. It was retired and sold in February 1931 to the Southern Sugar Company, which later became the United States Sugar Corporation, where the locomotive remained #98. It was later scrapped after being retired for a second time.

107     4-6-0   The steam locomotive was built as Durham & Southern Railway #105 by Burnham, Williams & Co. (Baldwin Locomotive Works) in October 1905, built with construction number 26544. In 1937, D&S #107 was scrapped, but the boiler was saved and used as a replacement on the frame of #105. This frame and boiler then became the new D&S #107 and was sold to the Birmingham Rail & Locomotive Company. On June 21, 1938, it became U.S. Sugar Corporation #107. Some sources state that

#107 was soon sold, while others show that it was scrapped at Clewiston during the 1940s.

USSC #107 is shown on March 22, 1940, waiting for its next assignment on the railroad. The locomotive was built by Baldwin in October 1905 as construction number 26544. It became Durham & Southern #105, and then was sold to Birmingham Rail & Locomotive Company. On June 21, 1938, it became U. S. Sugar Corporation #107. *U. S. Sugar engine number 107 in Clewiston. March 22, 1940.* State Archives of Florida, Florida Memory. https://www.floridamemory.com/items/show/7883.

**112  4-6-0**  The steam locomotive was built as Durham & Southern #112 by Baldwin Locomotive Works in February 1913, built with construction number 39325. When retired, #112 was sold to the Birmingham Rail & Locomotive Company. During August 1937, it became U. S. Sugar Corporation #112. The locomotive was later scrapped by USSC.

**113  4-6-2**  This steam locomotive was built as Florida East Coast #113 by Alco-Schenectady (American Locomotive Company) in 1913. Built with construction number 53902, #113 was part of the FEC

Class 151 superheated Pacific steam locomotives used to move fast trains across the railroad. It was retired and sold to Walter-Wallingford Company for scrap in September 1930. In 1938, it was resold to the United States Sugar Corporation where it remained #113.

This photo from the 1930s shows USSC #113 pulling carloads of sugarcane through a cane loader, moments before its trip to the mill. *United States Sugar Company train filled with sugarcane.* 1930 (circa). State Archives of Florida, Florida Memory. https://www.floridamemory.com/items/show/141815.

After working the cane fields for more than two decades, it was retired and eventually donated to the Gold Coast Railroad Museum in 1968. Located originally in Fort Lauderdale, the museum moved to a site near the Miami Zoo in 1984. #113 is currently on display, having last pulled a mainline trip in 1986 from the zoo location to Homestead and back.

*The Railroads of U.S. Sugar: History Through the Miles*

This photo from 1996 shows former U.S. Sugar #113 at the Gold Coast Railroad Museum near Miami, Florida.

**148** 4-6-2  This steam locomotive was built as Florida East Coast #148 by Alco-Richmond (American Locomotive Company) in April 1920. Built with construction number 61769, #148 was part of the FEC Class 151 superheated Pacific steam locomotives used to move fast trains across the railroad. It was retired and sold in June 1952 to the United States Sugar Corporation where it remained #148.

After working the cane fields for more than a decade, it was retired, one of the last three steam engines the company used. In 1968, it was the last steam locomotive sold, going to the Black River & Western in 1968, keeping #148 as its number. In 1974, the steam locomotive was sold to the Morristown & Erie, and then to D. M. Brown in Michigan in 1988. It never operated in Michigan, but was stored until sold to the Denver & Rio Grande Railway Historical Foundation in 2005. While some effort was made to restore #148, the work was not completed before #148 was sold to U.S. Sugar in 2016, where a full restoration soon began to return the steam locomotive to service where it operated the most during its career.

*Locomotives*

North Shop at Clewiston became the home of USSC #148, where it sits undergoing an FRA required inspection.

**153   4-6-2**   This steam locomotive was built as Florida East Coast #153 by Alco-Schenectady (American Locomotive Company) in May 1922. Built with construction number 63262, #153 was part of the FEC Class 151 superheated Pacific steam locomotives used to move fast trains across the railroad. It was retired and sold in January 1940 to the United States Sugar Corporation where it remained #153. After working the cane fields for more than two decades, it was retired and eventually donated to the University of Miami in February 1957. The University donated it to the Gold Coast Railroad Museum in November 1966. Located originally in Port Everglades, the museum moved to Fort Lauderdale in late 1966, and then a site near the Miami Zoo in 1984. #153 operated regular trips for the museum from March 1957 until November 1966, and is currently on display at the museum.

Locomotive #153 has a historical background. While serving on the Florida East Coast, it pulled a train carrying President Calvin Coolidge to Miami in 1928. In the 1930s, the locomotive often operated on the "Overseas Railroad" of the FEC to Key West. In 1935, #153 pulled one of the last trains off the line before the route was destroyed by the Labor Day Hurricane, which killed more than 400 people across the Florida Keys. On February 21, 1985, #153 was added to the National Register of Historic Places for its role in saving so many lives in Marathon, Florida.

**304**    **4-6-0**    This steam locomotive was built as Cape Fear & Yadkin Valley Railway #12 by the Pittsburgh Locomotive and Car Works (later Alco-Pittsburgh). Built in 1886, it carried construction number 877. The Cape Fear & Yadkin Valley operated between Wilmington and Mount Airy in North Carolina, and was sold under foreclosure in 1899. The route was soon divided between what became the Atlantic Coast Line and the Southern railways. CF&YV was renumbered #304 and assigned to the ACL, and reportedly operated on the Moore Haven & Clewiston. It was sold to the Southern Sugar Company on April 29, 1929. It was later owned by U.S. Sugar before being scrapped.

**502**    **0-6-0**    This steam locomotive was built as Florida East Coast #204 by Alco-Schenectady (American Locomotive Company) in October 1918. It was built with construction number 57552, and was one of two 0-6-0 locomotives built that year as part of the 201 Class of switchers. The FEC reportedly sold the locomotive in May 1923, one of three sold

*Locomotives*

that month. The locomotive went through several hands before becoming U.S. Sugar #502. It was used to switch the mill yard at Clewiston, where it was called "the big switcher." It was later scrapped.

**1504 4-6-2** This locomotive never operated for U.S. Sugar, but was acquired in 2021 as part of the company's steam program. It was built in August 1919 by the American Locomotive Company (construction number 59314) for the Atlantic Coast Line, and later preserved and put on display at the Atlantic Coast Line's corporate headquarters in Jacksonville, Florida, in 1960. In 1986, CSX donated the locomotive to the city and it was put on display at the Prime F. Osborn III Convention Center, the former Jacksonville Terminal Company train station. A restoration of the steam locomotive is planned by U.S. Sugar.

## Steam Locomotive #148

U.S. Sugar has recently taken advantage of its history by re-acquiring steam locomotive #148, which operated on the railroad for sixteen years. After several years of extensive rebuilding and restoration, No. 148 has been returned to service, used to support local tourism and charities, and to promote various activities of U.S. Sugar.

Why restore a steam locomotive? As has been explained by the company, Robert H. Buker, Jr., president and CEO of U.S. Sugar, is a history buff who loves "machinery and of anything historical, so to him it's fascinating." In an attempt to promote the company's history, a search began for a railroad steam locomotive, preferably one that had operated for U.S. Sugar. Fortunately, several of the steam locomotives had been saved by tourist railroads and historical societies, so a series of trips were made to inspect the options and to see if it was possible to bring one of these steam locomotives back to Clewiston.

USSC #148 is becoming the face of the outreach program of the United States Sugar Corporation.

*Locomotives*

After several visits, the team went to Monte Vista, Colorado, to inspect #148, a locomotive with a 4-6-2 (Pacific) wheel arrangement. This steam locomotive was built as Florida East Coast #148 by Alco-Richmond (American Locomotive Company) in April 1920. Built with construction number 61769, #148 was part of the FEC Class 151 of superheated Pacific steam locomotives used to move fast trains across the railroad. It was retired and sold in June 1952 to the United States Sugar Corporation where it remained #148.

After working the cane fields for more than a decade, it was retired, one of the last three railroad steam locomotives the company used. In 1968, it was the last steam locomotive sold, going to Mr. Sam Freeman and the Black River & Western Railroad (New Jersey) in 1968, keeping #148 as its number. After operations ended, it was moved to the New Hope & Ivyland Railroad for boiler and mechanical work. In 1974, the steam locomotive was sold to the Morristown & Erie Railway (New Jersey), and then was donated to the Connecticut Valley Railroad Museum after Mr. Freeman's death. It then was sold to D. M. Brown in Michigan in 1988. It never operated in Michigan, but was stored until sold to the Denver & Rio Grande Railway Historical Foundation in 2005. While some effort was made to restore #148, the work was never completed due to the 2008 economic downturn. As stated by U.S. Sugar, "Thanks to the vision of U.S. Sugar CEO Robert H. Buker, Jr., No. 148 was re-acquired by U.S. Sugar for restoration to operation in 2016." A full restoration at the Clewiston shops by a team of outside railroad preservation experts, plus more than two dozen U.S. Sugar employees, soon followed. The project was completed in April 2020, and the locomotive is now used for special events, such as Santa Claus trips, charity fund raising events, and harvest celebrations.

The tender of USSC #148 carries the slogan of "We Raise Cane!" that can be found more and more around the railroad.

Besides steam locomotive #148, the railroad has also restored boxcar #1225 for the Sugar Express operations.

## Locomotives

Shown at North Shop, this baggage car is also part of the *Sugar Express* operations.

### Steam Locomotive #1504

The purchase and restoration of locomotive #148 was a surprise to many, and the stakes were further raised with the acquisition of former Atlantic Coast Line #1504 in June 2021. Atlantic Coast Line (ACL) #1504 is a USRA Light Pacific (4-6-2) steam locomotive built by Brooks Locomotive Works of the American Locomotive Company in August 1919 (construction number 59314). The United States Railroad Administration (USRA) operated the nationalized United States railroad system during and after World War I, and designed a series of standardized steam locomotives. One of these was the Light Pacific, a locomotive design to be used for passenger service. On the Atlantic Coast Line, the locomotive was used on such high-profile trains as the *Florida Special*, the *Palmetto Limited*, the *Miamian*, the *Southland*, the *South Wind* and the *Dixie Flyer*. Diesel locomotives replaced it on these trains after World War II, and it handled freight trains until being retired in 1952.

Locomotive #1504 was chosen for preservation by ACL president Champion Davis, and the Head of ACL's Mechanical Department, John W. Hawthornethe. In 1960, the Atlantic Coast Line opened a new headquarters building in Jacksonville, and #1504 was restored and placed on display outside. After several mergers, the building later became the home of CSX. In 1986, the Jacksonville Union Station was rebuilt as part of the new Prime F. Osborn III Convention Center, named after former CSX chairman and CEO Prime F. Osborn III. ACL #1504 was cosmetically restored and moved to the convention center for display.

Atlantic Coast Line #1504, a 4-6-2 steam locomotive, was acquired by U.S. Sugar in 2021. For the previous 35 years, it was on display at the Prime F. Osborn III Convention Center in Jacksonville, Florida.

For years, the North Florida Chapter of the National Railway Historical Society (NRHS) maintained the steam locomotive. During this time, it was declared to be a National Historic Mechanical Engineering Landmark (1990) and placed on the National Register of Historic Places (2018). It was also awarded the *Trains* magazine Preservation Award in 2013. Much of this is because #1504 is considered to be the only surviving original USRA Light Pacific steam locomotive and is in almost original condition.

In June 2021, the Jacksonville City Council agreed to declare the locomotive as surplus property and transfer it to the North Florida Chapter of the NRHS, which had a contract to sell the locomotive to Sugar Express LLC, a division of U.S. Sugar Corporation. Plans are to move the steam locomotive to Chattanooga, TN, where it will be restored to operating condition.

## Diesel Locomotives

Even though U.S. Sugar Corporation operated steam until the mid-1960s, the lack of available replacements and the cost of operating and maintaining the older technology led the company to buy diesel locomotives for the cane railroad, and later the South Central Florida Express. As with most similar operations, the railroads of U.S. Sugar have used a number of diesel locomotives over the years. Many no longer serve the railroad, while others have gone through a number of coats of paint and have been rebuilt to allow them to still operate.

It should be noted that while the company once used different locomotives on the two rail operations, generally painted in different schemes, U. S. Sugar (USSC) and the South Central Florida Express (SCFE) now share a pool of locomotives, all of which comply with Federal Railroad Administration requirements. To simplify the locomotive fleet, and to add flexibility in their use, all are owned by U.S. Sugar and display USSC lettering and a U.S. Sugar logo. Using the reporting marks of USSX, the locomotives are all painted bright yellow with grey stripes. The red and blue combination paint scheme for which SCFE was known is no longer used.

This photo of USSC #503 shows the United States Sugar Corporation lettering that marks all locomotives owned by the sugar company.

The diesel locomotive fleet that operates today includes the following locomotives. Information about each includes their builder and construction number, build date and model, their frame number (FN), and when known, their history. Note that all of these locomotives were originally built by Electro-Motive Diesel (EMD). This firm started in 1922 as the Electro-Motive Engineering Corporation, based in Cleveland, Ohio. The firm soon became the Electro-Motive Company (EMC). In 1930, the company was acquired by General Motors, becoming the Electro-Motive Corporation (EMC). On January 1, 1941, General Motors created the Electro-Motive Division (EMD) to build diesel engines and railroad locomotives. In 2005, the locomotive manufacturer was spun off as Electro-Motive Diesel, Inc., and was then acquired by Caterpillar, through its Progress Rail Services Corporation subsidiary, in 2010.

This photo shows the cab of USSC 409 and the newer U.S. Sugar emblem being used on some locomotives.

While all of the locomotives were built by EMD, most have been heavily rebuilt and modernized, making them even more efficient and environmentally friendly. Please note that this roster was current as the book was being published, but can change quickly as changing company needs are met.

*The Railroads of U.S. Sugar: History Through the Miles*

On this April day in 2021, the North Shop is surrounded by a number of USSC diesel locomotives, waiting for their next assignment.

201   **USSC 201** is an SW1500 switch engine, built by Electro-Motive in June 1972 (#4608-59, FN 4608-59) as Southern Pacific #2649. After the Southern Pacific-Union Pacific merger, it was renumbered as Union Pacific #Y1212 in August 2001. When it was retired, it was sold to USSC.

202   **USSC 202** is an SW1500 switch engine, built by Electro-Motive in July 1972 (#4608-87, FN 4608-87). It was originally Southern Pacific #2677. After the Southern Pacific-Union Pacific merger, it was renumbered as Union Pacific #Y1222 in August 2001. When it was retired, it was sold to USSC.

203   **USSC 203** is an MP15AC, built by Electro-Motive. Only 246 locomotives of this model were ever built. Some USSC records state that USSC 203 was built in 1984, but that was at the very end of production of this model.

204   **USSC 204** is an MP15AC, built by Electro-Motive in December 1978 (#776128-3, FN 776128-3), as Kennecott Minerals Company #122. In January

*Locomotives*

1997, it was sold to Helm Leasing which leased it as Union Pacific #1429. In 2001, it was renumbered as Union Pacific #Y1429, and then retired in 2002. It was sold to USSC in 2004.

USSC #204 once operated in Utah for Kennecott Minerals, and then was sent to Union Pacific. Today it handles everything from switching the mill to handling sugar cane trains in South Florida.

**302**  USSC 302 is a GP11, a rebuilt Electro-Motive GP9 that was originally built in January 1956 (#20774, FN 5409-19) as Illinois Central #9136. It became Illinois Central Gulf #9136 in August 1972. It was rebuilt (GP11) and then became Illinois Central #8751. It was sold as South Central Florida Express #9029. It then became USSC #302.

**303**  USSC 303 is a GP11, a rebuilt Electro-Motive GP9 that was originally built in December 1958 (#25032, FN 5591-11) as Illinois Central #9380. It became Illinois Central Gulf #9380 in August 1972. In July 1980, it was rebuilt (GP11) as #8750 and became Illinois Central #8750 during February 1988. It was in storage by July 2000 and sold as South Central Florida Express #9032. It later became USSC #303.

**304**  USSC 304 is a GP11, a rebuilt Electro-Motive GP9 that was originally built in January 1957 (#22283, FN 5480-11) as Illinois Central #9198. It became Illinois Central Gulf #9198 in August 1972. In January 1981, it was rebuilt (GP11) as #8752 and became Illinois Central #8752 during February 1988. It was eventually sold to U. S. Sugar.

**305**  USSC 305 is a GP11, a rebuilt Electro-Motive GP9. It was built as Union Pacific #302 in August 1957 (#23658, FN 5552-3), and was retired in May 1978. It was sold to Illinois Central Gulf (ICG) in November 1978 and was rebuilt at Paducah in May 1979 as ICG #8703. After again being retired by Illinois Central, it was sold as South Central Florida Express #9023, which later became USSC #305.

USSC #305 heads north, passing the Clewiston Golf Course, with an empty sugarcane train on a sunny April 2021 day.

**307**   USSC 307 is a GP11, a rebuilt Electro-Motive GP9, that was originally built in December 1957 (#23811, FN 5553-12) as Illinois Central #9311. It became Illinois Central Gulf #9311 in August 1972. It was rebuilt (GP11) as #8726 and became Illinois Central #8726 during February 1988. It became South Central Florida Express #9027 and then U. S. Sugar #307.

**308**   USSC 308 is a GP11, a rebuilt Electro-Motive GP9, that was originally built in January 1957 (#22329, FN 5517-7) as Illinois Central #9206. It became Illinois Central Gulf #9206 in August 1972. It was rebuilt (GP11) as #8743 in May 1980 and became Illinois Central #8743 during February 1988. It was stored at Woodcrest Yard by July 2000. It later was sold as South Central Florida Express #9028 and then became U. S. Sugar #308.

**310**   USSC 310 is a GP11, a rebuilt Electro-Motive GP9, that was originally built in December 1957 (#23830, FN 5553-31) as Illinois Central #9330. It became Illinois Central Gulf #9330 in August 1972. It was rebuilt (GP11) as #8710 in August 1979 and became Illinois Central #8710 during February 1988. It was sold and became South Central Florida Express #9024 and then became U. S. Sugar #310.

**311**   USSC 311 is a GP11, a rebuilt Electro-Motive GP9 that was originally built in January 1957 (#22337, FN 5517-15) as Illinois Central #9214. It became Illinois Central Gulf #9214 in August 1972. In 1980, it was rebuilt (GP11) as #8746 and became Illinois Central #8746 during February 1988. It was sold to the South Central Florida Express as #9026, and later became U. S. Sugar #311 when the locomotive fleets were combined.

USSC #311 is seen crossing the Miami Canal at Lake Harbor, Florida.

**312** USSC 312 is a GP11, a rebuilt Electro-Motive GP9 that was originally built in December 1957 (#23831, FN 5553-32) as Illinois Central #9331. It became Illinois Central Gulf #9331 in August 1972. In May 1980, it was rebuilt (GP11) as #8741 and became Illinois Central #8741 during February 1988. It was in storage by July 2000 and sold as South Central Florida Express #9027. It became USSC #312 when the locomotive fleets were combined.

**404** USSC 404 is a GP38AC that was built by Electro-Motive in March 1971 (#36085, FN 5766-7) as Gulf, Mobile & Ohio #727. With the 1972 merger between the GM&O and Illinois Central, the locomotive became Illinois Central Gulf #9546. With the renaming of the railroad in 1988, it became Illinois Central #9546. When retired, the locomotive was sold as Helm Leasing Company #3678, who sold it to USSC in 2004.

405 **USSC 405** is a GP40-2, built by Electro-Motive in November 1979 (#786215-1, FN 786215-1). It was originally Detroit, Toledo & Ironton #422, and then became Grand Trunk Western #6422 in 1984. The locomotive was sold to Alstom in 2001, and then to Helm Leasing in 2004. It was sold to USSC and rebuilt in 2006.

406 **USSC 406** is a GP40-2, built by Electro-Motive in November 1979 (#786215-2, FN 786215-2). It was originally Detroit, Toledo & Ironton #423, and then became Grand Trunk Western #6423 in 1984. The locomotive was sold to Alstom in 2001, and then to Helm Leasing in 2004. It was sold to USSC and rebuilt in 2006.

407 **USSC 407** is a GP38-2 (GP38AC?), built by Electro-Motive in February 1970 (#35682, FN 5747-13) as Illinois Central #9517. It became Illinois Central Gulf #9517 in 1972, and was sold as Missouri-Kansas-Texas #341 in 1985. It became Union Pacific #1997 in 1991, and then was sold to USSC as SCFE #407, and later transferred to U. S. Sugar.

Here, USSC #407, a GP38-2, heads up the northbound Sebring Turn, waiting for the bridge to be turned at Moore Haven, Florida.

408 USSC 408 is a GP38-2 that was built by Electro-Motive in October 1974 (#74631-2, FN 74631-2) as Magna Copper Company #17. It became BHP Copper Company #17 in 1996, and later was sold to the Indiana Rail Road as their #36. It was renumbered #3806 in 2007. After an engine failure, it was sold to Metro East Industries in 2010. Metro East rebuilt the locomotive and sold it to USSC as SCFE #408, and it was later transferred to U. S. Sugar.

409 USSC 409 is a GP38 that was built by Electro-Motive in February 1970 (#36044, FN 7240-44) as Southern Railway #2796. It became Norfolk Southern #2796 through the 1982 merger. It then became Minnesota Northern #2796, Esquimalt & Nanaimo #2796, Puget Sound & Pacific #3876, and Coos Bay Rail Link #3876. It came to U.S. Sugar in 2021.

*Locomotives*

USSC #409 heads west on the Clewiston Mainline, bringing sugarcane to the Clewiston Sugar Mill.

501  **USSC 501** is a GP40 that was built by Electro-Motive in March 1966 (#31614, FN 7876-5) as Chicago, Milwaukee, St. Paul & Pacific #184. It was renumbered #2004 in 1968, and became Soo Line #2004 in February 1985. It became EMDX #196 and was rebuilt to GP40-2 specifications and sold to USSC.

502  **USSC 502** is a GP40 that was built by Electro-Motive in October 1966 (#32301, FN 7924-8) as Chicago, Milwaukee, St. Paul & Pacific #193. It was renumbered #2019 in 1968, and became Soo Line #2019 in February 1985. It became EMDX #197 and was rebuilt to GP40-2 specifications and sold to USSC.

503  **USSC 503** is a GP40-2 that was built by Electro-Motive in December 1977 (#776025-16, FN 776025-16) as Boston & Maine #315. It was retired and sold to Helm Leasing (HATX #508), which traded it to Canadian Pacific as #4654 in 1999. CP retired the locomotive in August 2012 and sold it to Metro East Industries, who sold it to USSC.

**504**   **USSC 504** is a GP40-2 that was built by Electro-Motive in December 1977 (#776025-13, FN 776025-13) as Boston & Maine #312. It was retired and sold to Helm Leasing (HATX #516). It went to U.S. Rail Partners as #516 and then returned to Helm Leasing (HLCX #4275). It was then sold to USSC.

USSC #504 heads west across the Miami Canal bridge in January 2015.

**505**   **USSC 505** is a GP40 that was built by Electro-Motive in January 1967 (#32621, FN 7944-13) as Seaboard Air Line #642. It became Seaboard Coast Line #1557, Seaboard System #6712, and then CSX #6712. It was rebuilt to a GP40-2 and then used as Virginia Railway Express #V-02, before becoming MPEX #102 in 2011. It was sold to USSC in 2014.

*Locomotives*

USSC #505 heads west past the sanding tower at North Shop after a day of moving sugarcane.

**506** **USSC 506** is a GP40 that was built by Electro-Motive in September 1968 (#34340, FN 7127-59) as Penn Central #3163, which became Conrail #3163 on April 1, 1976. It became Denver & Rio Grande Western #3163 in 1983 and was renumbered #3149 in 1985. In 1996, the DRGW became part of Union Pacific, which retired #3149 in 2000. The locomotive then went through the hands of a number of used locomotive dealers, including Locomotive Leasing Partners (LLPX), VMV, and National Railway Equipment Company (NREX). It was sold to Western Rail (WRIX) which rebuilt the locomotive to GP40-2 specifications and sold it to USSC in 2016.

*The Railroads of U.S. Sugar: History Through the Miles*

USSC #506 is shown operating long end forward and waiting for the St. Lucie Canal Bridge while hauling the Fort Pierce Turn.

## The Basics of Seeing the Railroads of U.S. Sugar

The railroads of U.S. Sugar have long been an attraction for rail enthusiasts. The combination of heavy traffic, unique freight operations, and the warm winter weather makes the Clewiston area a good vacation destination. However, most of the railroads of U.S. Sugar operate just out of sight, so knowing what access is available is important. While there are some public roads, the tracks are well maintained (many of the track maintenance employees have been through courses that the author teaches on the subject) and trains often operate about 40 miles per hour. Chasing these trains on narrow county roads is not advisable.

It must be pointed out that many cane roads do provide access to much of the railroad, but they are generally private property. Please don't trespass into the cane fields or down cane roads, as they are heavily used by large farming equipment. Also, the fields are generally burned before they are harvested. Fires can quickly consume a field, and the resulting smoke can make it difficult to see.

Most photographers figure out where the action is and then choose a favorite location, knowing that trains will come by frequently. Many start at the SCFE offices and locomotive shops located south of downtown Clewiston, where the ACL station once stood. Aztec Avenue is located just north of the mainline, and Basilan Crescent is to the south of the shops. A siding to the east is sometimes used to build the mainline trains. The area is clearly marked as private, but photos are available from these streets. Please respect the No Trespassing signs and help the next enthusiast get their pictures, too.

If you see cane being cut, you know that a nearby loader is busy. It is certainly worth stopping for a few minutes to watch the process to cut the sugarcane.

Signs like this can be found all along the railroad.

Once the direction of train traffic is ascertained, decisions can be made about photo locations. Northwest of Clewiston, the cane is loaded at a series of cane loading stations along the former ACL route. None are directly on the road, but County Road 720 crosses the tracks several times. The highlight along this line is the 130-foot through plate girder turn span of the Caloosahtchee Canal Swing Bridge at Moore Haven. The canal is part of the Okeechobee Waterway, which provides a short-cut between the Atlantic Ocean and the Gulf of Mexico. Train crews operate the bridge from a small control box, all visible from several local parks. Further north, the station at Lake Placid, and numerous wooden trestles and orange groves, provide plenty of reasons to take a picture.

Just east of Clewiston is the core of rail photography. A series of public roads encircle much of the sugarcane and cross the tracks at numerous locations. The first major street is Evercane Road, also known as Hendry County Road 835. This road crosses every track that heads east. At South Clewiston, the switch for the Ritta Line is next to the highway, and long views of eastbound trains with the sugar mill in the background are possible. Further south, Evercane Road crosses the primary sugarcane line in the area, the Clewiston Mainline. In many years, this can be the busiest sugarcane line near Clewiston, and is the future route for some trains to the Bryant lines.

Just to the south from Evercane Road, Rogers Road heads east into the land of sugarcane. This paved road crosses the SCFE line to the Okeelanta Sugar Mill, owned by the competing Florida Crystals Corporation, and the former Wetherald Line (named for Charles E. Wetherald, former president of U.S. Sugar). Heading on east, Rogers Road reaches Miami Canal Road. This road, while not paved, is part of a heavily used bypass around Clewiston, and large trucks are common. However, Miami Canal Road is wide and it provides access to the three U.S. Sugar bridges across the canal, once used for commercial navigation. To the south are the Clewiston Mainline and Okeelanta line bridges, while to the north is the SCFE bridge at Lake Harbor. The Lake Harbor and Clewiston Mainline bridges both see heavy traffic during the cane harvest season, but the road has recently been gated in this direction. The Lake Harbor bridge also has the advantage of the John Stretch Park and its restrooms, located not far to the north on Lake Okeechobee.

The former Eastern Division of the U.S. Sugar lines are east and north of Belle Glade, the home of the Glades Sugar House. While U.S. Sugar operates the sugar railroads, there are actually three sugar producers operating four sugar mills in the Clewiston-Belle Glade area, and all are served by, or near the SCFE. Florida Crystals Corporation operates the Okeelanta and Osceola Sugar Mills (east of Pahokee), Sugarcane Growers Cooperative of Florida operates the Glades Sugar House at Belle Glade, and U.S. Sugar Corporation operates the Clewiston Sugar Mill. Only the Osceola Sugar Mill doesn't have rail service.

The former Eastern Division was actually based at the large yard and growing industrial park at Bryant, just north of Pahokee. The Bryant area was once named Azucar (Spanish for sugar), and the Bryant Sugar House opened in 1962 on a series of sugarcane lines that date from the founding of the sugar company. The Bryant Sugar House closed in 2007 and was removed as all production was consolidated at Clewiston. However, cane production continues here. U.S. Sugar trains still operate over the lines to the north and south, and exchange loads and empties at the Bryant rail yard. This explains the need for the many SCFE Bryant Turn trains, which haul the cane from Bryant to the Clewiston Mill.

*The Basics*

Access to these sugarcane lines is very limited, but crossroads like Old Connors Road (FL-700), Muck City Road (FL-717), U.S. Highway 98, and Airport Road provide some access. Bryant Turn trains are easily photographed as they cross U.S. Highway 98/441 to get to and from Bryant Yard. These trains can be followed as they head to Clewiston, with numerous old mills and packing plants, sugarcane fields, and several cane loaders making perfect backgrounds. In Belle Glade, the bridge over the Hillsboro Canal and the former Florida East Coast office are favorite photo locations.

For those chasing the Fort Pierce Turn, one of the most popular photo locations is at Port Mayaca, not far north of Bryant. Here, the railroad crosses the St. Lucie Canal Bridge, a manual lift bridge operated by train crews. Like the Caloosahtchee Canal at Moore Haven, this is part of the Okeechobee Waterway. Other popular photography locations on the line include the CSX diamond at Marcy, the County Line Canal Bridge near Bluefield, and along Florida Highway 709 near Fort Pierce.

A final sugarcane line heads west from the Clewiston mill, and was recently extended to the Southern Gardens Citrus plant on Florida Highway 833. Access to this route is very limited, mainly at the Flaghole Road grade crossing,

It should be noted that most maps do not show all of these sugarcane lines. Even the most recent USGS topographic maps do not show all of the lines. The best advice is to use the satellite imaging that is available on many internet mapping sites.

## Table 11.
## MOORE HAVEN AND CLEWISTON.

| Mls | December 15, 1925. | 2 | |
|---|---|---|---|
| PM | LVE.] (*East. time.*) [ARR. | Noon | |
| 10 0 | ......Moore Haven...... | 12 00 | |
| 10 14.3 | ......Clewiston....... | †11 00 | |
| PM | ...ARRIVE] [LEAVE | A M | |

### Table 15—HAINES CITY BRANCH.

| | 375 | 191 | 183 | Mls. | December 15, 1925. | 194 | 182 | 376 | |
|---|---|---|---|---|---|---|---|---|---|
| | | PM | A M | | LVE.] (*East. time.*) [ARR. | PM | PM | | • Tuesday and Friday. ‖ Meals. + Coupon stations; ◊ Telegraph stations |
| | | *2 35 | *8 45 | 0 | +....Haines City....◊ | 1 35 | 7 15 | | |
| | | 2 46 | 8 57 | 5.3 | .....Lake Hamilton..... | 1 20 | 6 55 | | |
| | | 2 50 | 9 01 | 6.9 | .........Dundee......... | 1 16 | 6 50 | | |
| | | 3 10 | 9 20 | 15.4 | +.....Lake Wales.....◊ | 12 58 | 6 23 | | |
| | | 3 23 | 9 34 | 21.3 | ......Babson Park.....◊ | 12 45 | 6 10 | | |
| | | 3 37 | 9 48 | 27.8 | ........Frostproof.....◊ | 12 32 | 5 57 | | |
| | | 4 02 | 10 12 | 38.5 | .........Avon Park.....◊ | 12 09 | 5 33 | | |
| | | 4 20 | 10 30 | 46.5 | .........Sebring......◊ | *11 50 | 5 15 | | |
| | | P M | 10 50 | 55.6 | ......Istokpoga....... | A M | 4 56 | | |
| | | | 11 07 | 63.4 | ......Lake Stearns..... | | 4 40 | | |
| | | | 11 20 | 69.4 | .........Childs......... | | 4 27 | | |
| | Mix. | | 11 30 | 74.2 | .........Hicorio........ | | 4 17 | Mix. | |
| | P M | | 11 42 | 79.9 | ..........Venus........◊ | | 4 05 | A M | |
| | g2 07 | | 12 02 | 88.9 | .......Palmdale......◊ | | 3 46 | 8 25 | |
| | 3 00 | | 12 45 | 105.5 | .....Moore Haven...◊ | | *3 10 | h7 30 | |
| | P M | | P M | | ARRIVE] [LEAVE | | P M | A M | |

Historical passenger timetables for the Atlantic Coast Line Railroad's Moore Haven and Clewiston line and Haines City Branch. From *The Official Guide of the Railways and Steam Navigation Lines of the United States,* February 1926, page 557.

# Route Guide for the Railroads of the South Central Florida Express (SCFE)

The primary purpose of this book is to provide a description of the history and scenes along each rail line owned and operated by the United States Sugar Corporation and its subsidiaries. To do this, a route guide is provided for each line. However, this is complicated because of the history of many of the lines and the operating patterns of the sugar company. While most trains are based at Clewiston, it is not the logical start for many of these guides. For example, the two divisions of the South Central Florida Express actually divide at Lake Harbor, about ten miles to the east. A second challenge is that historically, the original owners of both of the lines considered Lake Harbor to be the south end of the line, so leaving Lake Harbor their trains operated northbound. A final challenge is that the western half of the South Central Florida Express uses track that once belonged to the Atlantic Coast Line, whose mileposts were from Richmond, Virginia. Meanwhile, the eastern half of the South Central Florida Express uses track that belongs to the Florida East Coast. These mileposts are the distance from Fort Pierce. Therefore, the mileposts change significantly at Lake Harbor.

Over the years, there have also been several changes. An excellent example is the line to Okeelanta. Here, the Atlantic Coast Line originally used the same origin for the mileposts as to Clewiston, but the line has since been renumbered by U.S. Sugar starting at Keela. Additionally, the cane lines recently were renumbered to avoid several conflicting mileposts.

Because of these issues, the reader will need to choose from several chapters to find the information for the line and route that they are interested in. Since the trains of the South Central Florida Express are based at Clewiston, the major routes will start here. This may mean that some trips following a line will require that the materials be read forward, while others may require the reader to cover the material in reverse.

Directions on this railroad will be based upon the railroad's own terminology. A train heading from Clewiston toward Sebring is heading railroad-north. A train heading east out of Clewiston is heading railroad-south until Lake Harbor, where it is then going railroad-north toward Fort Pierce. Directions on other lines are provided where needed. Note that every station and bridge location is also identified by a milepost location. Railroads identify locations along their routes by mileposts, much like highways do. For the rail lines of U.S. Sugar, most of the mileposts date back to the construction of the various railroads and lines. The mileposts for each location are included in this guide. There are signs every mile along the railroad that identify this distance, so watch for them if you wish.

## SCFE Sebring Subdivision
## Clewiston (FL) to Sebring (FL)

The railroad between Clewiston and Sebring is the Sebring Subdivision of the South Central Florida Express (SCFE). This route was built by the Atlantic Coast Line Railroad and the Moore Haven & Clewiston Railway, and was known as the Haines City Branch for many years. The railroad considers that trains heading from Clewiston to Sebring are going north.

The Atlantic Coast Line Railroad (ACL) played a major role in two of the lines operated by the South Central Florida Express. These are the line from Sebring to Clewiston and on to Lake Harbor (Sebring Subdivision), and the line to the sugar mill at Okeelanta (Okeelanta Subdivision) east of Clewiston. The Atlantic Coast Line started building toward the Clewiston area when it opened its line from Haines City to Sebring in 1912. Like several other rail projects of the era, the line was designed to reach the new winter vacation resorts opening up across southern Florida, and the many vegetable farms opening at about the same time. Once at Sebring, the railroad began looking ahead for business, and the port at Everglades City (southeast of Naples, Florida) promised access to the Cuban trade.

On March 13, 1916, a resolution was filed by the Directors of the Atlantic Coast Line Railroad to construct a line of railroad from Sebring to Immokalee, not far north of Everglades City. The plans became bigger two months later when the Board of Directors added a line to Moore Haven on Lake Okeechobee. A contract was soon awarded to Wade, Clower & Wade of Jacksonville, Florida, to build about 100 miles of track in about 18 months. Wade, Clower & Wade was an established firm in the general railroad construction business and had built other lines for the Atlantic Coast Line, and for other railroads across the region.

The construction techniques at the time were relatively modern, and much of the earthwork was performed using two Marion cranes, a set of 16-ton air side dump cars, and several steam locomotives. However, a significant amount of the work still required men moving dirt with wheelbarrows. The railroad was completed with 70-pound (per yard) rail and cypress ties, supplied by the Atlantic Coast Line Railroad. The line also required the construction of six miles of trestle. An article in *The Earth Mover* magazine (May 1917) reported on the work and included a number of photos.

According to *Poor's Manual of Railroads* (1921), the track from Sebring to Harrisburg (44.06 miles), and on to "Moorehaven" (15.64 miles), was placed in operation on April 29, 1918. With the ACL line south from Sebring to Moore Haven opened, the railroad allowed the development of vegetable and citrus farms, and a limited amount of logging and real estate development in the Lake Okeechobee region.

From Harrisburg, the ACL planned on having their line go in two directions, south to Immokalee and Everglades City, and east to Moore Haven and its water connections with Lake Okeechobee and much of the rest of south Florida. As stated, the first construction headed east, arriving in Moore Haven in early 1918. With the ACL so near Lake Okeechobee, developers chartered the Moore Haven & Clewiston Railway in 1920 and built their own line from Moore Haven east to their new town of Clewiston, Florida. Meanwhile, the ACL started building south from Harrisburg to Immokalee in 1921. It was later extended to serve the fruit and vegetable businesses around Everglades City by building some track and buying the Deep Lake Railroad. It also connected with the Lee Cypress Railroad at Copeland, which closed in the late 1940s.

This photo shows officials of the Atlantic Coast Line Railroad and the Moore Haven & Clewiston Railway riding a flat car to inspect new track in the Clewiston area. *The observation car with officials of two roads.* 1921. State Archives of Florida, Florida Memory. https://www.floridamemory.com/items/show/156713.

This 1921 photo from the Florida Memory collection shows sand being unloaded on the Moore Haven & Clewiston Railway to help stabilize the new grade. *Unloading sand for the siding.* 1921. State Archives of Florida, Florida Memory. https://www.floridamemory.com/items/show/156717.

## Moore Haven & Clewiston Railway

Construction on the Moore Haven & Clewiston Railway began in 1920, and the Railroad Retirement Board shows a start date of the company as being April 20, 1920. The February 3, 1921, issue of *Manufacturers Record* reported that tracklaying had begun, with "the first 7 miles to be completed by May 1." The line was described as going to be 14.5 miles long, and that Miller & Jackson of Jacksonville had the construction contract. The *Railway Age* issue of June 18, 1921, showed that progress on building the railroad was rapid. It stated that fourteen miles of the railroad had been completed, and only three more were left to finish. The article also reported that the "route is through rich trucking lands, and the railway is carrying produce at the rate of twenty carloads a day to the Atlantic Coast Line R. R. at Moore Haven."

Much of the construction of the Moore Haven & Clewiston Railway required significant work. Therefore, equipment such as this American Railroad Ditcher were used to build up the grade for the railroad, and to build adjacent drainage ditches. A note with this photo from 1921 states "Crossing the sleugh at an arm of Lake Okeechobee." *American Railroad Ditcher at work during the building of the Moore Haven and Clewiston Railway.* 1921. State Archives of Florida, Florida Memory. https://www.floridamemory.com/items/show/156701.

*Florida Memory*, part of the State Library & Archives of Florida, has a number of online photos of the construction of the Moore Haven & Clewiston Railway, some of which are used in this book. Among these are photos of Buckeye and American railroad ditchers, photos of bridge and track construction, and photos of early inspection trains.

The March 17, 1921, issue of *Manufacturers Record* had a large article about the development occurring in the Everglades at the time. The article, "An Empire in the Building – Reclaiming the Florida Everglades and Making Millions of Acres Available for Crops", written by Howard L. Clark, described the construction of the Moore Haven & Clewiston Railway.

> *Through the efforts of private capital, a new railroad, the first to be built entirely within the Everglades, is now under construction running from Moore Haven, 15 miles out into the Glades to Sand Point, where a settlement and townsite, known as Clewiston, will be developed. It is but logical to expect this road will ultimately be extended through to some Atlantic port, giving railroad transportation to all of the eastern portion of the Glades, which is developing rapidly. The Everglades line is the Moore Haven & Clewiston Railway, which is owned and being built by Capt. J. J. O'Brien of Moore Haven and A. C. Clewis, a prominent banker of Tampa. Several miles of track have been laid and it is expected the road will be built into Clewiston by June. The first locomotive to run in the Everglades proper came in to haul construction material on February 14. The spirit of the pioneer is exemplified by these men, who had the vision and the 'nerve' to undertake such an enterprise at this time. However, from all that the writer can gather, they are playing a 'safe bet.' The de-*

velopment of the territory is bound to come; it cannot be stopped. A feature of the construction of the road through the virgin Everglades is that the roadbed was built entirely with the aid of machinery. A ditcher, the same type that is used in digging most of the larger laterals, was run along the right of way, throwing up an embankment at one side and back up the other side throwing the second bank against the first, which was afterwards leveled off with a road scrape, making it ready for the laying of the crossties and rails. Upon the completion of this road thousands of acres of rich muck lands will be available for clearing and cultivating which otherwise could not be used to advantage because of the lack of transportation. Furthermore, there are vast possibilities offered for a railroad entering from the west up through the fertile Caloosahatchee Valley into the Everglades and Moore Haven section.

The initial service on the line was rather basic. A timetable dated October 1922 showed a daily except Sunday passenger train between Clewiston and Moore Haven. It left Clewiston at 11:45am and arrived at Moore Haven at 12:45pm. The return train left Moore Haven at 2:50pm, and was scheduled to return to Clewiston at 3:30pm. This schedule provided a connection with passenger trains on the Atlantic Coast Line, and included time to do some shopping at the larger community of Moore Haven.

The year 1925 saw a major change with the Moore Haven & Clewiston Railway. According to records of the State of Florida, the railroad had "14.13 miles of road, 0.88 miles of second main track, 0.66 miles of industrial trackage, 3.15 miles of yard track and sidings, 18.82 total." On April 22, 1925, the Atlantic Coast Line petitioned the Interstate Commerce Commission (ICC) for approval to control the

SCFE Sebring Subdivision

Moore Haven & Clewiston Railway Company. After several changes, the ICC decided the case on June 6, 1925. The approval allowed the ACL to purchase the capital stock of the MH&C, to lease the MH&C for 99 years, and to "assume obligation and liability in respect of $50,000 of first-mortgage bonds issued by the Moore Haven & Clewiston Railway Company."

The ICC report on the decision provides some interesting information about the Moore Haven & Clewiston. It stated that the railroad owned one engine and two passenger cars, and that all freight equipment was provided by the Atlantic Coast Line. The railroad was described as being "single track and laid with 60-pound rail." Furthermore, the rails were leased from the ACL, and the Moore Haven & Clewiston owed the larger railroad more than $80,000.

Due to the outstanding bonds and other legal issues, the Moore Haven & Clewiston Railway was leased by the Atlantic Coast Line in 1925. It was then extended to a junction with the Florida East Coast at Lake Harbor in 1929. In 1944, the Atlantic Coast Line completely bought out the Moore Haven & Clewiston Railway, creating the Haines City Branch between Haines City and Clewiston, and on to Lake Harbor. For several decades, the railroad primarily served the sugar and vegetable industries around Clewiston while the national railroad system suffered from over regulation and changing traffic patterns.

*The Railroads of U.S. Sugar: History Through the Miles*

This photo is entitled "Atlantic Coast Line cars full of sugar cane going to mills at Clewiston, Moore Haven or South Bay." It shows carloads of sugarcane heading to a sugar house somewhere on the railroad in the Clewiston area. *Atlantic Coast Line cars full of sugar cane going to mills at Clewiston, Moore Haven or South Bay.* 20th century. State Archives of Florida, Florida Memory. https://www.floridamemory.com/items/show/141811.

## Creating the Seaboard Coast Line and the South Central Florida Express

On August 18, 1960, the stockholders of the Atlantic Coast Line and its direct competitor, the Seaboard Air Line Railroad, voted to merge. In 1963, the Interstate Commerce Commission (ICC) approved the merger, but it wasn't until July 1, 1967, that a series of court cases and further ICC rulings finally made it official, creating the Seaboard Coast Line Railroad. This was just the start of a series of changes, as a merger with the Louisville & Nashville Railroad and Clinchfield Railroad on January 1, 1983, created the Seaboard System Railroad. About the same time, the line south of Harrisburg to Immokalee and on to Everglades City was abandoned.

## SCFE Sebring Subdivision

The Seaboard System Railroad and the Chessie System Railroad (a holding company that owned the Chesapeake & Ohio Railway, the Baltimore & Ohio Railroad, the Western Maryland Railway, the Baltimore & Ohio Chicago Terminal Railroad, and several other small railroads) were eventually controlled by the CSX Corporation on November 1, 1980. They were fully merged into CSX Transportation in December 1986. In Timetable No. 2 for the Tampa Division (October 25, 1987), the track between Sebring and Lake Harbor was listed as the Sebring Subdivision.

However, as the railroad got larger, this small rail operation on the north edge of the Everglades became less and less valuable to the railroad. Looking to raise capital and rid itself of low volume rail lines, the track from Sebring to Lake Harbor was sold to the Brandywine Valley Railroad, a Lukens Steel Company subsidiary, on June 2, 1990. With this, the route became the South Central Florida Railroad with the AAR reporting marks of SCFE. The line was then sold on September 17, 1994, to U.S. Sugar, who set the line up as the South Central Florida Express (reporting marks SCXF). U.S. Sugar already owned a series of lines into the sugarcane fields, and their two railroads began to cooperate, but remained legally separated for regulatory reasons.

Although the railroad was built from Sebring to Clewiston, this route guide follows the railroad from the railroad's headquarters at Clewiston northward to Sebring. The mileposts used date back to the Atlantic Coast Line, and later CSX, and are still used by the South Central Florida Express. Railroads identify locations along their routes by mileposts, much like highways do. There are signs every mile along the railroad that identify this distance, so watch for them if you wish.

## Passenger Service on the Haines City Branch

During the 1920s, several passenger trains operated over the Haines City Branch. Initially, the Atlantic Coast Line trains operated only to Moore Haven, where a connection was made with the Moore Haven & Clewiston. In May 1923, two roundtrip trains operated between Sebring and Moore Haven on the ACL. Nos. 181 and 184 operated Haines City-Moore Haven, with No. 181 leaving Haines City at 9:40am, and arriving at Moore Haven at 1:40pm. No. 184 headed back north at 3:15pm, arriving back at Haines City at 7:15pm. At the same time, a mixed train made a daily except Sunday run between Sebring and Moore Haven. It left Sebring as No. 175 at 7:00am and arrived at Moore Haven about 10:00am. The train turned as No. 178, heading north at noon, with a scheduled arrival time of 2:30pm at Sebring. Meanwhile, a Moore Haven & Clewiston Railway timetable dated October 1922 showed a daily except Sunday passenger train between Clewiston and Moore Haven. It left Clewiston at 11:45am and arrived at Moore Haven at 12:45pm. The return train left Moore Haven at 2:50pm, and was scheduled to be back at Clewiston at 3:30pm.

According to the December 15, 1925, ACL timetable, train No. 183 departed Haines City at 8:45am, and Sebring at 10:30am, arriving at Moore Haven at 12:45pm. Northbound No. 182 departed Moore Haven at 3:10pm and Sebring at 5:15pm, before a scheduled arrival time of 7:15pm at Haines City. Connecting to these trains were No. 1 (depart Clewiston at 11:00am, arrive Moore Haven at noon) and No. 2 (depart Moore Haven at 1:00pm, arrive Clewiston at 2:00pm). These separate trains were soon combined when the ACL acquired and leased the Moore Haven & Clewiston Railway.

At the same time, a unique passenger operation over part of the line was a pair of mixed trains between Palmdale and

Moore Haven. Mixed No. 376 headed north on Monday, Wednesday and Friday. It left Moore Haven at 7:30am and was scheduled to be at Palmdale at 8:25am. Meanwhile, mixed No. 375 headed south on Tuesday, Thursday and Saturday from Palmdale at 2:07pm, and arrived at Moore Haven at 3:00pm.

An interesting fact found while researching ACL timetables is that Immokalee Branch passenger trains (No. 373 south to Immokalee and No. 374 north to Palmdale) arrived and departed Palmdale at the same times. However, the days were flipped so that No. 373 headed south at 2:07pm on Monday, Wednesday and Friday, while No. 374 came north to Palmdale on Tuesday, Thursday and Saturday.

By May 1934, the Haines City-Clewiston service was down to one out-and-back train daily. No. 175 left Haines City daily at 6:15am and arrived at Clewiston at 9:50am. No. 176 then departed Clewiston at 6:00pm and arrived back at Haines City at 10:01pm. During that time, Sebring, Venus, Palmdale and Moore Haven were shown to be telegraph stations.

This basic schedule remained for the next decade, with no passenger service shown between Clewiston and Lake Harbor. A close examination of the schedule showed that the trains actually operated Lakeland to Clewiston as Nos. 102 (to Clewiston) and 101 (to Lakeland) on the Jacksonville-Tampa mainline. For a while during World War II, the trains were direct connections with the *Havana Special* at Jacksonville and carried Jacksonville-Clewiston coaches, plus an eight section-buffet sleeper. The sleeper was dropped mid-1949, and the through coaches were eliminated by 1951 when the Clewiston trains became tri-weekly. Finally, on June 21, 1954, Haines City-Clewiston passenger service ended. This left only a tri-weekly Palmdale-Everglades mixed train (Nos. 453-452), which was discontinued on October 1, 1955.

# SCFE Sebring Subdivision Route Guide Clewiston (FL) to Sebring (FL)

**947.9 CLEWISTON** – Clewiston is the home of U.S. Sugar Corporation and its railroads. Information about Clewiston is found in the *Welcome to Clewiston* chapter on Page 41 of this book. Information about the South Central Florida Express rail lines east of Clewiston can be found in the *SCFE Sebring and Fort Pierce Route Guide – Clewiston (FL) to Fort Pierce (FL)* chapter on Page 225.

Heading west from Clewiston, the railroad passes north of the Clewiston Golf Course. Just to the east of the golf course is the old Clewiston Municipal Airport, mainly replaced by the Airglades Airport west of town. The runways are still there and are used annually by the South Florida Ag Expo. The new Airglades Airport was once Riddle Field, a World War II British Flying Training School (BFTS). Officially BFTS #5, this facility was designed to provide extensive training in formation flying, acrobatic maneuvers, armaments and instrument navigation. BFTS #5 operated between September 1941 and September 1945, training more than 2000 Royal Air Force and 100 American pilots. There is a small museum at the airport to preserve the history of Riddle Field.

At the west end of Clewiston, the railroad turns north to pass Waring and cross U.S. Highway 27, here a four-lane divided highway that serves as the main street through Clewiston.

**946.3 BLOCK LIMITS** – Trains heading north from Clewiston are first in yard limits which cover the railroad between Mileposts 951.0 and 946.3. Then, trains enter the **Clewiston Block** at this location. The name of the block naturally comes from the nearby City of Clewiston.

The Clewiston Block protects about ten miles of track and the trains as they work the numerous cane loading facilities northwest of town.

**946.0 WARING** – In 1925, the timetable of the Moore Haven & Clewiston Railway showed a station that was located just south of today's U.S. Highway 27 grade crossing named Waring. There was no clear reason given for the name, but C. D. Waring was a noted railroad construction engineer who worked on a number of projects in Florida during the early 1920s. Several reports state that he was the engineer in charge of the location and construction of the Moore Haven & Clewiston. The station did not last long with it shown as being Highway Spur by 1933, and no sign of the location exists today.

For trains heading west from Clewiston, the line actually heads north for a short distance. For the railroad, trains heading in this direction are heading railroad-north, since the line's mileposts are the distance from Richmond, Virginia, via the original Atlantic Coast Line through Florence (SC), Savannah (GA), and Jacksonville (FL).

**945.9 U.S. HIGHWAY 27** – At the west end of Clewiston the railroad crosses U.S. Highway 27, here a four-lane divided highway that serves as the main street through Clewiston. Almost all of the nearly 500 miles of U.S. 27 in the state of Florida are

## SCFE Sebring Subdivision Route Guide

divided highway. The roadway is 1373 miles long and stretches between Fort Wayne, Indiana, and Miami, Florida. In Florida, U.S. Highway 27 has been declared to be the Claude Pepper Memorial Highway, named for long-time Florida U.S. Senator and congressman Claude Pepper.

**945.7 EPPS** – There was a spur track to the west at this location in 1949. The name Epps likely came from a family of the same name who has lived in the area since the early days of the region's settlement.

**944.9 SUGARTON #1** – Heading north toward Sebring, the railroad curves from heading north to heading west just before reaching this location, a small cane-loading facility with a 1327-foot siding. Located to the north of the tracks (railroad-east), this cane loader can only handle 28 cars on its siding, according to Seaboard Coast Line documents.

Passing through the sugarcane fields, you can see several different designs of sugarcane loading facilities. When the sugar industry first started in South Florida, small cranes were used to lift the cane off of wagons and place it in railcars for movement to the sugar mill. Today, two basic systems are used: elevators and ramps, with most elevator facilities also having ramps to help raise the cane above the elevator bins.

A majority of the cane-loading facilities on the U.S. Sugar railroads use elevators (conveyors) to raise the cane, and to then dump the cane into the railcars. Some simply include a ramp and an elevated area where tractor-hauled self-dumping cane wagons can directly pour their cane into the railcars. Sugarton #1 uses an elevator but no ramp.

Another type of loader used decades ago was a permanent crane. This loader could transfer an entire cane load from a field cart to a railcar in one move. This loader was in operation in February 1939. Wolcott, Marion Post, photographer. *Loading sugarcane into cars to be taken to the sugar mill of USSC United States Sugar Corporation. Clewiston, Florida.* Clewiston, Florida, Hendry County, Feb. 1939. Photograph. https://www.loc.gov/item/2017800318/.

While the name Sugarton has generally been used for this area, the early passenger station here was shown to be Sugartown. Not far to the west, the railroad has a grade crossing with County Road 720 at Milepost 944.1. Look for the cell and radio towers not much further west.

*SCFE Sebring Subdivision Route Guide*

Tractors hauling several trailers is the typical way that sugarcane is moved from the fields to the nearby cane loaders. Here, cane is being cut just north of Clewiston and will quickly be hauled to Sugarton #1 to be sent to the mill for processing.

County Road 720 is the key to following the railroad between Clewiston and Moore Haven. From U.S. Highway 27 just west of Clewiston, Hendry County Road 720 heads north, becoming Glades County Road just north of this location. It then heads northwest before connecting back to U.S. Highway 27 not far south of Moore Haven. At one time, this route was officially Florida Highway 720.

**944.1 GUNSON SIDING** – There was a station known as Gunson located in this area in the 1925 Moore Haven & Clewiston Railway timetable, and records of the Railroad Commission of the State of Florida show that name here through the 1930s. Records of the Atlantic Coast Line list a spur track to the east in 1949.

*The Railroads of U.S. Sugar: History Through the Miles*

Located west of Hendry County Road 720 and near where Gunson once existed, this photo shows USSC #310 heading south with a load of sugarcane.

**943.3 COUNTY LINE** – The county line is located at the sugarcane grade crossing at the north end of another 90-degree turn. For a train heading towards Sebring, heading north at this location the train exits **Hendry County** (to the south) and enters **Glades County** (to the north).

**Hendry County** has a population of 40,000, most of them in the Clewiston area, even though the county seat is LaBelle. The county was created in 1923 and named for Captain Francis Ashbury Hendry, a captain of Confederate calvary troops during the Civil War and one of the first area settlers. Hendry had been involved with the creation of Polk and Lee Counties, as well as the town of LaBelle. Because of his ranching experience, he was known as the "Cattle King of South Florida". With more than 1150 square miles, Hendry County is the eighth largest of the 67 counties in the state, and is located southwest of Lake Okeechobee. For reference, the State of Rhode Island has only 1212 square miles.

*SCFE Sebring Subdivision Route Guide*

**Glades County** was created with about 800 square miles in 1921, one of several counties created from parts of DeSoto County. With a population of about 13,000, its county seat is Moore Haven. The county was named for the Florida Everglades. The Glades County area has always been rural, initially with scattered Indian villages. The Spanish encouraged settlement by members of several Native American tribes, escaped slaves, and pretty much anyone who would settle the land and support the local militias. The Seminole Nation also played a major role in the area. Glades County celebrates this mixed history each year with what is claimed to be "Florida's oldest recurring festival," the Chalo Nitka Festival.

Since the railroad came before most of the development in the area, housing had to be provided for the construction workers. This photo from 1921 shows the construction camp at Nine Mile, near the Hendry-Glades County Line. *Construction camp at Nine Mile – looking east. 1921.* State Archives of Florida, Florida Memory. https://www.floridamemory.com/items/show/156698.

**942.3 SHAWNEE** – This cane loader is named for the Shawnee Farms, located to the east. Shawnee Farms is one of the independent sugarcane producers in the area, and they sell their cane to U.S. Sugar. For years after World War II, the farm had their own migrant worker facility known as Shawnee Camp. It was known for housing seasonal Jamaican workers who were experts at cane cutting. The farm has also produced fruits and vegetables over the years.

This sugarcane loader is to the east and railroad records show that it is designed to handle 44 cane cars and that the track is 2187 feet long. This is a very unique facility as it is not owned by U.S. Sugar or the South Central Florida Express. It is also unique because it uses only a ramp to transfer the sugarcane from the self-dumping cane wagons to the railcars.

Approximately 50,000 carloads of sugarcane a year come off of the cane loaders on the SCFE. Which ones are active changes from year to year, based upon the age of the nearby cane and whether the land was used for a few years for vegetable farming.

**941.0 LIBERTY POINT** – Coming in to Liberty Point, the railroad makes another sharp 90-degree curve to follow the field lines, curving back to the west. Generally known as Liberty Point #2, this cane loader was reportedly capable of handling 37 cars at a time. Today, there is still a 1416-foot siding to the north (railroad-east), but the permanent cane loading complex is gone and the site is no longer on the list of loading stations.

Liberty Point was a planned community that never developed. A post office opened in 1922 but closed the following year. The actual Liberty Point is to the north where the Mayaka Cut merges with the Rim Canal near Uncle Joe's Motel and Campground. Uncle Joe's was established in 1945 using cabins from nearby Riddle Field, built as a training ground for the British Royal Air Force during World War II.

This sign marks the entrance to Uncle Joe's Campground, where Liberty Point once was.

In this area was also the Liberty Point POW Camp, built to house German prisoners of war during World War II. The camp was built here to provide labor for area sugarcane fields, with the pay being $0.80 per day. The conditions were not good, and the International Red Cross described it in March 1945 as the "...worst in all America." Liberty Point was actually an agricultural branch of Camp Blanding, the first branch camp in Florida, and opened in February 1944. The initial occupants were members of Hitler's Afrika Korps. Reportedly, the camp had the third highest number of escapees and it was closed in September 1945.

**940.8   CAPAR** – This location was shown to be a railroad station during the first several decades of the line.

**939.8   BENBOW #3** – Benbow #3 is a ramp-only cane loader to the north (railroad-east) that can handle 41 cars. The SCFE shows that the siding capacity is 2043 feet.

A 1925 railroad timetable of the Moore Haven & Clewiston Railway showed a station of Frierson at this location. In 1949, the ACL showed a spur track to the west using the name Frierson. The Frierson family had a number of interactions with the Hendry family during the 1800s and early 1900s, as both were early leaders in the area. For example, both families had members serve as postmaster in nearby LaBelle, and both operated various businesses. Captain Francis Ashbury Hendry helped create several of the area counties, and the county just south of here uses his name. Part of Frierson's family settled near here at what became known as the Frierson Farm.

**939.6   LAAHOO** – Laahoo was listed by 1923 as a station on the Moore Haven & Clewiston. Track charts of the Atlantic Coast Line still showed the station of Laahoo in 1949, but there were no side tracks.

**938.8   BENBOW #2** – This cane loader is to the north (railroad-east) and consists of an elevator with a ramp. According to U.S. Sugar, both non-self-dumping truck trailers and self-dumping tractor-hauled cane wagons use elevators with ramps.

SCFE documents show that Benbow #2 is one of the longest cane loading sidings on the railroad, measuring 3527 feet long with a stated capacity of 37 cars.

Not far west of Benbow #2, the railroad turns to the northwest.

**937.4 GRAMLIN #1** – The Gramlin #1 cane loader is to the east, and according to 1983 records of the Seaboard System Railroad, can handle 37 cars. The South Central Florida Express states that the track is 1793 feet long and that the cane loader features an elevator with a ramp.

This photo shows the concrete ramp used to help load cane at Gramlin #1. During the past decade, U.S. Sugar has modernized many of the cane loaders to increase their efficiency and to allow multiple sets of equipment to be used.

The name Gramlin apparently came from the former Gramling syrup mill at nearby Moore Haven, a mill owned by the Moore Haven Syrup Company. According to the article "Sugar Development in the Everglades of Florida" in the November 26, 1921, issue of *The Louisiana Planter and Sugar Manufacturer*, this mill was the "largest sugar mill in the Everglades at the time." The article also stated that the mill was capable of grinding "about 150 tons of cane per day" and that "it has turned out only syrup in the past" with "a capacity of 3000 gallons of syrup per day."

The name Gramling originally came from Miami Judge John C. Gramling, who oversaw the planting of 125 acres of sugarcane in 1920 for the Moore Haven Syrup Company. Gramling was at the time Secretary and Treasurer of the syrup company. Later, Gramling was a leader in the Depression-era New Deal development of racially segregated public housing in the Miami area, designed to create communities of all-white and all-black residents and to allow the expansion of downtown Miami.

**937.0  BENBOW #1** – In this area are two cane loading facilities. To the west is Benbow #1, while to the east is the Gramlin #1 cane loader. In the *Seaboard System Railroad Employee Timetable* dated October 30, 1983, the railroad actually showed both the Gramlin and the Benbow facilities at Milepost 937.0. It also showed that the Benbow facility had a capacity of 72 cars, while the SCFE states that the Benbow #1 siding is 3370 feet long. It is interesting that older topographical maps show this area as Gramlin No. 2.

The reason that there are two cane loading facilities here is that Gramlin #1 is owned by U.S. Sugar, while Benbow #1 is owned by other sugarcane growers. There is a ramp and elevator complex at Benbow #1.

*SCFE Sebring Subdivision Route Guide*

It is rare to have two cane loaders across the tracks from each other, but U.S. Sugar and other cane growers have fields in this area. To keep the accounting on the volumes and quality of cane supplied by each, there are two cane loaders here.

This is a view of the cane loader at Benbow #1. Benbow #1 is one of the few loaders on the rail system that is not owned by U.S. Sugar. Instead, it is owned by other sugarcane growers who sell their cane to the larger company.

The Benbow facility is named for the Benbow family and their Benbow Farms. Their farm was considered to be the "most successful of the larger farming operations in the Moore Haven Glades section." On November 11, 1918, the Benbows began clearing 1500 acres in the area and later produced sugarcane for area mills, as well as various kinds of stock and vegetables. They were reportedly the first to grow hogs in the area for pork production. To the northeast off Glades County Road 720 is Benbow Village, which includes approximately 30 houses.

Proceeding north towards Sebring, the railroad heads northwest until near Palmdale. The railroad crosses County Road 720 at Milepost 936.5 and then a large canal on an eleven-span bridge at Milepost 936.1. Not far north is the Wedgworth's Fertilizer Lead switch.

Some farms sell their sugarcane to U.S. Sugar. A few have their own loaders on the South Central Florida Express and move the cane by truck or tractor. This truck is on Glades County Road 720 heading towards Benbow #1.

**936.5 BLOCK LIMITS** – This location is just south of the grade crossing with Glades County Road 720. To the south is the **Clewiston Block**, which protects the many cane loaders in this area. To the north is the **Moore Haven Block**. This block protects trains as they work the Wedgworth's Fertilizer Lead, several cane loaders north of Moore Haven, and while they operate the swing bridge over the Caloosahatchee Canal.

This sign for northbound trains notes the block limits between the Clewiston and Moore Haven blocks. It is located just south of Glades County Road 720.

The Sebring Turn passes the sign marking the boundary between the Moore Haven and Clewiston blocks on the South Central Florida Express.

Wildlife is a part of the adventure with the railroads of U.S. Sugar. Here, an osprey is checking out the whistle board (a warning about an upcoming grade crossing) that is located north of Glades County Road 720 near Roumania.

**936.2 ROUMANIA** – Roumania is an early spelling of the country of Romania. Some sources state that the word relates to being a Roman territory or artifact. It was a popular name for clubs and developments in south Florida before World War II. This station was listed in 1949 but no side tracks were shown.

USSC #310 hauls a sugarcane train southward just north of Glades County Road 720 where the former station of Roumania was once located.

**935.9 WEDGWORTH'S FERTILIZER LEAD** – This 1½-mile-long lead to the west once served the Glades County Sugar Mill, located next to U.S. Highway 27. According to the *Chicago Tribune* (August 19, 1962), the Glade County Sugar Growers' Cooperative Association built a $5 million sugar mill on U.S. Highway 27 two miles south of Moore Haven as a part of the sugar processing expansion after Fidel Castro confiscated the sugar mills in Cuba in 1961. Florida had only three sugar mills until the Cuban Revolution and subsequent rise of Fidel Castro and communism, but by the early 1960s there were many plans for more to be built. The three existing mills at the time were the U.S.

Sugar Corporation mill in Clewiston, and mills in Fellsmere and Okeelanta owned by Okeelanta Sugar Refinery. The new Glades Sugar Mill was a part of the expansion to replace Cuban sugar in the U.S. market.

The Glades County Sugar Growers Cooperative was incorporated on August 18, 1961. It was essentially created when Cuban immigrants Julio C. Iglesias and Dr. Carlos Sales Humara acquired 280,000 acres in the area, planting 150,000 acres with sugarcane. Iglesias, having served as the president of Shell Oil Company in Cuba, had many business connections in the States and the Cooperative soon had about 55 members. Production started in 1962, but after years of struggles, it was eventually sold to Gulf+Western, who closed it in 1977.

This photo shows the Moore Haven Sugar House, which once stood where Wedgworth's Fertilizer facility is now located. The site has been used over the years for several sugar mills. Strickland, George Washington, b. 1904. *View of the Moore Haven Sugar House.* 20th century. State Archives of Florida, Florida Memory. https://www.floridamemory.com/items/show/17204.

Today, the mill is gone, replaced by the Wedgworth's Fertilizer facility. The fertilizer company is part of a family-owned series of companies that include sugarcane production, ranching, and custom fertilizer production. The company started in 1932, is based in Belle Glade, and is the largest custom fertilizer dealer in Florida. They custom blend more than 200,000 tons of fertilizer per year.

This photo from the South Central Florida Express mainline shows today's Wedgworth's Fertilizer facility, located where the Moore Haven Sugar House once operated.

This sign is on the Wedgworth's Fertilizer facility near Moore Haven, but Wedgworth operates a number of facilities along the South Central Florida Express.

*The Railroads of U.S. Sugar: History Through the Miles*

**935.4 COBERT'S SIDING** – At one time there was a spur track to the east, located at an elevation of 22 feet. The location was listed during the 1930s by the Atlantic Coast Line as a station, using the simple name of Cobert.

**935.0 GRAM** – This station was shown to be 16.6 miles from Harrisburg. An early station, it was still listed on the railroad's track charts in 1949, but there were no side tracks.

The name Gram likely came from Frederick Gram and his family. Gram was a trained architect from Denmark who moved to Moore Haven in 1916. He immediately built a two-story vernacular (built in the local style of ordinary houses, rather than a grand architectural style) building at 3 Avenue J that became known as the Gram Building. It was one of the first buildings to be built in the Moore Haven commercial district. Gram and his family lived upstairs and leased two retail spaces on the first floor. Here was Peder Westergaard's drug store, the first in town. The building also housed the Langford Meat Market, the post office, a shoe repair business, and a restaurant. Gram later designed and constructed many of Moore Haven's commercial and residential structures. The Gram Building still stands within sight of the Caloosahatchee Canal Swing Bridge and is part of the Moore Haven Downtown Historic District, listed on the National Register of Historic Places,

**934.5 CASPUR** – Caspur was an early station on the railroad, but was gone by the 1940s. Some sources claim that the name came from Caloosahatchee Spur, and was a simplified spelling of the original name.

**934.3 CALOOSAHATCHEE CANAL SWING BRIDGE** – This is also known as the Moore Haven Railroad Swing Bridge, and is a popular railfan photography location, using several small parks around the Moore Haven Marina and the U.S. Highway 27 bridge. From the south end of the bridge, there are 10 concrete spans and then a short deck plate girder span. On the north end is a 130-foot through plate girder turn span.

The Caloosahatchee Canal Bridge is one of the favorite locations to photograph the South Central Florida Express. One of the reasons is that there are a number of locations to take these photos. This photo is from the small park near the Moore Haven marina and shows USSC #310 heading towards Clewiston with a trainload of sugarcane.

The bridge crosses the Caloosahatchee Canal, a five-mile-long canal built in 1881 to connect Lake Okeechobee to Lake Hicpochee. According to the canal's navigation information, the bridge has a closed vertical clearance of five feet, with 50 feet of vertical clearance in the center span when it is open.

The bridge is automated and remains open unless rail traffic is approaching. When a train arrives, the crew observes the canal for any boat traffic, and then, when the river route is clear, turns the bridge using controls on either end of the bridge.

The Caloosahatchee Canal turn span can only be described as slow. It takes several minutes to turn and then a few more minutes for the lift rail assembly to align. This photo shows the lift rail assembly before the rails lower to allow a train to cross.

## SCFE Sebring Subdivision Route Guide

The Caloosahatchee Canal Swing Bridge is opened by each train crew using the boxes on each end of the bridge. Here, the conductor of Cane #2 is opening the bridge on a sunny April day.

This photo of a northbound Sebring Turn as it crosses the Caloosahatchee Canal Swing Bridge is taken from the east side of the bridge from along the side of the canal.

A unique location to photograph the Caloosahatchee Canal Swing Bridge is from the U.S. Highway 27 bridge that crosses the canal just west of the railroad. Fortunately, a pedestrian walkway is perfectly located to take photos. This is Cane #2 heading south towards Clewiston.

The bridge is at Mile 78.3 of the Okeechobee Waterway. The Waterway, operated and maintained by the U.S. Army Corps of Engineers, starts at the Atlantic Intracoastal Waterway at St. Lucie Inlet, then heads west using the St. Lucie River to the St. Lucie Canal at South Fork. It then heads west to Lake Okeechobee at Port Mayaca. The route then crosses Lake Okeechobee and enters the Rim Canal at Clewiston, heads northwest to Moore Haven, and then enters the Caloosahatchee Canal. The canal heads west to Lake Hicpochee, and then the Okeechobee Waterway uses the Caloosahatchee River to the Gulf of Mexico near Fort Myers. The route saves 165 nautical miles when compared with sailing around the southern tip of Florida. However, most larger ships cannot fit through the system.

SCFE Sebring Subdivision Route Guide

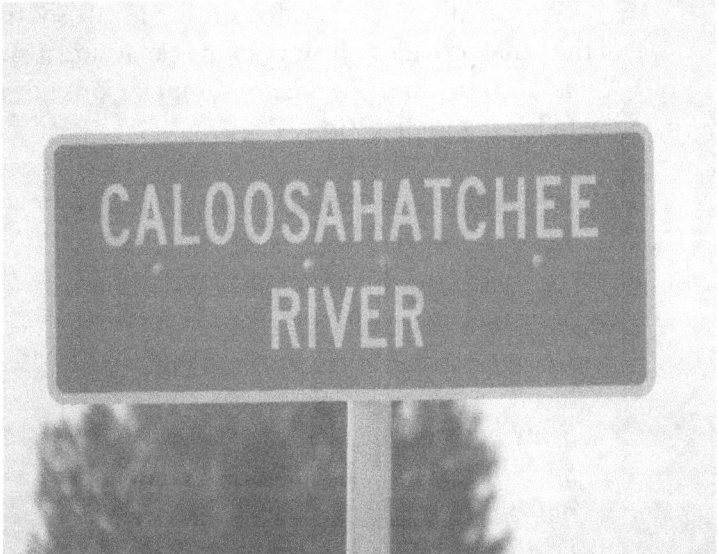

This sign identifies the Caloosahatchee River, which is used as part of the Okeechobee Waterway.

The name Caloosahatchee is used to describe the Indian culture that existed before about 1750 in southwest Florida. The culture featured a series of connected villages with mounds, generally obtaining their food by fishing. They also built a number of canals and causeways to connect their villages. Many of their communities were along this river near today's Fort Myers.

Lake Okeechobee, Florida's Inland Sea, is to the east, just beyond the Moore Haven Lock & Dam and Herbert Hoover Dike. Okeechobee means "big water" in the Seminole Indian language. The lake is the second largest natural fresh water lake in the Lower 48. Covering 730 square miles, or about half the size of the state of Rhode Island, the lake only averages nine feet in depth.

A historical marker located on the north shore of the canal provides a history of the canal and area. *"Lone Cypress" and Everglades Drainage* provides the following information.

> Shortly after Florida became a state in 1845, its leaders began to consider draining the swampy areas of south Florida to create prime farmland as an inducement to settlement. In 1850 Florida received title to all swamp and overflowed lands within its borders, but the young state did not have the funds to undertake drainage. Finally in 1881 the state convinced a wealthy northerner, Hamilton Disston, to drain the Everglades in return for half the acreage he could reclaim. One of his projects was to improve the Caloosahatchee River and connect it to Lake Okeechobee by a canal which enters the lake near here. A lone cypress tree standing at the entrance of this canal served as a navigational aid for boatmen using the new waterways. Early in the 20th century the town of Moore Haven, named for its founder James A. Moore, grew up around the "Lone Cypress" and canal entrance. By this time the state itself had assumed responsibility for drainage, and in 1917-18 it constructed a lock at the canal entrance. In recent years state and federal government have cooperated on the related problems of drainage, flood control, and navigation. As a result, the Caloosahatchee Canal and River have been continually maintained and improved.

**933.8 MOORE HAVEN WEST** – There is a short siding to the west, known as Moore Haven Siding by the Atlantic Coast Line. It is about 1200 feet long and is often used to hold fertilizer cars for area customers until needed. The Moore Haven railroad depot once stood in this area at Milepost 934.1, near the north switch according to a number of photos. Photos from the 1920s show a freshly painted wooden station at Moore Haven, with a light-colored wainscoat and dark paint at window level. It was a single-story building with a bay window for the agent. By 1982, the station had been modified and was painted all white. Photos show that the freight section was on the south end, and that the passenger end had been expanded. There was also a train order semaphore to alert train crews to any need to stop for new instructions.

This milepost sign stands near the south switch of the short siding at Moore Haven.

The siding at Moore Haven is often stuffed full of covered hoppers, generally carloads of fertilizer awaiting unloading at once of several railroad customers.

This photo from the late 1910s shows the Atlantic Coast Line Railroad (ACL) station at Moore Haven, soon after the railroad opened to this community. *Moore Haven railroad depot.* 1917 (circa). State Archives of Florida, Florida Memory. https://www.floridamemory.com/items/show/335406.

By the early 1980s, the station was closed and starting to deteriorate. However, this photo from July 1982 shows the building still with a white coat of paint and a set of train order signals. *Railroad depot in Moore Haven.* 1982. State Archives of Florida, Florida Memory. https://www.floridamemory.com/items/show/323582.

## Moore Haven

Moore Haven was actually a junction town between the Atlantic Coast Line and the Moore Haven & Clewiston Railroad for many years. When the ACL arrived here, it created a connection with steamboats serving the south Florida area via Lake Okeechobee and the Caloosahatchee Canal. However, to develop the land on the south side of Lake Okeechobee, several land owners and developers proposed to clear the land and build the railroad. The June 18, 1921, issue of *Railway Review* stated that "Fourteen miles have been completed of the Moore Haven & Clewiston R.R., which is being built from Moore Haven to Clewiston Fla., a distance of seventeen miles according to A. C. Clewis, of Tampa, Fla., vice-president of the company. The route is through rich trucking lands, and the railway is carrying produce at the rate of twenty carloads a day to the Atlantic Coast Line R.R. at Moore Haven."

This sign welcomes visitors to Moore Haven, Florida.

This water tower stands over downtown Moore Haven, and is located a block south of the Glades County Courthouse building.

Moore Haven is today a small town with a population of about 1600. It features a few convenience stores and gas stations, banks, a junior high school, marinas, and several retirement communities. However, when it was founded by James A. Moore, it was designed to be a manufacturing and industrial town, being located on the west side of Lake Okeechobee at the junction with the Caloosahatchee Canal. Its quick growth and location on the west side of a large lake temporarily earned it the title of "Little Chicago."

Early development included sugar production, and the Moore Haven Sugar Corporation was incorporated on March 17, 1921. According to the May 1921 issue of *Sugar*, to form the company, the Moore Haven Syrup Company and its 450 acres and several syrup making plants was acquired. Reports from several sources in the early 1920s state that the Moore Haven Sugar Corporation had arranged for 3000 acres of land contracts for the production of sugarcane, and that "an investment of $1,000,000 will be made in sugar production operations and that a sugar mill will be built." The Moore Haven Sugar Mill was reportedly the first mill built in the upper Everglades. In 1922, the mill produced some brown (raw) sugar, but soon went bankrupt due to expenses and unreliable cane crops.

To support these plans, the "Moore Haven & Clewiston Railroad will build immediately a two-mile siding for the sugar interest." The reports went on to state that "there are two other large sugar projects in process of development in the Moore Haven section." While some of the development did happen, the Great Miami Hurricane of 1926 changed things as much of the area was flooded and many buildings and houses were destroyed. Not long after rebuilding began, the 1928 Okeechobee Hurricane again destroyed much of the area, ending the grand future of "Little Chicago."

Without the planned industry, Moore Haven has relied upon area farming, including cattle, fruit and vegetables. Being the county seat of Glades County has also played an important role. Later, tourism played a big role with area fishing becoming popular. As a part of this, Moore Haven is now home to the Annual Chalo Nitka Festival, a Seminole term for "Big Bass." The event includes one of the largest fishing tournaments in the area, one that promotes the area's famous Black Bass.

The Glades County Courthouse stands in downtown Moore Haven, about ten blocks south of the tracks.

### SCFE Sebring Subdivision Route Guide

**932.7** **MOORE HAVEN #1** – This cane loader is to the east and serves the sugarcane fields just north of Moore Haven. It has the longest cane-loading siding on the Sebring Subdivision – 3741 feet long. The loader features an elevator and a ramp.

**931.9** **NEW HALL** – This area was once the community of Newhall. The town was created in the late 1910s by Marian Newhall O'Brien, the first mayor of Moore Haven, and her husband John O'Brien. The town was designed to be for "Englishmen" who stood out with their accents and customs. Many white workers lived here until black workers were brought in to work the fields, causing several years of violence between the two groups over wages and jobs. While peace eventually came, most of the white workers left and the town of Newhall died. Maps from 1932 still list the community, but it was gone by 1936. Nothing remains today but a few houses and the area is covered in sugarcane.

The railroad had a station to serve the community. The Atlantic Coast line still used the name New Hall for this location in 1949, but there were no side tracks at that time.

**931.8** **FLORIDA HIGHWAY 78** – Highway 78 once extended from the Gulf Coast of Florida to the northern tip of Lake Okeechobee. However, as other roads were built, it has been broken down into several disconnected sections. This part runs around the west side of Lake Okeechobee from U.S. Highway 27 west of Moore Haven to a connection with U.S. Highway 98 alongside the lake south of the City of Okeechobee.

**929.8 GRAHAM DAIRY FARM SPUR** – This short spur to the west is used for cattle feed, and is known as TGC (Graham Farms) Lead by the railroad. Graham Dairies Incorporated started operations in 1932 in northwest Dade County. The company was one of the most successful dairies in Florida, and was the last dairy to operate in Dade County. However, it was forced to move in the early 1950s as land development accelerated in the county. The firm moved to Moore Haven, where the dairy operates a herd of approximately 3000 dairy cows, producing 5.3 million gallons of milk per year.

This sign along U.S. Highway 27 points the way to the Graham Dairy Farm Spur.

The company actually has a direct connection to the South Florida sugar industry. Ernest "Cap" Graham moved to South Florida during the 1920s to manage some of the sugarcane operations for

## SCFE Sebring Subdivision Route Guide

the Pennsylvania Sugar Company. When the firm ceased operations, Graham acquired the land, livestock, and machinery of the company. In January of 1932, he opened Graham Dairy Incorporated, which became one of the largest dairies in Florida. When the firm moved to here, it created what would become the Graham Companies to develop the Dade County property as Miami Lakes.

The legacy of Cap Graham goes beyond his dairy and community. His three sons all became well-known. William Graham became the president of the company. Phil Graham served as publisher of *The Washington Post*. Finally, Bob Graham became the governor of Florida and also held the office of U.S. Senator. The firm also operates the Graham Pecan Farm and Graham Angus Farm, both in Georgia. They are also in the hospitality business, owning Shula's Hotel and Golf Club in Miami Lakes.

928.6   **MOORE HAVEN #3** – Located to the west of the tracks, this sugarcane loader handles the harvest from the most northwestern fields in the Clewiston area. This loader generally works north to south, with cars shoved south as they are loaded. This is complicated by a major sugarcane field road that crosses the tracks just north of the cane loader. The tracks north of this road can hold 21 cane cars, and the SCFE shows the siding as being 3517 feet long. Like most cane loaders in the area, it features an elevator with a ramp.

Some early timetables show this area to be Muckway, a small farming community in the swamps. For a number of years, the Atlantic Coast Line had a Muckway station near here. Land use changes here. It is generally the northwest end of sugarcane fields, and grazing, timber and citrus groves start to take over as you head north.

**927.5 BLOCK LIMITS** – This may be one of the least known block limit locations on the railroad because it is located away from roads and communities. At this location, **Moore Haven Block** is to the south, while **Boar Hammock Block** stretches northward to Palmdale. Boar Hammock is a local name for several clusters of tree-covered elevated areas just northeast of the U.S. Highway 27 grade crossing at Milepost 924.1.

A hammock is a regional term found in the southeastern part of the United States. It relates to an elevated area where a different ecosystem exists, generally hardwood trees in a swampy region. In this part of Florida, a few feet of additional elevation allows trees to grow that cannot survive in the adjacent wetlands. The name Boar Hammock likely came from the wild pigs found in the area as the term boar is used for male swine, but is also used for the adult male badger and raccoon.

Today, Boar Hammock is owned by Lykes Brothers, Inc., and much of it is leased to the Glades County Fish and Game Club for hunting, fishing, camping, and other outdoor activities.

**927.4 MUCKWAY** – Muckway is an interesting name. Many think that it relates to the mucky ground in the area. However, Muckway is also the last name of several families in south Florida. The station was located at 32 feet of elevation, 9.8 miles south of Harrisburg. There was a siding on the west side of the mainline between Mileposts 927.3 and 927.7.

*SCFE Sebring Subdivision Route Guide*

**924.1 U.S. HIGHWAY 27** – The railroad again crosses U.S. Highway 27, which stretches between Fort Wayne, Indiana, and Miami, Florida. The four-lane highway follows the South Central Florida Express from here to Sebring.

**921.3 LYKES BROTHERS POND** – To the west is a small wet-weather pond named for the Lykes Brothers, once owners of much of this land. To the east is a large sand pit, known as the Cemex Palmdale Sand Mine. Cemex is a global leader in the building materials industry and operates sand and gravel facilities worldwide.

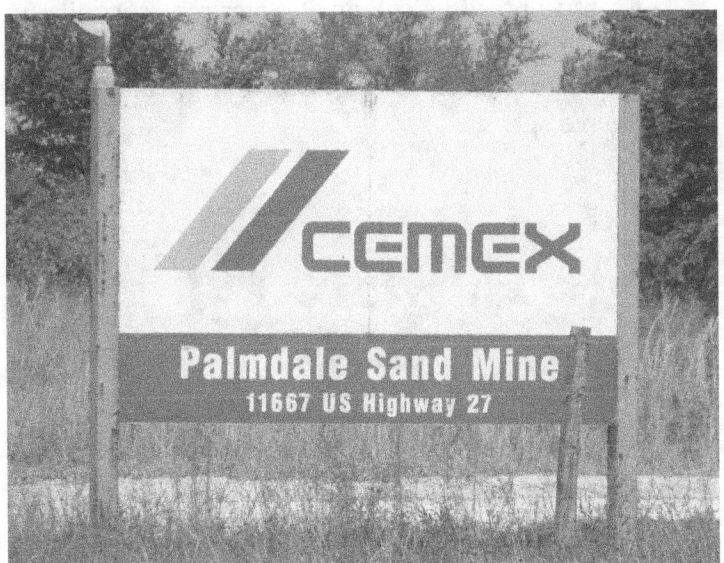

This CEMEX sign along U.S. Highway 27 marks the location of Lykes Brothers Pond.

To the east can also be seen the Herbert Hoover Dike. This dike was built in the 1930s, and expanded in the 1960s, as a flood levee around Lake Okeechobee. The Herbert Hoover Dike closely circles the lake everywhere except here, where the dike turns inland and parallels Fisheating Creek for several miles, leaving it the only remaining free-flowing tributary of Lake Okeechobee. The Dike also features a walking and biking trail, part of a 1000-mile-long Florida National Scenic Trail.

**920.5 GATORAMA** – To the east is Gatorama, self-proclaimed to be the "world's largest alligator farm" and the "home of the famous Alligator Hatching Festival." Opened in 1957, Gatorama was one of Florida's first alligator roadside attractions. In addition to the alligators, Gatorama has the largest captive breeding colony of American crocodiles in North America. This crocodile stock was brought to Gatorama in 1968 before they were an endangered species.

Gatorama is an opportunity to safely view alligators and American crocodiles, while still monitoring railroad action on the Sebring Subdivision.

Over the past several decades, the park has gone through the ownership of several generations of the Thielen family, and improvements and expansion have come with every change. Gatorama has been featured for years on various television shows, so the name and tourist stop is known around the world.

**918.6 HARRISBURG** – Approaching Harrisburg, look for the Palmdale Lookout Tower, an old fire tower still standing on the property of the Florida Forestry Service facility. At one time, Florida had far more than 100 observation towers, designed to watch for wildfires. Florida is known as "The Lightning Capital of the U.S." and has over 100 lightning storms that start wildfires every year. The towers have been closed due to the use of satellites and other technologies, but many of the towers still stand as monuments to the practice.

Harrisburg can be seen for miles due to this old fire tower.

Harrisburg is generally described as a ghost town, and is located at an elevation of 30 feet above sea level. Harrisburg came about because it was a railroad construction camp. Reportedly, the name Harrisburg came from the Harris Track-Laying Machine used to construct the railroad. The Harris Track-Laying Machine, originally designed by George Francis Harris in 1880, was a very popular track construction machine. The machine used a "railroad on a railroad" system where rail carts on the machine moved supplies to the front of the device. By 1887, one-fifth of all railway tracks in the United States were laid by the machine, according to *Appletons' Cyclopaedia of American Biography* (1901).

Harrisburg was once a water stop on the line, and in 1949 there was a 250-ton coaling station. This was also the actual junction with the Immokalee Branch, which ran as far south as Everglades City, Florida. Old maps show that there was a full wye here, but today there is only a simple switch to a short spur track, the remains of the branch. This track is now used by Lee Wood Timber, and also to unload rock for area levee projects. The spur holds about 22 railcars.

For trains heading towards Sebring, the line curves so trains are heading almost due north. During the late 1980s, CSX still showed a 24.4-mile-long Keri Spur heading south from Palmdale (actually Harrisburg). This spur track still served industry tracks at Goodno, Sears, and Keri.

**918.4 FISHEATING CREEK BRIDGE** – This bridge was built for two tracks, but the east track is gone. Look for the old piles still visible in the water. Fisheating Creek forms in wetlands west of Lake Placid, flows south to near here, and then turns east to flow into Lake Okeechobee. Much of this area is part of the Fisheating Creek Wildlife Management Area, which includes cypress swamps and hardwood forests. There is also a full-service campground. A bit of the wildlife often reported includes alligators, deer, wild boar, turkey, and black bear.

The bridge across Fisheating Creek provides an excellent photo opportunity from the shoulder of U.S. Highway 27. (Highway 27 is a busy road, so please use caution.) The Sebring Turn is heading north across part of the bridge on a sunny January day.

This sign marks the entrance to the Fisheating Creek Wildlife Management Area.

This two-track timber bridge is located at the grade crossing for the Fisheating Creek Wildlife Management Area, not far south of where the Palmdale train station once stood.

According to information from the Wildlife Management Area, the name Fisheating Creek comes from the Creek phrase *Thlothlopopka-hatchee* which means "the creek where fish are eaten." Mounds, ditches and earthworks along the creek show that the Belle Glade people were here between 1000 and 500 BC. The creek was a trade route between the ocean and Lake Okeechobee, and also a source of food. There are also indications that corn was grown along its banks, making the area one of the earliest agriculture communities in the pre-Columbian Eastern United States. Wooden platforms, bundles of human remains, and numerous wooden wildlife carvings have also been found. The area was still occupied by Native Americans when the Europeans arrived in the 16th and 17th centuries.

Fort Center, initially known as Battery Center, was built near here in the late 1830s as a part of the Second Seminole War and used to reduce raiding by parties from area villages. The fort was named for Lieutenant J. P. Center, adjutant of the 6th U.S. Infantry, who was killed in the battle of Okechobee, Florida, on December 25, 1837. The fort was again used during the Third Seminole War in 1855. During the early 1900s, the last of the Indian families along Fisheating Creek were replaced by sugar cultivation and cattle ranching. The Lykes family began buying the land as a private preserve, preventing further development, but they did operate a campground and a canoeing concession at Palmdale. After they closed their operation in 1989, the State of Florida fought to acquire the land and eventually got "an 18,272 acre corridor along the creek which became the Fisheating Creek Wildlife Management Area (WMA)."

South of this bridge is another long timber-span bridge. This one spans an overflow of Fisheating Creek.

917.7 **BLOCK LIMITS** – This is the north end of the **Boar Hammock Block** and the south end of the **Palmdale Block**. The Palmdale Block is named for the important train station and community that once was here. The Palmdale Block, almost twenty miles long, is mostly used to move trains to and from Childs and Sebring. However, there are several short tracks and potential rail shippers in the territory.

917.5 **PALMDALE** – Most trains of the South Central Florida Express pass right through Palmdale without stopping. However, there is some industry at Palmdale. To the west of the tracks is a bark mulch bagging plant, operated by The Scotts Company. While there is no track into this facility, the railroad has a 3250-foot siding on the east side of the mainline, with a long house track (765 feet) off the north end of the siding. This track is one of several in the area that have been used to unload rock for area levee projects. The siding stretches between Mileposts 917.7 and 918.3.

During April 2021, USSC #503 pulls Cane #2 northward through Palmdale.

The tracks at Palmdale can sometimes be hard to see through the brush, but this small building marks the location.

This sign for Scotts marks the major road crossing at Palmdale.

From 1951 until 1998, Palmdale was the home of Tom Gaskins' Cypress Knee Museum, which displayed hundreds of cypress knees and featured a ¾-mile cypress knee walk through the adjacent swamp. Gaskins had displayed some of his collection at the 1939-40 New York World's Fair and he got the Lykes Brothers to allow him to build a museum on their property. For years, Gaskins' signs lined the highway, but the museum closed in 1998 when Tom Gaskins died and the Lykes Brothers ended the property agreement. The property was soon sold to the State of Florida and is now managed by the Florida Fish and Wildlife Conservation Commission.

The Lykes Ranch has a number of facilities across the region, and this sign at Palmdale marks the way to the Sapp Pens complex.

According to several sources, "there may be no town or place in Florida that is further from the interstate highways than Palmdale, Florida. It is in the middle of the huge agricultural land holdings of Lykes Brothers, one of Florida's oldest family dynasties." There have been recent attempts to get the county to change zoning codes so an old general store can reopen because of the distance needed to travel to get to a store.

### The Atlantic Coast Line at Palmdale

While Palmdale is a small, unincorporated rural community, it once was an important station on this rail line. Palmdale was first settled as a part of the Florida Fruit Farm, which later became the Palmdale Land Company. Promoted as a winter resort for fishing and hunting, the town featured the

Palmdale Hotel. However, it was already a ghost of its past when the railroad arrived in 1916.

When the ACL arrived, they made Palmdale a passenger and freight station, building not only a depot but several side tracks. Stock pens were erected to ship cattle. Several section houses were also built to house track maintenance workers. A water tower and coaling tower were built nearby to support the locomotives working through the junction.

The depot was located on the east side of the mainline near the north end of the siding. While the station, at an elevation of 51 feet, was a simple one-story wooden building, it was listed as a Register Station for decades, and it housed current bulletin books for all train crews. This was done because several local mixed trains (freight and passenger service) were based here until the 1950s. Palmdale served as the junction station with the Atlantic Coast Line's Immokalee Branch, part of the Tampa District. Later the branch was renamed the Immokalee Subdivision of the Seaboard Coast Line.

The track arrangement at Palmdale was rather complex. A second track (now the siding) began not far north of the station and went as far south as the junction at Harrisburg. To allow trains to serve the depot, and for the tracks to also serve as a siding, there were several crossovers between the two lines. At Harrisburg, the track to the east went to Moore Haven while the west track went south as the Immokalee Branch.

*SCFE Sebring Subdivision Route Guide*

Palmdale was an important station along the line due to the nearby junction with the Immokalee Branch. Like most stations along the line, the depot was a one-story wooden structure with a passenger waiting room on one end, and a freight room on the other. *SCL depot – Palmdale, Florida.* 1979. State Archives of Florida, Florida Memory. https://www.floridamemory.com/items/show/139162.

### Immokalee Branch

The Immokalee Branch was opened by the Atlantic Coast Line Railroad (ACL) to Immokalee in 1921. It was later extended to serve the fruit and vegetable businesses around Everglades City by building some track and buying the Deep Lake Railroad on December 8, 1928. The Deep Lake Railroad was built in 1913 by Walter Langford and John Roach to move grapefruit from their farm to Everglades, later Everglades City. The railroad was 14 miles long and built to a gauge of three feet, narrow by industry standards. The availability of water transportation at Everglades made their groves valuable, but also attracted interest in their railroad. The railroad and the grapefruit groves were sold to Barron Collier in 1921. Collier added timber to the shipments, mainly pine and cypress to be cut at his sawmill in Everglades City.

The railroad also connected with the Lee Cypress Railroad at Copeland, which closed in the late 1940s. In 1949, ACL mixed train No. 453 left Palmdale at 9:25am after southbound passenger train No. 175 departed at 8:36am. Coming back north, mixed train No. 452 arrived at 5:30pm to connect with the 7:30pm No. 176. These mixed trains were not always on time as they handled both passengers and freight, and could be delayed by extensive switching during the harvest seasons.

The success of the Immokalee Branch didn't last much longer. The south 22 miles of the line between Everglades City and Sunniland were abandoned in 1957 as trucks began to take over the transportation of fruits and vegetables. The movement of fruits and vegetables remained heavy out of Immokalee into the 1960s and 1970s, with some days seeing more than two train loads of refrigerator cars shipped out. However, the business went away quickly and the rest of the line was abandoned and pulled up by the mid-1980s.

**911.6 DETJENS DAIRY ROAD** – Detjens Dairy bought land in the area during the 1940s, thus the name of the road. In 1949, track charts of the Atlantic Coast Line showed that there were once two spur tracks to the east. Today, this road also carries the name of Glades County Road 17.

This area is also noted as being the southernmost extent of the Lake Wales Ridge, which the railroad follows to Sebring. Heading north, the railroad and U.S. Highway 27 start to separate, but are generally within a mile or so of each other.

**911.2** **COUNTY LINE** – The county line is pretty easy to find, as the railroad crosses over a small stream that has been channelized. To the north is **Highlands County**, while to the south is **Glades County**.

**Glades County** was created in 1921, another county created from parts of DeSoto County. With a population of about 13,000, its county seat is Moore Haven. It was named for the Florida Everglades. The Glades County area has always been rural, initially with scattered Indian villages. The Spanish encouraged settlement by members of several Native American tribes, escaped slaves, and pretty much anyone who would settle the land and support the local militias. The Seminole nation also played a major role in the area. Glades County celebrates this mixed history each year with what is claimed to be "Florida's oldest recurring festival", the Chalo Nitka Festival, in Moore Haven.

**Highlands County** was also formed from part of DeSoto County in 1921 and named for its higher terrain when compared with surrounding areas. Its county seat is Sebring and the county has a population of about 100,000. The county advertises itself as having "gently rolling hills, orange groves and charming small towns" that "make this a relaxing country getaway." Reportedly, in 2012 the county had the fifth-oldest population in America. It is also the fourteenth largest county in the state with about 1016 square miles.

**908.8 VENUS** – Venus, an unincorporated community, is located where Highland County Road 731 crosses the tracks. A post office was here 1900-1907. While there are no SCFE tracks except for the mainline here today, Venus was a flag stop for passenger train Nos. 175/176 in 1949. In 1923, the Atlantic Coast Line Railroad had petitioned to the Railroad Commission of the State of Florida to move the railroad agency from Venus to Lake Stearns (Lake Placid). It was denied, and a new agency was opened at Lake Stearns. However, the Venus agency was later closed due to no local business.

In 1949, the ACL reported that it had a siding on the west side of the mainline. There was a crossover between the siding and mainline at the depot, located just north of the main grade crossing. Trains heading north have been climbing grades of 0.4% to 0.5% to reach the 117-foot elevation at Venus.

Reports indicate that in the late 1920s and early 1930s, the Crawford family operated a lumber business at Venus, Florida. Today, a greenhouse and an LP Gas dealer are in the area. Other major area activities include hunting and fishing. The small community of Old Venus, a cluster of a few houses and a church, is about a mile to the west.

Also to the west a few miles is the home of The Venus Project, a utopian project that took the name of the former railroad stop. Information about the organization states that it "proposes an alternative vision of what the future can be if we apply what we already know in order to achieve a sustainable new world civilization. It calls for a straightforward redesign of our culture in which the age-old inadequacies of war, poverty, hunger, debt and unnecessary human suffering are viewed not only as avoidable, but as totally unacceptable. Anything less will result in a continuation of the same catalog of problems inherent in today's world." Their website shows a futuristic ringed community in the middle of water and woods. Among the group's public stances are that wealth is criminal and cannabis is the "King Of All Plants."

The railroad has a small curve south of Venus. Heading north, the tracks will be straight until a small curve near Archbold. Citrus groves start to become a common sight.

**905.3 JAMES B. HENDRIE/H&H DAIRY LEAD** – Look for the short spur track to the east at the Blueberry Hill Road grade crossing. This track was once used to deliver feed for area dairy facilities.

Signs like this used to be found at many grade crossings, but this one at the Blueberry Hill Road grade crossing is a rare reminder of those days.

This part of the state is a mix of citrus groves, grazing, logged woods, and undeveloped South Florida woodlands. To the east about a mile is U.S. Highway 27, allowing a few scattered farms and businesses to exist in the area.

At Milepost 906, the large Costa Farms facility is to the west. This facility was earlier owned and operated by Delray Plants. Delray Plants was founded in 1968 by Jacob Koornneef and by 2016 was the 13th largest grower in the United States. It had 3,868,116 square feet of environmentally controlled greenhouses, 119 acres of shade greenhouses, and 20 acres of field production. The firm grew almost 150 different varieties of plants from ferns to grasses, to lilies and orchids, and just about everything in between. The firm sold potted foliage crops, flowering potted plants, and some vegetable plants to home improvement chains, mass merchandisers, supermarket chains, wholesale florists, and independent garden centers.

An announcement was made on March 10, 2017, that Costa Farms had acquired Delray Plants. Costa was founded in 1961, and by 2016, was the second largest grower in the United States. It had 15,071,760 square feet of environmentally controlled greenhouses, 747 acres of shade greenhouses, and 1,484 acres of field production. Based in Miami, the firm has thriving indoor and bedding plant divisions, and handles young-plant production and merchandising. The firm has operations in Florida, North and South Carolina, the Dominican Republic, and the Far East.

## SCFE Sebring Subdivision Route Guide

Commerical nursuries are common across much of southern Florida, and the large Costa Farms facility is west of the tracks at the switch to the H&H Dairy Lead.

**902.9  HICORIA** – For many years, Hicoria (a Latinized version of the word Hickory) was a major station on the line, handling a number of passengers and a large volume of freight. However, the station was no longer listed by the railroad by 1949. There are several conflicting histories about Hicoria, however, John Kunkel Small is credited with the name. During the winter of 1918-19, Small explored the area documenting the vegetation, although logging and cattle had already begun to alter it. Small found a great deal of Scrub Hickory in the area, then known as Hicoria floridana, now Cary floridana. Small suggested the Hicoria name to honor the small tree, and the railroad replaced the original name of Red Hills with Hicoria.

According to the National Register of Historic Places, Hicoria Siding was "immediately north of where Old State Road 8 now crosses the railroad line." The first settler was reportedly James Carlton, who homesteaded the area in 1908 after the U.S.

government opened the area to homesteaders. He and two sons started clearing land and planting orange trees.

By 1917, much of the area land was surveyed and divided as the town of Hicoria by the Atlantic Land and Improvement Company, a subsidiary of the Atlantic Coast Line Railroad. The first industry was the turpentine operation of the Consolidated Land Company (Consolidated Naval Stores), started in the early 1920s and employing several hundred people. In 1928, the W. C. Sherman Lumber Company moved its Sherman (Okeechobee) mill to Hicoria and the company began to cut timber off land belonging to the Consolidated Land Company. Between the mill, the woods crew, and the logging railroad, hundreds were employed and Hicoria boomed to a population of more than 600.

The sawmill suffered with the Great Depression of the 1930s, spending long periods of time closed until a lumber order was received. It closed completely after it burned in 1935. With the closure, just seasonal turpentine work remained, which also soon closed. Hicoria was essentially abandoned over the next several years. A post office was in service at Hicoria from 1915 to 1943. Just a few foundations in the brush are still visible today. One of the mill's stationary steam engines is on display at the Lake Placid Historical Society's Depot Museum.

In 1949, the Atlantic Coast Line still showed a short spur track on the east side of the mainline. The elevation at Hicoria was shown to be 154 feet, and the track crossed a number of low hills, creating a rolling profile.

*SCFE Sebring Subdivision Route Guide*

Heading north, County Road 17, Old State Route 8, follows the tracks to Lake Placid.

**900.5 ARCHBOLD** – There is not a siding or spur track here, and Archbold was not listed as a station by the Atlantic Coast Line, but it certainly is a point of interest. To the east is the Archbold Biological Station, the primary division of Archbold Expeditions, and a 5000-acre ecosystem research facility created in 1941 by Richard Archbold. Archbold was actually conducting research in New Guinea but fled to Florida as New Guinea was impacted by the Japanese during World War II. This is one of several Archbold facilities, protecting 19 federally listed threatened species, 13 endemic plant species, and an extensive area of Florida scrub, a highly threatened ecosystem.

This sign marks the Old State Route 8 entrance to the Archbold Biological Station.

Visitors are welcome and they can tour displays about the facility, hike a nature trail, and even picnic. Educational programs are also offered at the facility. On July 20, 2007, this facility was added to the National Register of Historic Places. Nearby are the organization's ranch, the MacArthur Agro-ecology Research Center, and the Archbold Reserve, an effort to restore worked land.

**899.0  GP LEAD** – South of Florida Highway 70 is a long spur track to the east. This track was once known as the St. Regis Lead, but then became the GP Spur after Georgia Pacific bought the mill on the line, and then GP Lead by the South Central Florida Express. The GP mill is now closed. However, there are two shippers on the line. First is Howard Fertilizer & Chemical, which started business in Orlando in 1932. In 2012, the company opened this agricultural fertilizer blending facility, which promotes their rail service as a feature of the plant.

Signs like this on the former Georgia Pacific facility certainly make the plant look closed.

This water tower carries the name of Howard Fertilizer & Chemical, a rail shipper on the GP Lead south of Lake Placid.

Howard Fertilizer & Chemical is one of a number of rail shippers located on the South Central Florida Express. Located on the GP Lead, the plant is served by the Sebring Turn.

At the end of the line is The Andersons Plant Nutrient facility. There are actually three offices here: Ag Retail, Industrial, and Florida Turf Distribution. The farm center "specializes in liquid fertilizer production for citrus fertigation and nutritional applications. In addition, the plant produces pasture grade fertilizer that is applied in surrounding beef cattle and dairy operations." This facility handles both dry and wet chemicals and products.

To the west is Lake Annie, a 90-acre sinkhole lake acquired by the Archbold Expeditions in 1983. It is reportedly at an elevation of 111 feet above mean sea level, and is the "southernmost of a series of sinkhole lakes extending 200 miles north along and beyond the Lake Wales Ridge." There is a research buoy on the lake used to monitor the water quality as part of a long-term study.

**898.3   CHILDS** – This is the location of what was known as Childs Station, named after Lake Childs, the original name of what is now known as Lake Placid. Most maps show Childs at the grade crossing with Florida Highway 70 at Milepost 898.75, but the Childs Station actually stood here. There has been a 2590-foot siding (2887 feet in 1937) to the west for years. During the 1930s, a small sawmill operated here. Later, the siding was used for fertilizer for area citrus farmers. Much of the fertilizer was actually made from human waste, a process used at many waste treatment plants.

Childs was once the home of a number of section houses, used to provide housing for track workers who maintained the railroad in this area. The region is noted for sandy rolling hills, orange groves, and a growing sugarcane industry. The higher elevation makes the area drier, but with a number of small lakes. The track climbs a number of grades in the area, with an elevation of 133 feet at the north siding switch shown in 1949, and 123 feet at the south siding switch.

During the 1930s, a small sawmill operated at Childs. Reportedly it was owned by Mr. Warren, a resident of Fort Meade, Florida. The operation was about as basic as could be, with no lights or toilets, and only one water pump for the entire complex. Workers reportedly built their own homes from old lumber. Wolcott, Marion Post, photographer. *Sawmill. Childs, Florida*. Childs, Florida, Highlands County, Jan. 1939. Photograph. https://www.loc.gov/item/2017799789/.

In early 2018, improvements were made at Childs to construct a new 4000-foot siding using steel ties. Additionally, a new sugarcane loading facility was built consisting of a mechanical elevator and truck ramp. This new cane loader was built to serve sugarcane growers in the Lake Placid area who previously were forced to truck their cane to market.

According to U.S. Sugar, this facility can use both non-self-dumping truck trailers and self-dumping tractor-hauled cane wagons. The cane is dumped into a large bin and then moved up the elevator to be poured into the railroad cane cars. These cane elevators are essentially large incline conveyors custom designed to handle cane that has been cut into short lengths. With Old State Route 8 immediately to the east, the operations of this cane loader can easily be viewed.

The Childs cane loader was built to handle trucks that once hauled sugarcane long distances. Trucks such as this now move the came to this nearby loader during the harvest season.

The sugarcane loader at Childs uses a modern design with a permanent ramp and a large elevator to load the cane into railcars.

For the type of loader located at Childs, trucks drive up onto the ramp. There, a small crane tilts the cane onto the elevator, which raises and then dumps the cane into the railcars.

**898.0  BLOCK LIMITS** – Located just south of the Childs cane loader are a pair of large signs that mark the limits of the Palmdale and Sebring blocks. The **Palmdale Block** is to the south while the **Sebring Block** is to the north. The Sebring Block is named for the city at the north end of the railroad and it protects much of the switching at Childs, at several shippers near Sebring, and the interchange movements between the South Central Florida Express and CSX.

The new cane loader at Childs is located just north of the Palmdale-Sebring Block Limits sign. This area is also used to park cane trucks at night and when they are not being used. Fueling of the trucks also take place here.

The Palmdale-Sebring Block Sign can easily be found just south of the Childs cane loader, located next to the Milepost 898 sign.

**896.0 VIEW** – In 1949, there was a spur track to the east that used the name View. In this area, the railroad is almost thirty feet higher than Lake Placid, located just to the west. As the name implies, the views can be great.

**893.3 DASHER ROAD BRIDGE** – The railroad crosses this small road using a six-span timber trestle that measures 62 feet long. Through this area, the railroad is often on a high fill between lakes. To the east is Lake McCoy, while to the west is Lake Pearl. Both are small, 50-acre round lakes surrounded by houses. Just west of Lake Pearl is Lake Sirena, while to the east of Lake McCoy is the larger Lake Huntley.

This area is full of lakes. Coming from the south, the railroad passes Lake Placid to the west before arriving at Dasher Road. To the east and just out of sight is Grassy Lake. Leaving the City of Lake Placid, the railroad passes Lake June in Winter.

**892.0 LAKE PLACID** – Welcome to "The Caladium Capital of the World" where 98 percent of the world's caladium bulbs come from, or the "Town of Murals" and its more than 40 murals painted on buildings throughout the town. Lake Placid is a small town of about 2000 residents, but its many murals document its interesting history, one that made it *Readers Digest's* "2012 Most Interesting Town."

Besides the various nicknames, Lake Placid has had a number of other names, including Weco (post office 1919) and Lake Stearns (post office 1919-1927). This area was used for raising cattle by the Creeks, and later by the Seminoles. After a series of wars, European settlers began to move in. Reportedly, the first of these settlers was Thomas Knight, who arrived here in 1869, bringing with him citrus trees, starting the citrus revolution in the area. The area lake became known as Lake Stearns, and the small community took the same name.

Signs like this welcome visitors to Lake Placid, Florida.

In addition to ranching and citrus production, the area woods soon attracted another industry, the turpentine and pine resin industry. The large number of yellow pine trees in the area was perfect for this, and soon most pine trees in the area carried the "cat face" scar, a cut that allowed sap to flow down through the cut and into a container for collection, allowing the production of pine gum. This gum was distilled into turpentine, and to make pitch to fill holes on ships and coat the rigging for extended wear. This attracted the Consolidated Naval Stores Company, a major user of the products. Its president, Walter Coachman, was also Chairman of the Board of the Consolidated Land Company, which began developing area real estate.

In the early 1900s, the community took on the name of Weco, also spelled Wicco and Wico. The railroad arrived in 1916. Several years later, a post office opened. The nearby lake, known today as Lake Placid, also went through several names, being called Lake Buck, Lake June, and then Lake Stearns. The last name had once been used for the community that became Weco, and it again became the name in 1924 when promoters A. H. DeVane, E. C. Stuart, and E. Morrow arrived and began another round of citrus and land promotions, officially chartering Lake Stearns on December 1, 1925.

Another change took place when a new promoter arrived in 1927. In that year, Dr. Melvil Dewey, the inventor of the Dewey Decimal System and the founder of the Lake Placid Club in Lake Placid, New York, arrived on the scene. Wanting to create a Florida resort to partner with his New York resort, Dewey opened another Lake Placid Club here and also petitioned the government of Lake Stearns to change its name to Lake Placid. With the promise of more development and the tourist trade, the Town of Lake Stearns became the Town of Lake Placid on June 6, 1927.

The New York Lake Placid Association immediately began to promote this new Lake Placid as a winter resort. Members of the association soon built two hotels for tourists and worked with the Atlantic Coast Line to make it easy for guests to arrive, bringing Pullman sleepers and regular coaches from New York City and other northeastern cities. This effort also resulted in a new train station at Lake Placid. However, the Great Depression and then World War II halted most of the effort, but the community again began to see the tourist trade in the late 1940s.

Fortunately, the late 1930s also saw a new industry develop in Lake Placid – caladiums. Captain

Theodore W. Webb discovered some caladiums while visiting Tampa. He brought some bulbs home and planted them, and then began to sell them, creating a worldwide market worth millions of dollars. Caladiums, known as Elephant Ear, Heart of Jesus, and Angel Wings, originally came from the tropical Amazon River Valley. From these single plants there are now more than 1000 named versions cultivated by growers. The annual Caladium Festival is held in late July.

Today, Lake Placid, located at 170 feet above sea level, is again a tourist community, many of whom are "snow birds" who come for the winter. Fishing is also an attraction with 27 freshwater lakes in the area. The town is also known for its "Happiness Tower" that was built in 1960. The tower, originally known as the Placid Tower, is 270 feet tall and is made of about 90,000 concrete blocks from Texas. It was the tallest concrete-block structure in the world at the time of its construction. It featured a restaurant, a lookout deck, and "Florida's highest pay phone." The tower didn't become the hoped-for attraction, so it was renamed and remarketed as the "Happiness Tower" in the late 1960s, but was also called "The Tower of Peace." It closed in 1982 due to unpaid taxes and reopened in 1986. It closed sometime in the early 2000s (no one knows for sure, it was just open less and less until it didn't open again) and today stands as a big landmark for Lake Placid.

Lake Placid is also the home of the American Clown Museum and School, and the city claims to have more clowns per capita than any other town in the world.

## The Railroad at Lake Placid

Railroads took a serious step towards the Lake Placid area when in 1912, the Atlantic Coast Line Railroad Company started buying land here, as part of a plan to build into south Florida. Construction began at Haines City, east of Tampa, and the line reached Sebring on June 12, 1912. In 1916, further construction began and the railroad passed through Lake Placid (known as Weco by the railroad when it arrived). A wooden depot was built here, but was replaced by a bigger station in 1926. The old station was sold to a nearby citrus packing house. Unfortunately, this original station burned in 1954.

This photo shows the track-side of the former Atlantic Coast Line depot at Lake Placid. Today, the building is used by the Lake Placid Historical Society.

This view shows the south and east sides of the depot at Lake Placid.

Besides the station, the railroad also built a number of section houses at Lake Placid. These houses were here through at least the late 1940s and were the home of track forces that maintained the railroad. There was also a large water tank that provided water for these houses as well as steam locomotives that operated along the line.

The new station remained active for many years, but the route was never a mainline for the ACL, so passenger service never reached the level of their other Florida routes. Passenger service ended in the mid-1950s and the station closed on July 15, 1975. The railroad then leased the building to several companies, but finally sold it to the Lake Placid Historical Society in 1982, which opened it as the Depot Museum. The museum features information about the area and displays include a caboose (Seaboard Air Line 20932, later Seaboard Coast Line 0932), the 1920s Lake Placid jail, and a portable steam engine used at several area sawmills.

SCFE Sebring Subdivision Route Guide

Seaboard Air Line caboose #20932 is located next to the Lake Placid depot.

Nearby is the Railroad Depot Mural. Completed in 1995 and a part of the Lake Placid Mural Society project, the mural includes the sound of a steam locomotive and lit crossing gates.

During January of 1993, the station was added to the National Register of Historic Places. The application described the station as "a one-story, masonry vernacular building constructed in 1926. The basically rectangular structure was designed to provide passenger and baggage facilities for regular railroad traffic passing through the city of Lake Placid. The building is covered by a gable roof and is distinguished by a loggia (roofed open gallery) on three elevations. Although a number of changes have been made to the building, the depot still retains many of its original and distinctive features." The report further states that the "depot is 80 feet long by 25 feet wide, not including the 10 foot wide loggia found on three of its elevations. The building has four major rooms. Because of the policy of racial segregation which existed when the station was constructed, there are two waiting rooms (one white and one black), a ticket agent's room, and a baggage room. There were also originally four rest rooms."

There is a short 407-foot siding just north of the station. Downtown Lake Placid is to the east of the station, while Devane Park and Park Drive which circles it, are to the west. Devane Park is a nice urban park which features a gazebo, gardens, and lots of benches. Heading north, the railroad starts to pass through a chain of communities, most with stores, restaurants and hotels, and then open farmland.

This marker on the Lake Placid depot notes its place on the National Register of Historic Places.

*SCFE Sebring Subdivision Route Guide*

USSC #407 pulls the Sebring Turn northward pass the Lake Placid depot on a sunny spring day.

**891.2 PARKSON** – Parkson was once located just north of an overhead highway bridge. The new bridge at this location is today used by Highlands County Road 17. In 1949, there was a spur track to the east. Today, the area is the site of the Town of Lake Placid Maintenance Barn.

**890.8 U.S. HIGHWAY 27 BRIDGE** – This four-span beam bridge crosses the four-lane U.S. Highway 27. The highway connects Fort Wayne, Indiana, with Miami, Florida. It generally operates through the center of the state and closely follows the railroad from South Bay to Sebring. That is Lake June in Winter to the west.

**885.2 JOSEPHINE CREEK BRIDGE** – Josephine Creek flows out of Lake Josephine about five miles to the west, and flows into Lake Istokpoga less than a mile to the east. Lake Josephine consists of three small bodies of open water, connected by narrow channels to form one 1300-acre lake. Wolf Creek and Jackson Creek flow into the lake, and waters exit through a concrete dam built in 1965. The railroad crosses Josephine Creek on a long 25-span timber trestle, shown as being 230 feet long in 1949.

Heading north, trains are coming down a long, steady grade as the line has climbed over the Lake Wales Ridge. This ridge is more than 200 feet higher than the surrounding areas, and has become the location of a chain of communities wishing to locate above the swampy lands on either side of the ridge. Also known as the Mid-Florida Ridge, it is a sandy ridge that runs north-south for about 150 miles. It is named after the City of Lake Wales, which is located in the middle of the ridge. The ridge's highest elevation is at Sugarloaf Mountain (312 feet). The ridge dates back about two million years when most of Florida was underwater, except for a chain of islands that later became the Lake Wales Ridge.

**884.6  ISTOKPOGA** – This was a regular station location for the Atlantic Coast Line and Seaboard Coast Line, located at an elevation of 60 feet. A siding of about one-half mile long was located to the east of the mainline, and it was a regular stop for passenger train Nos. 175/176 in 1949. There are no side tracks here today. Currently, this area is just a few open pastures and fields. The name of the station comes from the nearby Lake Istokpoga, the fifth largest lake in the state of Florida and located to the east. While the lake is approximately 5 miles wide and 10 miles long, the average depth of the lake is only 4 feet. There are a number of public boat ramps and docks, as well as fishing camps, on the lake. The name Istokpoga is reported to be Seminole and means "a lake where someone was killed in the water." The legend says that the name came about when "a group of Seminole Indians attempted to cross the lake and were bogged in the mire and swallowed by whirlpools."

Lake Istokpoga is known by bird watchers as a good place to observe the snail kite. The snail kite is related to eagles and hawks, and the males are very colorful. They have dark blue-gray plumage with darker flight feathers, with red legs. The female is more brown with yellow or orange legs. South America, especially Brazil, is the primary home of the snail kite, but this part of Florida also has them, their only regular site in the United States. Why the name snail kite? Their favorite food is the large apple snail.

Not far north of Istokpoga, the railroad turns to the northwest and heads toward Lake Jackson at Sebring, Florida.

**881.8 U.S. HIGHWAY 98** – The South Central Florida Express crosses U.S. Highway 98 at grade. Large gates and flashers protect this crossing. U.S. Highway 98 was established in 1933 and is today almost 1000 miles long, connecting Palm Beach, Florida, with Meadville, Mississippi. It was originally much shorter, being a route between Pensacola and Apalachicola, Florida.

**881.3 THE SPANCRETE GROUP** – Located north of U.S. Highway 98 and to the west of the tracks are several large industries, none of which are shippers on the railroad. Next to the railroad is the former Florida Precast Industries facility, acquired in

March 2007 by Spancrete. Spancrete manufactures precast and prestressed concrete products for all sorts of projects. To the south is Jahna Concrete, based in Avon Park, Florida. This is their Spring Lake (Sebring) cement plant.

**881.0 BLOCK LIMITS** – North of this location to Sebring, trains operate under yard limit conditions. To the south is the **Sebring Block**. This block covers seventeen miles of track to near Childs.

**879.1 DE SOTO CITY INTERCHANGE** – Squeezed between DeSoto City Road (Milepost 878.64) and County Road 17S (Milepost 879.74) is the DeSoto City Interchange Yard, the primary interchange location between CSX and the South Central Florida Express. This mile-long yard has two tracks to the west, with the first track generally being used for SCFE traffic to CSX.

The old Atlantic Coast Line DeSoto station was at Milepost 879.8, and was a flag stop for passenger train Nos. 175/176 in 1949. There was a simple spur track on the west side of the mainline, and the elevation was shown to be 110 feet above sea level. Not far to the south can be seen an old boxcar in the woods, there since at least 1997. Sometimes old railroad equipment is not even worth the time and money it would take to drag it out of the woods.

**877.9 SALLY SIDING** – Sally Siding is relatively new, installed in 2008 and built just more than ½ mile long. The siding was named for Sally Cochran, former vice-president of the South Central Florida Express, who retired in 2009 with more than 35 years in the shortline railroad industry. The siding

## SCFE Sebring Subdivision Route Guide

is located on the east side of the mainline and is often used for interchange with CSX. The siding is surrounded by citrus groves.

At the south switch at Milepost 878.1 is a spur track to the south that serves Amerikan, a subsidiary of Myers Industries Inc. Amerikan was incorporated in 2004 and manufactures blow-molded plastic nursery and horticultural containers – yes, those black plastic containers that nursery plants come in. There is a great deal of business for these products in Florida.

**877.1 HIGHLANDS AVENUE GRADE CROSSING** – For trains heading towards Sebring, the railroad turns to the north and crosses the highway in the middle of citrus groves. However, this area is being overcome by subdivisions, so how long citrus groves will remain here is anybody's guess. Just to the south is Jim's Import Auto Salvage, acres of wrecked cars from around the world.

Heading north, the railroad is on the west side of Highlands Avenue almost all the way to CSX near the Sebring Amtrak station.

**876.4 KENILWORTH BOULEVARD** – This is an important through street in Sebring, and also serves as Florida Highway 17 to the east. Just north of the street and on the west side of the railroad is the Highlands County Fair Association complex, which includes a convention center, baseball field, football field and track, and of course, the fairgrounds.

**875.9 SEBRING** – The South Central Florida Express crosses Highlands Avenue as the road curves to the northwest and becomes Sebring Parkway. The

SCFE then connects to CSX not far south of the Sebring Amtrak station, located at an elevation of about 140 feet.

Sebring is a town of more than 10,000 residents in Highlands County, Florida. Sebring was built on the eastern shore of Lake Jackson, founded by pottery manufacturer George E. Sebring. This is actually the second Sebring that George E. Sebring created, the other is in Ohio where the pottery manufacturing began. The Florida Sebring was created in 1912, chartered in 1913, and became the county seat of Highlands County in 1921 when the county was created.

The author's introduction to the railroads of U.S. Sugar was this photo taken from Amtrak #1 – the *Sunset Limited* – back in 1996. South Central Florida Express locomotives 9016, 9017, and 9018 were parked at the Sebring junction with CSX.

George Sebring heavily marketed his Florida community as an escape from winter, both as a permanent home and as an excellent vacation spot. The arrival of the railroad through town made it boom. According to the National Register of Historic Places, "In January, 1925, a cross-state train dubbed the *Orange Blossom Special* made its initial journey through Sebring, which immediately proclaimed itself the 'Orange Blossom City.'

Sebring was designed and built in an interesting fashion. It is laid out in a circle, giving it the nickname "The City on the Circle". This original downtown area, located just a few blocks west of the rail junction, is now recognized as the Sebring Downtown Historic District. Sebring is probably best known today as the home of the 12 Hours of Sebring, a major sports car endurance race. The track was built in 1950 on a retired airbase and is used for numerous events.

### The Atlantic Coast Line at Sebring

The Atlantic Coast Line (ACL) was the first railroad to build to Sebring, Florida. The railroad opened their 42-mile-long Haines City to Sebring line in 1912. The line was then extended southward toward Palmdale in 1916. The line was further extended to Moore Haven, where steamboat connections across Lake Okeechobee and along several canals provided connections to West Palm Beach, and even Miami.

Initially, the ACL had their Sebring station north of downtown at the northwest end of Pine Street, at the end of the Haines City-Sebring tracks. When the line on to Moore Haven was built, this station was located on a spur track at the end of a wye track. Today, this area is the Sebring City Water Plant, but the grade for the wye is still clearly visible.

In 1917, a new ACL stucco combination freight and passenger station was built on the extended mainline around the north side of Sebring, located between Pomegranate Avenue and Ridgewood Drive. The station was on the south side of the tracks along Eucalyptus. Nearby were several section houses for track maintenance forces.

In 1967, the Atlantic Coast Line and Seaboard Air Line merged. A few years after the merger, the ACL tracks through Sebring were abandoned and all trains began to use the Seaboard Air Line route. In 1999, an effort was made to save the ACL depot, which was then owned by Sebring and Highlands County. The former ACL grade was being used for the new Sebring Parkway and the station had to be moved. Unfortunately, the station could not be saved and was eventually torn down.

**The Seaboard Air Line at Sebring**

Sebring is the western outside connection for the South Central Florida Express. Located at Milepost 875.9, it connects with the CSX line to Miami and south Florida. This line was built by the Florida Western & Northern Railroad (FW&N), controlled by the Seaboard Air Line Railroad. Construction started in the 1920s at Coleman, northeast of Tampa, Florida. The line headed south-southeast to Auburndale, Sebring, and West Palm Beach as a part of a plan by Seaboard president S. Davies Warfield to enter the South Florida market and end the monopoly of the Florida East Coast Railway. The line was extended a few years later when the Seaboard-All Florida Railway built on to Miami, Homestead and Florida City.

The line remained a major route through the mergers that created the Seaboard Coast Line Railroad, and then CSX. During the late 1980s, the

## SCFE Sebring Subdivision Route Guide

route from Coleman to Auburndale was abandoned as alternative routes existed, but the line from Auburndale to Miami continues as a major freight and passenger route. Once the Miami Subdivision, for CSX this is the Auburndale Subdivision. Amtrak's *Silver Meteor* and *Silver Star* trains use the line daily as a part of their Atlantic Coast Service.

The South Central Florida Express connection heads north onto the CSX line. Heading south, the SCFE crosses Highland Avenue, also known as the Sebring Parkway, and follows it southeast out of town. The CSX line makes a major turn from heading south-southeast to due east.

Just north of the junction between CSX and South Central Florida Express is the Sebring Amtrak station, known as SBG by Amtrak. The station is reportedly one of six stations erected when the FW&N built through central Florida in 1924. Known by many as the "Old Seaboard Air Line Depot", the building was added to the National Register of Historic Places on March 16, 1990. The National Register of Historic Places describes the station as a "one story masonry vernacular building...the station has such railroad station features as a passenger waiting room, baggage room, and the ticket agent's office. The agent's office is centrally located and incorporates a projecting track side bay. Other distinguishing features include a projecting roof supported by brackets and the shed roofed platform running parallel with the track."

Near the junction between the South Central Florida Express and CSX at Sebring is the Amtrak station, originally the Seaboard Air Line depot.

## SCFE Sebring and Fort Pierce Subdivisions Clewiston (FL) to Fort Pierce (FL)

Because most South Central Florida Express (SCFE) trains moving sugarcane from the loaders west of Clewiston operate to the USSC Clewiston Yard to deliver the cane to the sugar mill, the SCFE Sebring Subdivision actually goes as far east as Ritta. There, the track becomes the Fort Pierce Subdivision, which includes a few miles of ACL track and the track that is leased from the Florida East Coast Railway. Trains heading towards the USSC Clewiston Yard are heading south, both from Sebring and from Fort Pierce.

The railroad east from Clewiston and then north to Fort Pierce was built by the predecessors of two railroads, but actually by a number of different companies at different times. The track from Clewiston east to Lake Harbor was built by the Atlantic Coast Line Railroad (ACL) in the name of the Moore Haven & Clewiston Railroad, while the track on north to Fort Pierce was built by the Florida East Coast Railway.

The Atlantic Coast Line Railroad played a major role in two of the lines operated by the South Central Florida Express. These are the line from Sebring to Clewiston and on to Lake Harbor (Sebring Subdivision), and the line to the sugar mill at Okeelanta (Okeelanta Subdivision east of Clewiston). The track west of Clewiston was built by the Moore Haven & Clewiston Railway, which was leased by the Atlantic Coast Line in 1925. About this time, the Florida East Coast (FEC) had reached nearby Belle Glade, Florida. The two railroads watched each other for several years, and then each extended their line to Lake Harbor in 1929.

By 1944, the ACL completely bought out the Moore Haven & Clewiston Railway, creating the Haines City Branch between Haines City and Clewiston, and on to Lake Harbor.

On August 18, 1960, the stockholders of the Atlantic Coast Line Railroad and its direct competitor, the Seaboard Air Line Railroad, voted to merge. In 1963, the Interstate Commerce Commission (ICC) approved the merger, but it wasn't until July 1, 1967, that a series of court cases and further ICC rulings finally made it official, creating the Seaboard Coast Line. This was just the start of a series of changes, as a merger with the Louisville & Nashville Railroad and Clinchfield Railroad on January 1, 1983, created the Seaboard System Railroad.

The Seaboard System Railroad and the Chessie System Railroad were eventually controlled by the CSX Corporation on November 1, 1980. They were fully merged into CSX Transportation in December 1986. However, as the railroad got larger, this small rail operation on the north edge of the Everglades became less and less valuable to the railroad. Looking to raise capital and rid itself of low volume rail lines, the track from Sebring to Lake Harbor was sold to the Brandywine Valley Railroad, a Lukens Steel Company subsidiary, on June 2, 1990. The line was then sold on September 17, 1994, to U.S. Sugar, who set the line up as the South Central Florida Express.

## Florida East Coast K-Branch (Fort Pierce-Lake Harbor Branch)

The South Central Florida Express (SCFE) route from Lake Harbor northeast to Fort Pierce is the Florida East Coast Railway Fort Pierce-Lake Harbor Branch (also known as the K-Branch). The line still belongs to the Florida East Coast (FEC), but is leased to the SCFE west of Milepost 15.0, with additional haulage rights on into the

## Sebring and Fort Pierce Subdivisions

rail yard at Fort Pierce, with the lease agreement reached on March 2, 1998.

The line involved is actually the result of two different construction projects. The first project was the Kissimmee Valley Line which started near New Smyrna (later New Smyrna Beach) and built south to Okeechobee and beyond, reaching Belle Glade by 1923. When the Atlantic Coast Line built east from Clewiston, the FEC extended their line to a junction at Lake Harbor in 1929. Both lines were built to support the growing sugar industry.

On August 4, 1928, the Florida East Coast Railway Company filed an application to build 9.5 miles of track "from a point at or near Belleglade-Chosen to a point on the west bank of the Miami Canal at Lake Harbor." The stated purpose of the track was "to transport sugar cane to two factories of the Southern Sugar Company and to provide transportation for the further extension of cane growing to supply these factories." One detail was that Southern Sugar provided a free right-of-way for the line. Other details in the Interstate Commerce Commission report were that the line was laid with 70-pound rail, its maximum grade was 0.3 per cent, and the maximum curve was 3 degrees. Approval for the new line's construction was given on September 1, 1928, and construction started almost immediately.

The second part of the FEC line was the Fort Pierce Cutoff, built from Fort Pierce to the old Kissimmee Valley Line at Mantola, and opened on March 8, 1947. This line was built to provide a shorter route to the Belle Glade and Lake Harbor area, and to avoid the hundred empty miles of railroad north of Mantola. Soon, the line north of Mantola was abandoned or sold.

The concept of the original K-Line was to open miles of Florida real estate, land that was given to companies and individuals that turned swamps into useable lands. For railroads, Florida would give as many as 8000 acres for every mile of railroad built. The FEC would eventually claim more than 2 million acres through this process, making land development a major part of the company. The Kissimmee Valley Line was designed to provide a route west of the mainline of the Florida East Coast and through the swamps surrounding Lake Okeechobee, with the goal of developing the land and then hauling the business that the development created. On November 7, 1910, the Kissimmee Valley Construction Company and FEC forces began construction southward, with grading starting at Maytown on February 25, 1911. The line was built to the south, passing not far east of Orlando, and reaching Okeechobee in early 1915.

The construction of the railroad resulted in the company owning lots of land, but with little value. To sell the land, the FEC established a number of real estate companies such as the FEC Land and Industrial Development Department, the Model Land Company, the Perrine Grant Land Company, and the Chuluota Land Company. However, sales were disappointing, and even the agricultural business that did locate along the line did not provide the business hoped for. Seeing the boom starting around Lake Okeechobee in the 1920s, the railroad decided to build on south. A part of this plan was to build south from Lake Harbor alongside the Miami Canal to reach the Miami market. While the lower end of the line was never built, the line reached Belle Glade and then Lake Harbor in the 1920s, just in time for the Depression of the 1930s.

During the 1930s and 1940s, it became clear that the northern end of the line was too far north for reliable agricultural development, and the only major business on this part of the line was timber. Towns didn't develop, and the last passenger service over the line, a mixed freight and passenger train, operated in 1941. With most of the freight being on the south end of the line, a new shortcut was built from the division point of Fort Pierce to Mantola, south of Okeechobee.

Opened on March 8, 1947, this provided a shorter route to the growing sugarcane industries and vegetable farms in the Everglades Agricultural Area along Lake Okeechobee, and allowed the abandonment of more than 150 miles of railroad later that year.

At that time, the line north of Mantola was being used by the Peavy Wilson Lumber Company. The firm started in 1916 when A. J. Peavy started logging in Natchitoches, Sabine, and Vernon Parishes in Louisiana. He partnered with an experienced lumber mill manager, R. J. Wilson, and created the mill town of Peason (PEAvy and wilSON) and the Peavey Wilson Lumber Company. Their Peason mill was known as the largest pine lumber operation west of the Mississippi River. The company ran out of timber and closed their mill in 1935, and moved to Holopaw, Milepost 71 on the original Kissimmee Valley Line. The company ended its operations in 1952 and the line was then removed.

The line to Belle Galde and Lake Harbor saw a steady growth in business, from just a few thousand cars of produce a year in the 1920s, to almost 10,000 a year by the end of the 1940s, and 15,000 by the mid-1950s. Much of this growth was initially winter vegetables, but shipments related to the sugar industry also became significant. The Fort Pierce Cut-off actually produced little new business for the railroad, but it did create enormous savings for the company. Today, most of the shipments of winter vegetables are gone and the South Central Florida Express mainly hauls products related to the sugar industry.

The Florida East Coast Railway started as several small railroads, organized as the Jacksonville, St. Augustine & Indian River Railway Company in 1893. On September 7, 1895, the property became the Florida East Coast Railway

Company. The growth of the railroad is due to Henry Morrison Flagler, described as an American tycoon, real estate promoter, railroad developer and John D. Rockefeller's partner in Standard Oil. The railroad often partnered with land and hotel companies to develop the territory where it operated. The tracks went as far south as Key West in 1912, but they were cut back after the line was heavily damaged by the Labor Day Hurricane of 1935. Unfortunately, the railroad had declared bankruptcy and was in receivership by September 1931, so the Key West line was not rebuilt.

Today, according to the company, the FEC "is a Class II regional railroad that owns all of the 351-mile mainline track from Jacksonville, FL, down to Miami. It is the exclusive rail provider for Port Miami, Port Everglades and Port of Palm Beach." For those wanting to learn more about the Florida East Coast, check out the book *Speedway to Sunshine – The Story of the Florida East Coast Railway* by Seth Bramson.

### Passenger Service on the Kissimmee Valley Line

The Atlantic Coast Line never operated scheduled passenger trains between Clewiston and Lake Harbor, but records show that a few unscheduled trains did operate over this route. For example, on December 2, 1936, the Florida East Coast delivered a special passenger train to the ACL at Lake Harbor. The train was taken to Clewiston for the night, and then on to Jacksonville, Florida, on December 3rd.

However, the Florida East Coast did operate scheduled passenger service north of Lake Harbor on the Kissimmee Valley Line. In January 1926, the Florida East Coast published a schedule with a pair of daily New Smyrna-Okeechobee passenger trains. These trains provided local service over that part of the line, northbound No. 132 in the morning, and southbound No. 131 in the late afternoon and evening. South of Okeechobee, daily No. 134 departed Canal Point at 5:00am, arriving at Okeechobee thirty minutes before the 7:00am departure of No. 132. Southbound, No. 133 departed Okeechobee at 10:00pm, thirty minutes after the arrival of No. 131. The train finished up at Canal Point at 11:30pm.

The FEC line was completed to a junction with the Atlantic Coast Line at Lake Harbor in 1929, and it wasn't long until the passenger service was also extended. By 1934 during the Great Depression, the Florida East Coast was serving the entire New Smyrna-Lake Harbor route using a pair of daily mixed trains operating on a somewhat unfriendly schedule. Northbound No. 132 departed Lake Harbor at 6:00pm and made an almost hour stop at Okeechobee before departing at 10:00pm. The train finally arrived at New Smyrna at 3:10am, where a several hour wait was required to connect to the *Havana Special* to Jacksonville. Southbound No. 131 was a bit more friendly as it was scheduled to depart New Smyrna at 12:50pm, shortly after the arrival of the *Daylight Express*. The mixed train was scheduled to arrive at Okeechobee at 6:30pm, and then depart at 7:45pm. Arrival back at Lake Harbor was shown to be at 11:30pm. This schedule continued for almost a decade with only minor changes until it was ended by 1942, making the line "freight service only."

The Fort Pierce Cut-Off, also known as the Glades Cut-Off, opened on March 8, 1947. No scheduled passenger train service ever operated on this line.

*The Railroads of U.S. Sugar: History Through the Miles*

# SCFE Sebring and Fort Pierce Route Guide Clewiston (FL) to Fort Pierce (FL)

**947.9 CLEWISTON** – Clewiston is the home of U.S. Sugar Corporation and its railroads. Information about Clewiston is found in the *Welcome to Clewiston* chapter on Page 41 of this book. Information about the South Central Florida Express rail lines west of Clewiston can be found in the *SCFE Sebring Subdivision Route Guide – Clewiston (FL) to Sebring (FL)* chapter on Page 135.

For trains heading east from Clewiston, the line actually heads south for a short distance before turning east. For the railroad, trains heading in this direction are heading railroad-south for a short distance since the line's mileposts are the distance from Richmond, Virginia. Once at Lake Harbor, the South Central Florida Express changes from former Atlantic Coast Line Railroad track to track built by the Florida East Coast Railway. Therefore, trains heading towards Fort Pierce are considered to be heading railroad-north.

**948.7 CLEWISTON WYE** – This wye was used to turn the steam locomotives off of ACL passenger trains. It was also used by freight trains to reach the docks on Lake Okeechobee. Today, the only industry left on the port line is Andersons Plant Nutrient, and most of the port line is abandoned. The wye area is used as a material storage yard by the railroad.

*The Railroads of U.S. Sugar: History Through the Miles*

Steam locomotive #148 pulls a special passenger train for invited guests on Friday, January 28, 2022. The location is at the Davidson Road grade crossing, just south of the Clewiston Wye.

**949.5   SUGAR JUNCTION** – This wye connects the mainline with the large sugar mill to the west, the base of employee-owned United States Sugar Corporation (USSC). This is also a junction with the Clewiston Mainline Division of the private railroads of U.S. Sugar. The private lines head south, with the Flaghole Mainline then turning west to reach Southern Gardens Citrus west of Airglades Airport, and the Clewiston Mainline to South Bay and Bryant heading further south before turning east.

Just south of the wye is a new switch and crossover that allows freight trains to enter the USSC sugar lines and head west to reach the Southern Gardens Citrus facility at the west end of the new line to the west of Flaghole Road.

**951.0   BLOCK LIMITS** – This is the south end of the yard limits from Clewiston. From here south to Lake Harbor, the railroad is included in the **Keela Block**.

The name Keela comes from the junction where the Okeelanta Branch breaks off from the mainline and turns south.

**951.4 SOUTH CLEWISTON** – This is the switch to a spur into the Weekley Brothers Industrial Park, located just west of Evercane Road, County Road 835. This industrial park has several large warehouse buildings and is the home of BioNitrogen, a company that converts biomass into urea fertilizer. This facility can be viewed from nearby Evercane Road, also known as County Road 835.

During the mid-1970s, the Florida Department of Transportation turned a number of rural state highways over to various counties. Parts of Florida Highways 832 and 846 were transferred to Hendry County, which created Hendry County Road 835.

**951.5 RITTA** – Located just west of Evercane Road, County Road 835, the switch at Ritta leads to a U.S. Sugar Corporation line that turns due east. The line heads east about two miles to serve a single cane loading facility. About a mile further east is the community of Ritta Village, identified in several sources as being worker housing owned by U.S. Sugar. It is also a base for farm equipment used in fields in the area.

In 1951, the Interstate Commerce Commission produced a report that included a description of the Ritta Sugar Line. "Switching at Ritta is performed on a 2-mile loading track having a hoist track and a storage track each with 20 car capacity. This is the largest loading track on the Coast Line. Such switching is especially complicated, as there is no track at Ritta to move the engine around the cars." A description of today's Ritta Sugar Line is included here.

**0.0  SOUTH CLEWISTON/RITTA SWITCH** – This short private cane line is unique in that it is only accessed from the former Atlantic Coast Line just east of Clewiston, and that it only serves a single cane loading facility. The cane loader at Ritta is also unique in that it has a short siding, requiring a cane train to stay at the loader to switch cars during loading.

**0.1  EVERCANE ROAD** – Evercane Road, also known as County Road 835, heads south from the Clewiston area into the sugarcane fields to the south. It, along with County Road 846, form a route south and west to Immokalee, Florida.

**1.1  COUNTY LINE** – The county line is located not far west of the only sugarcane loading facility on this line. To the west is **Hendry County,** and to the east is **Palm Beach County.**

Hendry County has a population of 40,000, most of them in Clewiston, even though the county seat is LaBelle. The county was created in 1923 and named for Captain Francis Ashbury Hendry, a captain of Confederate calvary troops during the Civil War and one of the first area settlers. Hendry had been involved with the creation of Polk and Lee Counties, as well as the town of LaBelle. Because of his ranching experience, he was known as the "Cattle King of South Florida".

**Palm Beach County** was established in 1909 from part of Dade County. It was named for one of the oldest and largest communities in the area – Palm Beach. The county has had its borders changed several times, the latest in 1963, but it is still the second-largest county in Florida with 1969 square miles of territory. The county has a population of about 1,400,000 people, making it the third-most populous county in Florida. It is also Florida's wealthiest. Palm Beach County also leads the State of Florida in agricultural productivity, the second largest industry in the county. The largest is real estate.

1.7 **RITTA #1** – Located on the north side of the line, this cane loader siding holds about seven cars on either side of the loader. There is a cane field road crossing just west of the siding at Milepost 1.5.

The design of this cane loading facility is the most common used by U.S. Sugar operations. It has a ramp that allows non-self-dumping truck trailers and self-dumping tractor-hauled cane wagons to unload their cane into a bin. From there, an elevator is used to raise the cane and to load it into railcars.

2.1 **END OF TRACK** – The track ends here, with enough track lead to work the cane loader. About a mile further east is the community of Ritta Village, identified in several sources as being worker housing owned by U.S. Sugar and once being known as Ritta Plantation Village. Photos indicate that this employee village was built about 1937. It is also a base for farm equipment used in fields in the area. You can drive to Ritta Village today, on what can only be described as the roughest paved road the author has ever driven.

The sign for Ritta Village Road marks what might be the roughest paved road anywhere.

This area west of the Miami Canal is the Ritta Drainage District, established on July 1, 1945, to build and maintain canals for drainage and irrigation. The name Ritta comes from an island at the southern end of Lake Okeechobee, located several miles north of here. A small town developed there, along with the Ritta Hotel. Everything was destroyed by the 1928 Hurricane.

During February 1939, Marion Post Wolcott photographed the sugarcane harvest of U.S. Sugar for the Farm Security Administration. The location of this photo was not identified, but it does show a migrant worker's home and a company commissary at one of approximately a dozen worker villages that were in existence that year. Wolcott, Marion Post, photographer. *Commissary and home for Negro workers in cane fields.USSC United States Sugar Corporation, Clewiston, Florida.* Clewiston, Hendry County, Florida. Feb. 1939. Photograph. https://www.loc.gov/item/2017801033/.

**951.8 BARE BEACH** – ACL track charts from 1949 show a siding on the east side of the mainline, located just east of the county road. For a few years, this was the siding of Bare Beach. This was not the first Bare Beach in this area, but this one was a part of U.S. Sugar. The sugarcane loading facility was Bare Beach, while the nearby worker village was Bare Beach Plantation, one of fourteen that were operating during the late 1940s and early 1950s.

To the north alongside Lake Okeechobee was the original Bare Beach. With the lake having been moved with the construction of the Herbert Hoover Dike, the site is now on the south side of U.S. Highway 27 about five miles east of Clewiston. Today the area is used by what was once known as the Lakeview Trailer Park.

The community of Bare Beach started in 1916 as a farm growing winter tomatoes. The farm was a partnership of Steve and William Hooker, as well as the Alderman Brothers. In 1917, Isaac H. Stone opened a store, followed by a drug store, four tomato packing houses, an electric plant, a garage, two church houses and a school, and several other businesses. A post office opened in 1920.

Bare Beach can't be found today as the loading track and nearby worker village are now gone. However, during the 1940s, it was one of eight cane loading facilities on the Atlantic Coast Line. *U.S. Sugar Corp. field harvest prepared to be loaded onto railcars at the Bare Beach Plantation in Clewiston, Florida. 1947. State Archives of Florida, Florida Memory. https://www.floridamemory.com/items/show/255908.*

*Sebring and Fort Pierce Subdivisions Route Guide*

The name Bare Beach came from the fine, but hard sandy soil, perfect for the tomatoes. Several docks were built on Lake Okeechobee to ship product to Miami and other markets. There was even a cemetery. However, the lake was also the community's weakness as high water flooded the area in 1922 and 1923. Soon after, much of the land was acquired for the production of sugarcane, and the post office closed in 1925. During the 1930s, much of the land was part of the Joe Jones Plantation Farm.

**953.1 COUNTY LINE** – The county line is located at the sugarcane grade crossing north of Keela Wye. To the west is **Hendry County,** while to the east is **Palm Beach County.**

**Hendry County** has a population of 40,000, most of them in Clewiston, even though the county seat is LaBelle. The county was created in 1923 and named for Captain Francis Ashbury Hendry, a captain of Confederate calvary troops during the Civil War and one of the first area settlers. Hendry had been involved with the creation of Polk and Lee Counties, as well as the town of LaBelle. Because of his ranching experience, he was known as the "Cattle King of South Florida".

**Palm Beach County** was established in 1909 from part of Dade County. It was named for one of the oldest and largest communities in the area – Palm Beach. The county has had its borders changed several times, the latest in 1963, but it is still the second-largest county in Florida with 1969 square miles of territory. The county has a population of about 1,400,000 people, making it the third-most populous county in Florida. It is also Florida's wealthiest. Palm Beach County also leads the State of Florida in agricultural productivity, the second largest industry in the county. The largest is real estate.

**953.7 KEELA - WYE JUNCTION** – Keela, sometimes known as Wye Junction, is the junction with the Atlantic Coast Line Okeelanta Branch, now generally known as the SCFE Okeelanta Lead. The mainline curves to the east while the Okeelanta Lead heads off to the southeast before curving due south.

Today there is a wye at this location, but an ACL track chart from 1949 shows that there was not an eastward leg at that time. Information about the South Central Florida Express rail line to Okeelanta can be found in the *SCFE Okeelanta Lead – Keela (FL) to Okeelanta (FL)* chapter on Page 319.

**954.7 MOTT #1** – Mott #1 is an elevator and ramp cane loading facility, shown to have a 66-car capacity in Seaboard System documents, and a 3281-foot siding by the SCFE. The cane loader and siding is to the compass-south. Passing through the sugarcane fields, you can see several different designs of sugarcane loading facilities. Many include a ramp and an elevated area where tractors and trucks can dump their cane into the railcars. Others use conveyors (elevators) and similar systems to raise the cane, and to then dump the cane into the railcars.

The Mott name has a great deal of significance with United States Sugar Corporation employees. Charles Stewart Mott was an engineer who became president of the Weston-Mott Company, his family's bicycle-tire manufacturing firm. After the company began manufacturing automobile tires, it merged with Buick in 1905. General Motors eventually bought Weston-Mott and Mott briefly served as vice president of GM, and served on its board of directors for the rest of his life.

In 1931, General Motors acquired the financially failing Southern Sugar Corporation, and assigned Charles Mott to restore the newly named United States Sugar Corporation. Mott worked with farming techniques, sugarcane varieties, and drainage issues, and the company turned a profit by 1941 and became Florida's leading sugar producer by the early 1980s. The son of Charles Stewart Mott, Charles Stewart Harding Mott, succeeded his father as chairman of the company and diversified into citrus and vegetables, purchasing South Bay Growers in 1980. Today, the Charles Stewart Mott Foundation provides charitable contributions to many local causes, as well as scholarships to students.

956.6 WATSON – Watson is a short track (1740 feet long) to the north that was sometimes used to load cane. *Seaboard System Railroad Timetable No. 1*, dated October 30, 1983, showed the track as having a capacity of 17 cars. Recently, the track has been used to store freight cars until they are needed, or while switching the nearby Calcium Silicate Corporation facility.

957.0 CALCIUM SILICATE CORPORATION – Just east of Watson is another siding, this one serving the Calcium Silicate Corporation (CSC) facility to the north. Founded in 1987, this is the company's main office, with a second facility in Columbia, Tennessee. The initial goal of CSC was to provide the agricultural industry with a high quality and spreadable source of silicon. They have since moved into the construction and manufacturing industries, processing and selling 150,000 tons of product annually, making it the largest provider of silicon nutrients for agriculture in the world.

This siding, which measures 4680 feet long, is officially known as Long Cane. It has grown over the years and stretches between Milepost 956.6 and Milepost 957.6.

The Calcium Silicate Corporation facility features a number of conveyors to move the various agricultural products that the railroad delivers.

**957.5 WEST LAKE HARBOR WYE** – For years, the Atlantic Coast Line had a wye here to turn their steam locomotives after exchanging trains with the Florida East Coast. The tail of the wye went towards downtown Lake Harbor and ended near the Miami Canal, serving the rice mill that once stood there. Remains of a few buildings that once received shipments on the track still exist. A second spur track once broke off this leg of the wye and crossed over the east leg to reach more customers. A few of these grades can still be found in the brush.

**957.7 LAKE HARBOR** – Lake Harbor dates from the early years of navigation on Lake Okeechobee. There is also evidence that the area was sometimes settled by Native Americans years before Europeans arrived in the area. As the area began to develop, land near the lake was more in demand and farming began. Farm products like beans, cabbage, and other vegetables were soon being grown. Because of this, Lake Harbor was an early location for migrant worker houses. When the Miami Canal was built, Lake Harbor was where it connected with Lake Okeechobee, making the town even more important as it also had access to the Atlantic Ocean at Miami. Early maps show several warehouses on the canal, and there are still remains of a lock.

This area was originally known as Ritta Shore, using the name from Ritta Island in Lake Okeechobee. The community was originally promoted by developer Richard J. Bolles, who built a hotel here in 1911. There was a Ritta post office 1912-1931. When the Miami Canal and its lock opened, the community took the name Miami Locks. However, it soon became Lake Harbor. In 1945, two post offices opened in the area – Southshore Rural Station and Ritta Rural Station – which closed in 1977 and 1978, respectively. In 1931, the Lake Harbor post office opened. In the 2000 census, the population of Lake Harbor was 195.

To the north alongside the Lake Okeechobee dike is the John Stretch Park. John Stretch was the director of recreation and conservation for the flood control district between 1963 and 1970, and the park displays a number of parts from various flood control facilities such as valves and pipes, and several historic diesel engines. The park features a number of covered picnic tables, restrooms, a lake, and open grassy areas. There is also access to the Lake Okeechobee Scenic Trail.

Where the Miami Canal once connected with Lake Okeechobee, there is now a large pumping station that allows water to flow in or out of the lake and canal.

The vegetable and fruit business that once was at Lake Harbor is remembered by this Ice Plant Road sign.

John Stretch Park, operated by Palm Beach County, is north of the tracks at Lake Harbor.

John Stretch Park at Lake Harbor features a number of displays of equipment used to move water back and forth through the Hoover Dike, and on the area's various canals.

## The Atlantic Coast Line at Lake Harbor

Lake Harbor (elevation 20 feet) was the east end (railroad-south) of what was called the Miami Canal Extension from Clewiston. This was the junction between the former Atlantic Coast Line and Florida East Coast lines. Because of the junction, there was a wye on each railroad; the Atlantic Coast Line just west of the Miami Canal bridge, and the Florida East Coast wye to the east.

The ACL had a long siding to the east between Mileposts 956.5 and 957.6. Charts showed that the mainline turned north into Lake Harbor, where there were a number of tracks and a siding. The railroad's depot and a number of section houses for track forces were also located here.

**957.8 = K70.9 MILEAGE CONVERSION** – This is the property limits between the former Atlantic Coast Line Railroad to the west, and the Florida East Coast Railway to the east. The former ACL milepost of 957.8 was based upon the distance from Richmond, Virginia, via the original Atlantic Coast Line through Florence, Savannah and Jacksonville. The Florida East Coast milepost of K70.9 is based upon the distance from Fort Pierce, Florida.

**K70.9 BLOCK LIMITS** – This is the dividing line between the **Keela Block** (towards Clewiston) and the **Lake Harbor Block** towards Belle Glade. Interestingly, because this is a junction between two railroad construction projects, the railroad operates northward in either direction.

At 3.4 miles long, the Lake Harbor Block is the shortest mainline block on the railroad, only the Citrus Block on the Flaghole Line is shorter. The

Lake Harbor Block is short because it protects several cane loaders in this area, but allows trains in another block to reach the Okeelanta Lead and several cane loaders and shippers to the west. To the east of the block are several more cane loaders and shippers in the Belle Glade area. The short Lake Harbor Block allows trains to serve all three areas at the same time.

Located at the west end of the Miami Canal Bridge, this sign marks the divide between the Lake Harbor and Keela blocks. It also marks the boundary between the Florida East Coast and former Atlantic Coast railroad tracks.

**K70.8 MIAMI CANAL BRIDGE** – This bridge consists of, from the west, five wooden spans, one deck plate girder span, and seven wooden spans. The Miami Canal is a major connection between Lake Okeechobee and the Atlantic Ocean at Miami. Also known as C-6 Canal and even the South New River Canal, it was built during the early 1900s as a part of the effort to drain and irrigate the Everglades Agricultural Area. Some of the last dredging took place in 1913, and a final lock was completed in 1915. While the plans were for the canal to be 90 feet wide and 13 feet deep, it was never fully completed to these standards.

The Miami Canal connects with Lake Okeechobee at Lake Harbor and heads south more than 75 miles to the Miami River, which flows five more miles to the Atlantic Ocean. The word Miami reportedly is an Indian word meaning "sweet water." The Miami River received this name because it was fed from a series of natural springs instead of purely from the Everglades, as many other area streams were watered.

One challenge with the Miami Canal was that much of it was not dug to the originally planned depth because of a layer of limestone rock. This reduced the amount of water that could be moved by the canal, and the loads that boats could carry on the canal. Because of this, boat service ended as the railroads built into the area.

This location features roads, waterways and railroads – a true intermodal location. Steamboats once operated on the canal and the remains of a lock are still visible at Lake Harbor, just to the north of the bridge. Next to the canal is Miami Canal Road, a popular route into the area for fishermen, and a shortcut often used by trucks to get around the south side of Clewiston. For the two railroads – Atlantic Coast Line and Florida East Coast – the Miami Canal at Lake Harbor was the south end of their line, so technically, it is railroad-north from here no matter which way the train is heading.

## Sebring and Fort Pierce Subdivisions Route Guide

The Miami Canal bridge at Lake Harbor is one of the most popular photo spots on the railroad. This is due to the great access, regular traffic, and scenic location that the canal and bridge provides. Here, USSC #404 heads west across the bridge pulling the Fort Pierce Turn.

Because of the public access, the railroad has clearly marked the Miami Canal Bridge as private property – no trespassing.

North of the tracks are the remains of one of the Miami Canal Locks.

The records of the State of Florida's Internal Improvement Fund show that an agreement was made with the Tatum Land Company in 1917 that would allow the land company to build a railroad along the Miami Canal. The railroad route was to cover the entire distance from Miami to Lake Okeechobee, and the agreement also allowed the construction of a road. The right-of-way provided was "fifty feet wide for main line railroad construction, and 120 feet wide for sidings, turn outs, station houses and other necessary constructions and erections."

The Tatum Land Company was just one of many land development companies owned by the Tatum Brothers Company. J. H. Tatum and B. B. Tatum created a large number of companies to develop communities, transportation systems, and other facilities during the early boom years of South Florida. They were also involved with the Pennsylvania Sugar Company.

**K70.4 EAST LAKE HARBOR WYE** – This was the Florida East Coast wye at Lake Harbor. Like the ACL wye, the tail headed north into town to serve several customers. However, unlike the ACL wye, this one still exists, although its tail has been greatly shortened and only holds several cars or locomotives. The FEC train station was once located on the tail of the wye. In 1957, there was an "engine pit track" according to FEC documents. The railroad still has a siding here between the wye switches, measuring just over 1000 feet long, according to SCFE records.

This photo of the Florida East Coast's station at Lake Harbor dates from the mid-1960s. While the paint is peeling, the photo shows the covered freight platform. At the far end was a two-story section which housed the passenger waiting room and the railroad office on the first floor, and housing for the station agent on the second floor. *FEC Railway station at Lake Harbor, Florida.* 1965 (circa). State Archives of Florida, Florida Memory. https://www.floridamemory.com/items/show/259695.

To the south are several paved roads, the remains of a small base of farming for the area known as Miami Locks. On the north side of the mainline is a large egret rookery, or nesting colony of breeding birds.

**K69.8 MIAMI LOCKS #1** – In 1967, this was shown to be a 26-car siding used for loading sugarcane by U.S. Sugar. The facility was active by the 1940s, but is gone today.

**K69.2 U.S. SUGAR MIAMI LOCKS** – This is the railroad-north switch to a sugarcane loader, located to the south of the tracks, but actually located railroad-east. The ramp loading facility is known as Miami Locks #2. Facilities like this require tractor-hauled self-dumping cane wagons to pour the cut sugarcane into the rail cars from an elevated ramp.

In a 1957 Florida East Coast timetable, Miami Locks was shown to hold 73 cars. The timetable also stated that "conveyors have been constructed by U.S. Sugar Corpn. at Runyon, South Shore and Miami Locks which do not clear a man on side of car." Today, this cane loading facility features a large permanent ramp to allow cane to be poured into railcars directly from field wagons. The name for this loader location comes from nearby Lake Harbor's earlier name of Miami Locks. SCFE shows that the siding for the sugarcane loader is 3360 feet long.

Heading towards Fort Pierce, the railroad is actually heading to the southeast. Just southeast of Miami Locks #2, the railroad curves so that it is heading due east. In all directions there are views of sugarcane.

This 1946 photo shows sugarcane being moved from field cars to railcars for transport to the sugar mill in Clewiston. The location is at the Miami Locks Plantation. *U.S. Sugar Corp. hoist at the Miami Locks Plantation moving cane from field cars to railcars for transport to sugar mills in Clewiston, Florida. 1946.* State Archives of Florida, Florida Memory. https://www.floridamemory.com/items/show/255910.

**K67.5  BLOCK LIMITS** – To the south (towards Clewiston) is the **Lake Harbor Block**, while to the north to Runyon is the **South Bay Block**. This block protects several cane loading facilities on the Florida East Coast Line, plus the industry and storage tracks at Belle Glade.

**K67.5  BUKER PASS** – To the south (railroad-east) are two tracks that stretch between Mileposts K67.0 and K68.0. The track closest to the mainline is Buker Pass (5175 feet long), named for U.S. Sugar President and CEO Robert H. Buker, Jr. Buker is a 1981 graduate of the University of Florida at Gainesville law school and first worked in agricultural law. He was named President and CEO of U.S. Sugar Corporation in May 2005.

The second track is known as Wade Siding (4875 feet long). It was named for Malcolm S. Wade, Jr., Senior Vice President, Corporate Strategy and Business Development of U.S. Sugar. Wade has been involved in developing and overseeing the company's environmental programs. This pair of tracks is frequently used for trains to meet during the sugarcane harvest.

U.S. Sugar built a number of worker villages across the region, allowing workers to live close to where they worked. These villages included simple housing, a commissary store, and often recreational and other facilities. This view of an unidentified village appears to show a new community, with young trees, newly painted houses, and a well-graveled street. Wolcott, Marion Post, photographer. *USSC United States Sugar Corporation village for Negro workers in cane fields.* Clewiston, Hendry County, Florida. Feb. 1939. Photograph. https://www.loc.gov/item/2017801031/.

Some older documents show this to be South Shore Station, named for its location on the south shore of Lake Okeechobee. To the north of the tracks is another U.S. Sugar work base, once known as South Shore Village. A few buildings remain as offices and maintenance facilities, but there were once a number of homes here also.

K65.8 **SOUTH SHORE #2** – South Shore is actually a complex of facilities about a mile west of U.S. Highway 27. Heading from Clewiston to Fort Pierce, there is first an elevator with a ramp cane loader to the south at Milepost K66.1, what is considered to be railroad-east, as the line is considered to be running north from Lake Harbor to Fort Pierce. This was another cane loader that the 1957 Florida East Coast timetable warned employees about by stating that "Conveyors have been constructed by U.S. Sugar Corpn. at Runyon, South Shore and Miami Locks which do not clear a man on side of car." In 1957, the FEC showed that there was a track here that held 71 45-foot-long rail cars, and SCFE shows the track to have a capacity of 3365 feet of freight cars.

Next, at Milepost K65.8, is a connection with the U.S. Sugar private rail line that is used to load sugarcane, and also as a possible bypass of the former Florida East Coast mainline. This is the east end of the line that connected at the sugar mill at Sugar Junction. Earlier known as the Wetherald Line of the Western Division, this is now the Clewiston Mainline and serves more than a half-dozen cane loaders and can be very busy during harvest season.

**K64.5 SOUTH BAY** – The railroad has several storage tracks just west of U.S. Highway 27 (Milepost K64.6) that are used to hold cars until needed. From west to east, there is the 1715-foot South Storage Track, and then the 1700-foot North Storage Track, both on the railroad-east, compass-south, side of the tracks. The third track is the South Bay Team Track which measures a bit more than 1000 feet and is located on the railroad-west side of the mainline.

The City of South Bay is promoted locally as the "Crossroads of South Florida" because it is at the intersection of Florida Highway 80 and U.S. Highway 27, near the southeastern shore of Lake Okeechobee. Most highway traffic in the region must pass through South Bay. The name South Bay came from the bay it sits on along the south coast of Lake Okeechobee, and a post office opened here using that name in 1919.

The history of the city started with the construction of canals to drain the northern side of the Everglades, and to manage the waters of Lake Okeechobee. One of these canals was the North New River Canal, known as Canal L-18, opened in 1912. A dozen families lived here by 1917, and a number of similar small communities grew along with the agricultural development. The hurricanes of the 1920s almost destroyed the community. One locally famous incident took place during the 1928 Hurricane when Aubrey "Orb" Walker and his brother Haughty "Haut" Walker loaded their families onto a barge in the canal to survive the high waters.

By the 1930s, the communities were merging to form larger towns, and South Bay was incorporated in 1941. Orb Walker was chosen as the first mayor.

The city survives on the local agriculture, as well as a bit of tourist trade. Its population is about 5000 and growing. A few of the local industries include the Glades Precooler and the TruGreen facilities.

**K64.2 NORTH NEW RIVER CANAL BRIDGE** – The North New River Canal, Canal L-18, was built as part of an effort to drain parts of the Everglades. The canal was also a transportation route for steamboats between Fort Lauderdale and Lake Okeechobee, and then on to Fort Myers via the Caloosahatchee River. Locks were built on the canal, and Lock No. 1 at the south end of the canal was the first to be built in South Florida. It is now listed on the National Register of Historic Places. Regular service on the canal ended in 1926 and the locks were deactivated.

The bridge consists of three short deck plate girder spans, totaling less than 100 feet in length. Heading towards Fort Pierce, the railroad curves to the northeast.

This bridge crosses the North New River Canal, and can be reached on NW First Avenue at South Bay, Florida.

NW 1ST AVENUE
272318Y
K64.28

This sign identifies the grade crossing just south of the North New River Canal.

The South Central Florida Express Local heads north across the North New River Canal near Belle Glade.

**K63.0 DAHLBERG #1** – This is another sugarcane loading facility, located to the east of the tracks. This facility includes an elevator that is loaded from an adjacent farm road. Self-dumping wagons use this facility as there is not an elevated ramp.

This facility was upgraded after World War II with an elevator and was listed as a clearance issue in the 1957 FEC timetable. However, this facility has not been upgraded with the large ramps often used to transfer sugarcane directly from field wagons to railcars. Today, Dahlberg is simply identified as "an unincorporated community in Palm Beach County, Florida." However, the name has a great deal of significance with U.S. Sugar.

Bror Gustave Dahlberg was a Swedish immigrant who started work in the railroad industry, moved to the paper industry, and then created Celotex, an insulating board. This led to the creation of the Celotex Corporation, a company that Dahlberg led until his death. One of Dahlberg's ideas was to use bagasse – sugarcane stalks from which cane juice has been extracted – to make insulated board. After experiments, Celotex bought several sugar companies in Louisiana, only to discover that the industry was failing due to an illness in the sugarcane.

Dahberg hired experts to research the problem, finding that inbreeding of the cane had allowed the development of several diseases. Dahberg then funded research to create a number of new strains, saving the industry. He invested further, moving his efforts to Florida. There, he bought into the industry. The company that he bought was Florida Sugar and Food Products, which had been reorganized as the Florida Sugar Company. In 1925, Bror Dahlberg bought control of the company and incorporated it as the Southern Sugar Company. This company later became U.S. Sugar, and this station honors Dahlberg.

**K61.3 HILLSBORO CANAL BRIDGE** – The bridge over the canal measures less than 100 feet long and consists of three short deck plate girder spans. The Hillsboro (spelled Hillsborough during the early 1900s) Canal (Canal G-08) stretches from Lake Okeechobee to the southeast to the Atlantic Ocean at Deerfield Beach. The canal actually replaced a river that could range from a few puddles to a roaring stream throwing alligators into the Atlantic Ocean. Early maps called the river by many different names, including the Sharkstail River, Rio Seco, Rio Nuevo, and the Potomac River. In 1820 it took the name of the Hillsboro River, named for the Earl of Hillsborough, the British Secretary of State for the U.S. colonies in the 1770s.

In the early 1900s, efforts were made to drain this part of Florida and the Hillsboro River was dredged over a ten-year period. The canal is credited with making much of Palm Beach County liveable, including the land west of Boca Raton and Pompano Beach, which would otherwise be under water. Construction of the 55-mile-long canal was finished by the early 1920s, and narrow canal boats began operating along the Hillsboro Canal, handling mail, freight, and even passengers.

Two floodgates were included as part of the project, one at Deerfield Beach, and the other just west of here at Belle Glade. Others were added in 1949 as part of more flood prevention projects. A final part of the project was the creation and preservation of the Loxahatchee National Wildlife Refuge, where the marshy characteristics of the original Hillsboro River were maintained.

The Hillsboro Canal Bridge consists of three short deck plate girder spans.

**K61.2 BELLE GLADE** – The Hillsboro Canal passes through the center of Belle Glade. The railroad has generally shown that the station of Belle Glade was just north of the canal, although the 1957 Florida East Coast timetable showed the station of Belle Glade-Chosen to be at Milepost K61.6 at the NW Avenue D grade crossing. At that time, the railroad had a trainmaster assigned to Belle Glade to handle the Fort Pierce-Lake Harbor Branch.

For many years, the FEC used the station name of Belle Glade-Chosen for this location. Belle Glade remains, but the community of Chosen is no longer shown on maps. A post office operated with the name Chosen from 1921 until 1955. It was at the site of a Calusa Indian mound which was excavated in the 1930s by the Smithsonian Institute.

Located near Belle Glade, the community's name was selected by J. R. Leatherman, a preacher from Virginia, for the Biblical reference of the "chosen" land. Much of the town was destroyed by the 1928 Okeechobee Hurricane, and the remains were slowly absorbed by Belle Glade.

The area just north of the Hillsboro Canal was once full of railroad-served fruit and vegetable packing houses that handled products like celery, radishes, and beans. These included Hooker & Thomas, Keesee Company, the Florida Pre-Cooling Company, Knight & Company, Lord's Packing House, Pioneer Growers, and the Wedgeworth Packing and Pre-Cooling Plant. In addition, there were several ice houses, seed and fertilizer warehouses, and oil companies located to the east of the tracks. The railroad also had a "Freight Depot" here, according to several Sanborn maps from 1942. Today, there is a siding and several spur tracks in the area.

Belle Glade, like most area communities, came about due to the drainage efforts to allow this part of the Everglades to be farmed. In particular, the Hillsboro Canal caused the creation of the community of Hillsboro in 1918 at the head of the Hillsboro Canal. In 1921, the Everglades Experiment Station was created just east of today's Belle Glade to help local farmers. This included working with vegetables and sugarcane, as well as livestock, in an attempt to make the region productive. Today, the station is the University of Florida Agricultural Research and Education Center.

By 1925, the town was renamed Belle Glade, short for "Belle of the Glades," and incorporated in 1928. The population reached about 500 before the town was almost destroyed by the 1928 Okeechobee Hurricane. However, thanks to the developing sugar industry, Belle Glade quickly rebuilt. During World War II, due to local labor shortages, a prisoner-of-war (POW) camp was built at the Everglades Experiment Station to provide workers for a bean-canning factory and the sugarcane fields. Some prisoners also worked on improving the nearby Lake Okeechobee Dike.

The city carries the nickname of "Muck City" for the area muck soil that sugarcane grows in, and often uses the motto "Her soil is her fortune." Today, more than half of the sugarcane grown in the United States is from the Belle Glade-Clewiston area. The cane sugar mill of the Sugarcane Growers Cooperative is located just east of Belle Glade, employing more than 500 workers during the harvest season. Because of this, the community is a base for workers in the industry and is the largest city on the southern rim of Lake Okeechobee with a population of almost 20,000. The town features a number of fast-food restaurants, but hotels and gas stations are located to the west along U.S. Highway 27.

Belle Glade and nearby Pahokee are centers of the National Football League (NFL). More than sixty players have come from just these two communities. These players include Reidel Anthony, wide receiver for the Tampa Bay Buccaneers; Kelvin Benjamin, wide receiver for the Carolina Panthers; James Lee, offensive lineman for the Tampa Bay Buccaneers; Fred Taylor, running back for the Jacksonville Jaguars; and Andre Waters, safety for the Philadelphia Eagles and Arizona Cardinals.

This photo from the Farm Security Administration – Office of War Information Photograph Collection (Library of Congress) shows that Belle Glade was once also known for its vegetable production, including "The Best Beans Grown." The photo was taken in January 1937 by Arthur Rothstein, one of America's premier photojournalists. This photo was part of his work for the Resettlement Administration, where he documented the struggles of farmers and the creation of a number of new farming communities for urban and rural families. Rothstein, Arthur, photographer. *Sign in Belle Glade, Florida.* Belle Glade, Palm Beach County, Florida, Jan. 1937. Photograph. https://www.loc.gov/item/2017761371/.

**K61.0 FEC OFFICE** – To the west at the NW Avenue D grade crossing is a small modern metal building labeled "FEC Belle Glade." Several sidings and industry tracks are still in this area. For example, to the north is a two-track yard, known as North Yard by train crews. North Yard is often used to swap freight cars between the SCFE Local, which switches the facility of the Sugar Cane Growers Cooperative of Florida, and the Fort Pierce Turn.

This large Florida East Coast station at Belle Glade featured a two-story section for the waiting room and railroad offices, plus an upstairs housing area for the station agent and his family. The other end of the station featured a freight house. The station was expanded with the one-story structure, used as offices and as a bunkhouse. Note the semaphore train order signal, used to alert train crews of the need to stop and receive new train orders or other instructions from the agent. *FEC Railway station at Belle Glade, Florida.* 1965 (circa). State Archives of Florida, Florida Memory. https://www.floridamemory.com/items/show/259677.

The former Florida East Coast office still stands at Belle Glade, as shown by this photo.

**K60.3 BELLEGLADE PIGGY-BACK** – Following World War II, many of the growers and packers of fruits and vegetables started moving their shipments by truck, and the railroads responded by building loading ramps for trailer-on-flat-car (TOFC, or Piggy-Back) movements. Later, the railroads closed most of their local ramps and concentrated the business at larger and more modern terminals. Note that the name Belle Glade was spelled as one word for this location.

**K60.2 GLADES SUGAR HOUSE SPUR** – To the east of the mainline is the north end of the two-track North Yard plus a 1½-mile-long spur to the Sugar Cane Growers Cooperative of Florida sugar mill. Known as the Glades Sugar House mill, it is one of the largest mills in the world and can grind as much as 26,000 tons of sugarcane a day. This mill is served by trucks and doesn't use rail for the delivery of sugarcane. However, the railroad does serve the mill to move bulk raw sugar, molasses, and other products produced by the mill, and to move inbound products as needed. The mill has at least one car mover to handle their own switching. Some railroad documents show that the spur is also known as the Sugar Cane Growers Lead. A description of the line is included here.

USSC #305 shoves a cut of tank cars into the Sugar Cane Growers Cooperative. On this day, #305 is pulling the Local for the South Central Florida Express.

**0.0 SCFE/FEC K-BRANCH** – This is the switch with the mainline of the South Central Florida Express, also known as the Florida East Coast K-Branch, or the Fort Pierce-Lake Harbor Branch. It is at Milepost K60.2 of that line. This spur track serves the Sugar Cane Growers Cooperative of Florida, located on the east side of Belle Glade, Florida. The South Central Florida Express handles a limited number of loads, primarily molasses.

**0.6 HIGHWAY 15/80** – This highway, also known as North Main Street, is the main route through Belle Glade. It connects U.S. Highway 27 at the southwest edge of town, with U.S. Highway 441 on the north side of Belle Glade.

The track to the east of the highway is actually owned by the Sugar Cane Growers Cooperative of Florida. However, sometimes the track forces of the South Central Florida Express can be found making some of the track repairs under contract.

**1.2 INTERCHANGE YARD** – There are two tracks here that are used to interchange railcars between the railroad and the private rail operation at the Glades Sugar House mill. The mill has its own red car mover to handle switching of the plant, so the South Central Florida Express only delivers and picks up cars from the sugar mill.

**1.6 WEST SUGAR HOUSE ROAD** – This is the road in front of the Sugar Cane Growers Cooperative. The Cooperative dates back to the 1950s when a number of area farmers met to form a sugar cooperative in the Glades Area – basically the area west of West Palm Beach and southeast of Lake Okeechobee. In July 1960, 54 farmers chartered the Sugar Cane Growers Cooperative of Florida and immediately started plans to build their own sugarcane processing mill. The Glades Sugar House mill opened on November 22, 1962, and has been updated and expanded since then to produce more than a half-billion pounds of raw sugar per year.

Their website states that the "Cooperative is comprised of 45 small to medium-sized member farms that grow sugarcane on approximately 70,000 acres of what is among the most fertile and productive farmland in America, located in the Everglades Agricultural Area (EAA)." The mill produces more than 350,000 tons of raw sugar annually, enough to meet the demand of more than 9 million people. The raw sugar produced is then sold to one of the sugar refineries owned by the ASR Group.

This is a view of the tracks that head into the Sugar Cane Growers Cooperative of Florida mill at Belle Glade, Florida.

In 1998, the Sugar Cane Growers Cooperative of Florida and Florida Crystals (operator of the nearby Okeelanta Sugar Mill) created the American Sugar Refining Group (ASR), now owned by Florida Crystals. ASR Group became the world's largest cane sugar refining company, and it owns and operates sugar refineries in Louisiana, California, New York, Maryland, Canada, Mexico, England, Italy and Portugal. Its products are sold through the Domino, C&H, Florida Crystals, Redpath, Jack Frost, and Tate & Lyle brands.

Unlike U.S. Sugar, the Sugar Cane Growers Cooperative of Florida has its cane delivered by truck. Signs like this mark the area.

**K60.0 CANAL BRIDGE** – Look for the seven-span timber trestle. This canal drains many of the sugarcane fields to the east. To the northwest is the former Glades Correctional Institution. The men's prison opened as Florida Farm #2 in 1932, and was renamed the Glades State Prison Farm in 1951. It became the Glades Correctional Institution in 1962 and was closed in 2011. The facility was sold in 2014 and part of the complex is now used as warehouse space.

K59.0 STOCK PENS – Florida East Coast documents show that in 1957 there were stock pens here, served by a four-car spur track. These stock pens were used to load and unload livestock, especially cattle that were moved to the area for winter grazing. Today, this area houses a large number of Palm Beach County offices and the local hospital.

K57.7 BLOCK LIMITS – The sign for these block limits is located next to U.S. Highway 98 north of the Runyon #1 cane loader. **South Bay Block** is to the south while the **Canal Point Block** is to the north.

K57.6 RUNYON #1 – This was another of the cane loaders on the Florida East Coast with the warning that "Conveyors have been constructed by U.S. Sugar Corpn....which do not clear a man on side of car." Today, the elevator (conveyor) operates without a large ramp. The track that serves the loader is long, the SCFE states that the cane loader siding is 3390 feet long. This may be the easiest cane loader to view without trespassing on U.S. Sugar or other private property, as it is alongside U.S. Highway 98.

*The Railroads of U.S. Sugar: History Through the Miles*

The Runyon #1 cane loader, which is located immediately beside U.S. Highway 98, is one of the most accessible for those following the railroad.

When not in operation, cane loader sidings are often used by the track maintenance forces and the railroad for other purposes. Here a cut of ballast cars are stored on the Runyon #1 siding.

Milepost K57.6 was used for Runyon #1 during the 1950s by the Florida East Coast. The milepost is actually the north switch to the sugarcane loader, located to the west of the mainline at Milepost K58.0. Some documents show Runyon to be at Milepost K58.5, which is where Runyon Village is located.

Not far to the south of the loader is Runyon, also known as Runyon Village. This is another former U.S. Sugar housing development, now owned and managed by Alston Management, Inc. It was built to house the seasonal workers needed to plant, maintain, and harvest the local sugarcane fields.

Heading north, the railroad passes a number of sugarcane fields and crosses a series of drainage canals.

This sign for Runyon Avenue is located a short distance south of the Runyon #1 cane loading facility.

**K55.6 CARDWELL** – Cardwell is another railroad location that has moved around. In 1957, the FEC had it at Milepost K55.6. Other documents have shown it to be at Milepost K56.5, a mile to the south. Up until at least the 1960s, the FEC had a section tool house here, identified in 1965 as FEC Building No. 745. The railroad's timetable stated that the "Telephone at Cardwell is located near Section Foreman's tool house."

In 1943, a siding was located on the west side of the mainline and was used to serve the packing houses of P. M. Cates and L. L. Stuckey. There was also a fertilizer warehouse and several smaller storage facilities.

**K52.8 PAHOKEE** – Although the City of Pahokee is actually off to the west on Lake Okeechobee, the railroad freight house and station stood at the grade crossing with U.S. Highway 441/98 until at least the mid-1960s. No side tracks or structures remain here. However, this was once a very busy location with a number of shippers. A spur track south of the grade crossing once headed south between the tracks and the highway. On this track was a Florida Power & Light powerhouse, the City Ice & Fuel Company, a Gulf Oil bulk plant, and the Hull Packing Company. To the north of the grade crossing was a siding to the west. A spur track off of it was used to serve customers like the Unity Farms packing house, the P. M. Cates warehouse, and the Pope-Johnson Company packing house.

This photo, taken as part of a survey of railroad structures during the mid-1960s, shows the depot at Pahokee. Note the sagging freight platform that once was so important for the Florida East Coast Railway. *FEC Railway station in Pahokee.* 1965 (circa). State Archives of Florida, Florida Memory. https://www.floridamemory.com/items/show/259662.

Pahokee went through a number of different names, including East Beach and Ridgeway, before the name Pahokee became final. The name Pay-ha-o-kee is reportedly the Seminole name for the Everglades and means "grassy waters." Much of the land had been sold to the Southern States Land and Timber Company, which allowed farmers to use the property without payment. Eventually, much of the land became owned by the Pahokee Realty Company, which began to sell it in smaller parcels. The area became famous when a February 1917 frost damaged crops north of Pahokee, but the crops at Pahokee were saved by a slight change in elevation. This caused the vegetable business to boom and the area to become known as the "Winter Vegetable Capital of the World." A Pahokee post office opened in 1918, and Pahokee was incorporated in 1922. The same year, the Pahokee Drainage District was created to make more land available for farming.

The 1928 Okeechobee Hurricane flooded and destroyed much of the town, but the new Pahokee High School survived, sheltering many of the local residents. The school is now listed on the National Register of Historic Places. The town continued to boom through the 1930s, reaching a population of more than 2000, but changes in agriculture and the move toward sugarcane changed the community. The sugarcane crops brought with them the name "The Muck," a name still used by Muck City Road, Highway 717. Today, citrus, corn, and grass sod are also grown in the area. The population of Pahokee is about 7000 today, with a boom thanks to the tourism business related to Lake Okeechobee and the Pahokee State Park.

With Belle Glade, Pahokee is part of the National Football League (NFL) center of gravity. A large number of professional football players came from the local high school and community, including Reidel Anthony, wide receiver for the Tampa Bay Buccaneers; Rickey Jackson, Hall of Fame linebacker for the New Orleans Saints and San Francisco 49ers; Pernell McPhee, linebacker for the Chicago Bears; Alphonso Smith, cornerback for the Detroit Lions; and Antone Smith, running back for the Atlanta Falcons.

In early 1941, a new migratory labor camp was built at Pahokee to handle the laborers needed for the vegetable harvest, and the growing production of sugarcane. Wolcott, Marion Post, photographer. *Migratory labor camp under construction. Pahokee, Florida.* Pahokee, Palm Beach County, Florida, Jan. 1941. Photograph. https://www.loc.gov/item/2017806639/.

Pahokee was also the boyhood home of country musician Mel Tillis, who was born in Tampa, but his family moved here soon after.

This sign marks Mel Tillis Boulevard at Pahokee.

**K52.5 PELICAN LAKE** – The unincorporated community of Pelican Lake is actually about two miles to the east on Muck City Road (Florida Highway 717), but this was the railroad stop for service to that community. Pelican Lake had a post office from 1939 to 1964, when it was replaced by the Pelican Lake Rural Station that finally closed in 1992. Records show that Pelican Lake, also known as Pelican Lake Village, was a worker community for U.S. Sugar. For a number of years, the company had a commissary there, as well as a welcome sign that read "Pelican Lake Village – a housing community for agricultural employees of United States Sugar Corporation." Today, it is a small well-kept community noted for the large trees and flowering bushes around its entrance.

**K51.1 PAHOKEE FARM MARKET** – To the east of the tracks was once the Pahokee State Farmers Market celery packing facility. In 1967, the Florida East Coast reported that there was a 70-car track here to serve this agricultural business. Today, this area is simply the north end of a series of sugarcane fields.

At Milepost 50.5 are the remains of an old packing house and cold warehouse. Facilities like this used to be located in almost every town along the railroad.

USSC 311N, the SCFE Local, heads north near Pahokee pulling tank cars, a common load.

**K50.3  USSC JUNCTION** – This is the junction with the Bryant/USSC Lead that connects to a series of U.S. Sugar Corporation private rail lines at Bryant Yard. At Bryant, the line splits with one leg turning south, serving almost a dozen sugarcane loaders, and originally ending on the east side of Belle Glade. The other leg turns north and then southeast to serve a number of sugarcane loaders north of Old Conners Road. Both are now part of the new Clewiston Mainline Division. For details on these lines, check out the information about the Clewiston Mainline on page 341.

At the junction, known as Canal Point by the SCFE, the railroad has several long tracks that are used to hold railcars and to switch trains. One is the 3450-foot-long Storage Track, located on the west side of the mainline, while the shorter 1550-foot-long track is to the east and is known as the Team Track. In the FEC's 1967 employee timetable, a 3-car spur track named Rinker was also shown to be here.

During April 2021, the Canal Storage Track is stuffed full with covered hoppers. Cars like this are used for fertilizers and for bulk shipments of sugar.

This is as far north as the sugarcane trains operate on the South Central Florida Express mainline. The Florida East Coast had a warning about this connection in their *Employee Timetable No. 4*, dated December 12, 1957. It stated: "Curvature in track at Canal Point is such that hand signals cannot be used to govern movements of cane trains between F.E.C. main track and tracks of the United States Sugar Corporation."

Immediately to the west is the Herbert Hoover Dike, with the waters of Lake Okeechobee just a few feet further west. On top of the dike is the Lake Okeechobee Scenic Trail, designated as being part of the Florida National Scenic Trail in 1993. The trail circles the lake and is about 110 miles long. The U.S. Army Corps of Engineers states that "more than half of the trail is paved, and the remainder consists of a two-track gravel roadway on top of the 35-foot-high Herbert Hoover Dike." Often being the highest land in the area, the trail is known for its great views of the lake and the surrounding land, but also for its lack of shade.

Signs like this can be seen in a number of places along the South Central Florida Express. They point to various parks and access locations to the Lake Okeechobee Scenic Trail.

## Bryant Lead

The Bryant Lead goes through Bryant Yard and ends at the north and south wye switches, for a distance of just more than two miles. While the line is technically a part of the SCFE, operations over the line require approval from the Bryant Yardmaster. Details about Bryant Lead are included here.

**0.0 USSC JUNCTION** – This is the switch with the mainline of the South Central Florida Express, also known as the Florida East Coast K-Branch, or the Fort Pierce-Lake Harbor Branch. It is at Milepost 50.3 of that line.

USSC #503 shoves a Bryant Turn across U.S. Highway 441 at USSC Junction near Pahokee.

In 1957, the FEC had clear instructions about this interchange location with U.S. Sugar, and the sharp curve involved. Their timetable read:

> *Curvature in track at Canal Point is such that hand signals cannot be used to govern movements of cane trains between F.E.C. main track and tracks of the United States Sugar Corporation.*
>
> *Two color light signals, each visible both north and south when lighted, are located on west side of main track, one 1050 feet south of and the other 200 feet north of station building. These signals are normally dark.*

The timetable also included a long set of instructions on how to use the signals to control train movements. It also mentioned that all train movements over the highway grade crossing "must be made at a speed of not exceeding four (4) miles per hour."

**0.3 U.S. HIGHWAY 98/441** – U.S. Highway 441 runs 939 miles from Miami, Florida, to Rocky Top (formerly Lake City), Tennessee. U.S. Highway 98 is an east-west highway along the Gulf Coast from near Natchez, Mississippi, to Palm Beach, Florida. It is almost 1000 miles long. In this area, the two highways share the same route and run along the east side of Lake Okeechobee. Here, it is also known as East Main Street.

Operations at Bryant Yard are under the control of the Bryant Yardmaster. South Central Florida Express trains cannot cross this highway and enter the yard without authorization.

Another trainload of empty cane cars is being delivered to Bryant in January 2018. The traditional method of getting cane cars between Clewiston and Bryant has been the use of a series of Bryant Turns that operate over the South Central Florida Express.

**0.8  BRYANT YARD WEST SWITCH** – The yard at Bryant includes several short and long sidings and yard tracks, and then a seven-track yard next to the old Bryant Sugar House. There are also a number of old mill tracks that are being used to repair and rebuild freight cars.

This is the SCFE Local delivering two carloads of molasses to the new bulk tank farm complex at Bryant.

**1.1  BRYANT MILL SWITCH** – This switch separates the railroad into two routes. The south route leads into the primary rail yard at Bryant. The north track leads to a new bulk tank farm complex for molasses. The several tracks at the tank farm are switched by a car mover.

**1.5  BRYANT** – The yard here has six tracks plus a through track. It is south of the former Bryant Sugar House mill, closed on April 11, 2007, after producing almost 20 billion pounds of raw sugar. The mill is now nothing more than a large number of foundations, but the U.S. Sugar Corporation is developing the mill area into an industrial park. Besides the tank farm,

GBW Railcar Services once had a railcar repair shop here, using some of the old mill tracks. GBW Railcar Services was jointly owned by The Greenbrier Company and Watco, a railroad and rail services company. The firm was created in 2014, but was dissolved in 2018 because the "market never fully materialized."

This sign on Florida Highway 700 lets you know when you are in Bryant, Florida.

Bryant was originally known as Azucar (Spanish for sugar), and was from its origin a sugar-based town with housing for workers. A post office was here and named Azucar from 1930 until 1946. In that year, the town was renamed Bryant to honor Frederick Edward Bryant, who died in 1945. Bryant first showed up in Florida in 1908 when he began developing agricultural concepts for the Everglades.

With the sugar shortage caused by World War I, Bryant encouraged research on sugarcane, including the creation of a U.S. Department of Agriculture sugarcane breeding station at Canal Point. Bryant and his business partner, G. T. Anderson, formed the Florida Sugar and Food Products Company and built the first sugar mill in the Everglades in 1921. He soon merged the company with the Southern Sugar Company, which became the United States Sugar Corporation in the 1930s. He continued to manage their Eastern Division operations until his death in 1945. The company renamed Azucar to Bryant to honor him.

The Bryant Sugar House opened in 1962 and was considered to be the most modern mill in the world. However, as the efficiency of mills improved, excess capacity within the company led to the closing of the sugar mill in 2007. The mill, and the company town that supported it, were soon torn down, leaving just a series of streets and foundations. Like many company towns, Azucar/Bryant had a mixed reputation. Frederick Edward Bryant spent a great deal of money trying to provide comfortable housing, recreation, and schools for his workers. Critics complained that the company town trapped workers to the company. Nevertheless, most workers who lived at Bryant had fond memories and many were reluctant to move after the mill and town were closed.

This old building was once part of the Bryant complex, and it still stands alongside Florida Highway 700.

**1.8 WEST BRYANT WYE SWITCH** – This is the east end of Bryant Yard. The wye connects the line west to the South Central Florida Express mainline, and the U.S. Sugar lines that head north and south from Bryant.

**2.1 SOUTH BRYANT WYE SWITCH** – This switch connects the Bryant Yard area with the Clewiston Mainline Division.

**K49.7 CANAL POINT** – Canal Point is the name used by SCFE for this area (K50.5), and the name used by the FEC (K49.7) for the series of tracks at the U.S. Sugar connection. However, the community has had a number of names over the years. Reportedly, it started as New Town, noted in 1909 as being the first white settlement on the east side of Lake Okeechobee. The name soon changed to Long

Beach and then Nemaha. With the construction of the canal, the post office at first used Canalpoint when it opened in 1918, but quickly changed it to Canal Point.

When the West Palm Beach Canal was completed in the late 1910s, this area became a logical location for a community with the drained fields, the connections to both Lake Okeechobee and the Atlantic Ocean, and the support of local landowners. Almost immediately, farmers were shipping their products on the canal and the Southern States Land and Timber Company was planting various varieties of sugarcane here. Additionally, in 1920, the U.S. Department of Agriculture established a Sugarcane Field Station to supply sugarcane stalks for Louisiana and local farmers. The first sugar mill in the Everglades opened near here in 1922. The paved Conners Toll Highway reached here in 1924, opening up further markets.

In 1920, the U.S. Department of Agriculture established a Sugarcane Field Station at Canal Point, and this sign marks the location of the current facility.

## Conners Toll Highway

One of the challenges for early farms and industry along the east and southeast side of Lake Okeechobee was the lack of transportation. There were a few canals and poor trails, but none were useable throughout the year, especially for heavy loads. This changed when William J. "Fingey" Conners arrived in the area and bought about 4000 acres during the early 1920s. He wanted to develop the property and realized that transportation was the key.

In 1924, Conners applied to the Florida State Legislature for permission to build a toll road to the lake, and received permission in 2 hours and 20 minutes. On October 16, 1924, construction began. Like most heavy construction in the area, the toll road was built using a number of dredges that threw up dirt from what became ditches. Eventually, a temporary railroad was built on the grade to spread materials. After spending $1,800,000, the 52-mile toll road opened on June 25, 1925. It was an immediate success, raising $2000 a day in tolls at $0.03 a mile.

The road between Twenty Mile Bend and Canal Point was paved, and it provided an economic boom to the region. Conners died on October 5, 1929, and the road was sold to the State of Florida for $660,000.

## The Peak and Decline of Canal Point

As stated, Canal Point was the location of one of the first large sugar mills in Florida. The South Florida Sugar and Products Company built a mill with a designed capacity of 400 tons of cane daily. The mill was built from parts of a mill acquired in Louisiana. The location of the mill was described as being "approximately one and one half miles from Lake Okeechobee on the south side of the West Palm Beach Canal near Canal Point." It was to open in February 1922 so that some cane could be crushed late that season as a test. The reason for the location was that there were plans to move the cane on the canal from fields beside the West Palm Beach Canal. The mill was later bought to be used as parts for the new Southern Sugar Company mill in Clewiston.

Canal Point reached its peak during the 1930s, but the closure of the mill in the late 1920s hurt the community. Then, as the railroad and highway took away the freight and passenger business, the facilities and businesses that served the water trade slowly closed, with the canal boat traffic ending in the 1930s during construction of the Herbert Hoover Dike around Lake Okeechobee. The local high school closed in 1988, and Hurricanes Francis (2004), Jeanne (2004), and Wilma (2005) destroyed most of the historic buildings in Canal Point. Today, it is an unincorporated rural community for workers in nearby cities, and a collection of vacation and winter homes along Lake Okeechobee.

**K49.0 BLOCK LIMITS** – The sign for this location is immediately south of the West Palm Beach Canal Bridge. To the south is the **Canal Point Block**. To the north is the longest block on the railroad (33.5 miles), the **Fort Pierce Block**.

Many of the original Florida East Coast concrete mileposts are still located along the line. This one is just south of the West Palm Beach Canal Bridge.

This sign alerts southbound trains that they are entering the Canal Point Block and leaving the Fort Pierce Block.

**K49.0 WEST PALM BEACH CANAL BRIDGE** – This bridge is about 100 feet long and has a through plate girder span over the main channel of the canal, with smaller deck plate girder spans on each end. When the canal was active, this bridge included a vertical lift span to allow boats to pass under the tracks. Note that the center span remains from this lift bridge – look for the lifting eyes on each corner of the through plate girder span.

The West Palm Beach Canal Bridge was once a lift bridge, but it is now locked in place with the lifting mechanism removed.

The West Palm Beach Canal, also known as the C-51 Canal, was built in the early 1900s to lower Lake Okeechobee and drain a part of the Everglades in order to farm the land, today part of the Everglades Agricultural Area. The canal starts at Canal Point on Lake Okeechobee, and flows southeast to Twenty Mile Bend, immediately adjacent to U.S. Highway 98. The canal flows through acres of sugarcane, providing drainage for the farms. At

Twenty Mile Bend, the Ocean Canal flows into the West Palm Beach Canal and the combined canal then flows to the southeast as the northern boundary of the Loxahatchee National Wildlife Refuge. It flows south of the Palm Beach International Airport and then into the Lake Worth Lagoon, a part of the Intracoastal Waterway at Palm Beach.

Notice the former lifting eyes on the West Palm Beach Canal Bridge that show it once was a lift bridge like the one at the St. Lucie Canal.

Note the old canal lock just to the east of the U.S. Highway 98 bridge. This was West Palm Beach Canal Lock #1. A small park and pedestrian bridge over the canal have recently been built here. The Conners Toll Highway was located on the south bank of the canal and was later replaced by U.S. Highway 98. The former toll gate was just east of the lock and lock tender's office.

This West Palm Beach Canal lettering is on the highway bridge next to the railroad's bridge.

This photo from the State Library and Archives of Florida shows the West Palm Beach Canal bridge in a raised position as a small boat enters Lake Okeechobee. *Florida East Coast railroad bridge – Canal Point, Florida.* 1920 (circa). State Archives of Florida, Florida Memory. https://www.floridamemory.com/items/show/138326.

Along the south side of the canal and several blocks to the east of the tracks is Triangle Park. This park is managed by Palm Beach County Parks & Recreation, and includes parking, restrooms and shaded picnic tables. Just north of the bridge is public access to the Canal Point Recreation Area, which has access to Lake Okeechobee, covered picnic tables, and plenty of parking. For about the next ten miles heading north, the railroad will be next to Lake Okeechobee. However, the Herbert Hoover Dike around the lake prevents views of the water.

This sign marks Triangle Park, located just a short distance from the West Palm Beach Canal Bridge.

Heading north, the U.S. Department of Agriculture's Agricultural Research Service has their Sugarcane Field Station to the east. The facility works with a similar Louisiana facility to create sugarcane that is resistant to disease, and to improve disease detection and screening techniques.

**K45.1 SAND CUT** – During the 1950s, the railroad had a siding that held 75 cars. Today, there is not much here but sugarcane, some trees, and new work on

Lake Okeechobee's Herbert Hoover Dike. Sand Cut was once a small migrant workers community, but it was removed to allow expansion of the levee.

To the north at Milepost K44.9, the railroad bridges another canal just before it connects to Lake Okeechobee. This canal is the L-8 Canal. The L-8 Canal flows from Lake Okeechobee at Sand Cut and heads southeast to the West Palm Beach Canal at Twenty Mile Bend. The canal first passes through citrus groves, sugarcane, and corn, and then flows between the sugarcane fields of U.S. Sugar and the J. W. Corbett Wildlife Management Area.

**K42.9 DORSET** – In 1957, the FEC had an 11-car track here. A short 460-foot siding is still located to the east, that has been used for delivering large stone for work on the nearby Hoover Dike. Just north of here the railroad crosses U.S. Highway 441 at grade, and then cuts north and away from Lake Okeechobee. Less than a mile to the east is a rock and sand quarry operated by Mayaca Materials.

There is another parking area to the west that provides access to the Lake Okeechobee Scenic Trail. It is known as the Lake Okeechobee Connector Natural Area and consists of eight acres managed by Palm Beach County. The park provides a connection between the DuPuis Management Area and Lake Okeechobee while hiking on the Ocean to Lake Trail, a part of the Florida National Scenic Trail system.

**K42.1 COUNTY LINE** – The county line is located at the canal to the east that separates sugarcane fields to the north and citrus groves to the south. To the south is **Palm Beach County,** and to the north is **Martin County.**

**Palm Beach County** was established in 1909 from part of Dade County. It was named for one of the oldest and largest communities in the area – Palm Beach. The county has had its borders changed several times, the latest in 1963, but it is still the second-largest county in Florida with 1969 square miles of territory. The county has a population of about 1,400,000 people, making it the third-most populous county in Florida. It is also Florida's wealthiest. Palm Beach County also leads the State of Florida in agricultural productivity, the second largest industry in the county. The largest is real estate.

**Martin County,** like Palm Beach County, stretches from the beaches of the Atlantic Ocean to Lake Okeechobee. However, unlike Palm Beach County, Martin County doesn't include any of the major cities on the Atlantic coast. Also, unlike Palm Beach County, Martin County is rather small, covering only 543 square miles (54th largest in Florida). The county's population is about 150,000, ten percent of what Palm Beach County has. Its county seat is Stuart, the only incorporated city in the county. Martin County was created in 1925, using parts of St. Lucie and Palm Beach Counties. It was named for John W. Martin, the Governor of Florida at the time. The creation of Martin County also included a change in the county lines of several other counties. At the time, Palm Beach County included all of Lake Okeechobee, giving it a larger share of state and federal road tax revenues. This was changed so that the lake was divided among the counties that it bordered.

**K40.5 PORT MAYACA** – In 1957, the Florida East Coast reported that Port Mayaca had an 8-car spur track and a telegraph station. It also showed the station milepost to be K40.0. However, earlier, the community of Port Mayaca was a cluster of houses and businesses just south of the St. Lucie Canal and between today's Highway 78 and Lake Okeechobee to the west. Today, a few houses still stand along the lake, while there are a number of active sand and gravel pits to the east.

Today's sparsely populated Port Mayaca is far from what was planned for the community. In 1925, Bessemer Properties established the Mayaca Corporation to develop a city on the eastern shore of Lake Okeechobee. 6500 acres were purchased between the William Conners Toll Highway (completed in July 1924) and the St. Lucie Canal (completed in 1925), and professional city planners were hired to design a city for the location. A water system was built, including fire hydrants and lines for houses south of Conners Highway, and between the business district and the canal. Along the lake, there were plans for bathing beaches, a yacht basin, golf courses and bridle paths.

In 1927, the Mayaca Corporation brought in Paul M. Hoenshel, a successful developer, to manage the promotion of the new town. While the original plans were for a community that would rival posh communities like Coral Gables, Hoenshel's efforts focused on making Port Mayaca a citrus and vegetable farm region. Soon, 500 acres were put to use as an orange grove, using irrigation water from the adjacent St. Lucie Canal. The adjacent pine forests were also sold to timber companies. This was a fortunate plan for the company as the Florida land boom ended with the hurricanes of the 1920s and the Great Depression of the 1930s.

On June 7, 1928, a post office opened at Port Mayaca. The town was almost destroyed on September 17th by the Okeechobee Hurricane of 1928. However, the town survived and during September 1935, the Cypress Lodge, a two-story colonial-style cypress-frame country inn, was opened in town. The lodge was built to high standards, especially for during the Depression, and it featured a hotel kitchen, dining hall and two lobbies on the first floor, and eight guest rooms with private baths on the second floor. The lodge, now known as the Cypress Plantation, still stands near Lake Okeechobee and is on the National Register of Historic Places. Another noted landmark is the Port Mayaca Cemetery, chosen in 1928 as the site for the mass burial of over 1600 unidentified people who lost their lives in the September 1928 Lake Okeechobee Hurricane.

The city of Port Mayaca never developed, and the post office closed on June 30, 1958. What growth did occur is mainly due to vegetable crops, cut flowers and citrus groves established by Minute Maid and Tropicana. Today, Port Mayaca, named for the Mayaca Tribe and pronounced port my-ak-kuh, is simply a cluster of a few houses and businesses along U.S. Highway 441 and State Highway 78 on the south side of the St. Lucie Canal.

## Okeechobee Hurricane of 1928

The Okeechobee Hurricane of 1928 was one of the deadliest hurricanes recorded, and the third deadliest hurricane in the United States. After hitting a number of Caribbean Islands, the hurricane made landfall near West Palm Beach, Florida, on September 17, 1928. The storm had slowed down, and many people had returned home after earlier receiving a warning to evacuate. A storm surge traveled up the many waterways to Lake Okeechobee and water poured over the south bank, flooding hundreds of square miles of farmland, and a number of towns and small communities. An estimated 2500 people died from flooding in the United States, almost all in the Lake Okeechobee area.

Towns like South Bay (nearly all houses destroyed and at least 160 fatalities), Okeelanta (abandoned), Belle Glade (heavily destroyed), and Canal Point (much of the community swept away) were under as much as twenty feet of water. Most of the area crops and farms were also destroyed.

There is no clear answer as to how many people died in the Lake Okeechobee area. Obtaining a solid number is difficult due to the large number of migrant workers who were in the area to harvest crops, and the many settlers who simply left the region for good. Another issue was that many bodies were washed into the Everglades, where they were never recovered. An initial Red Cross estimate was 1836 fatalities, but that was officially increased to "at least 2500" in 2003. Two mass cemeteries were used for the bodies. The first mass graves were created at West Palm Beach, where about 70 white victims and 674 black victims were buried in two different mass graves.

About two miles east of the railroad at Port Mayaca is the Port Mayaca Cemetery. Here, a mass grave contains the bodies of 1600 victims of the hurricane. The gravestone states "In Memoriam to the 1600 pioneers in this mass burial who gave their lives in the 1928 hurricane so that the Glades might be as we know it today." Meanwhile, a historical marker is nearby on State Road 76. It states:

> On September 16, 1928, a hurricane came ashore near the Jupiter Lighthouse and traveled west across Palm Beach County to Lake Okeechobee. This deadly hurricane destroyed hundreds of buildings and left millions of dollars of property damage. Many of the 1,800 to 3,000 casualties occurred when the Lake Okeechobee dike collapsed, flooding the populated south side of the lake. Approximately 1,600 victims were buried in a mass grave near Port Mayaca in Martin County. Approximately 743 victims were buried in mass graves in West Palm Beach. Many other victims were never found.

*The Railroads of U.S. Sugar: History Through the Miles*

About two miles east of the railroad at Port Mayaca is this historical marker which notes the mass burial of many of the victims of the Hurricane of 1928.

**K40.1 ST. LUCIE CANAL BRIDGE** – This bridge is a manual lift bridge operated by train crews. It is normally in the open position, displaying flashing green lights to indicate that vessels may pass. Located at Mile 38.0 on the St. Lucie Canal, when open it provides 56 feet of horizontal clearance and 49 feet of vertical clearance. Built 1925-26 by the Florida East Coast Railway, the bridge consists of a through plate girder lift span with deck plate girder spans off each end. The lifting tower is essentially a series of truss spans designed to handle the weight of the lift span.

This sign explains the process of raising and lowering the St. Lucie Canal Bridge.

This lift bridge over the St. Lucie Canal near Port Mayaca is a major attraction along the line. Here the lift span is shown moving down so a train can pass over it.

The U.S. Sugar Fort Pierce Turn heads north across the St. Lucie Canal Bridge in January 2018.

The St. Lucie Canal (also known as the C-44 Canal) was built 1916-1924 between Lake Okeechobee and the South Fork of the St. Lucie River, creating a link to the Atlantic Ocean. With the Caloosahatchee Canal, it creates the Okeechobee Waterway across Florida. However, the original purpose of the canal was to remove floodwaters from Lake Okeechobee.

The initial construction didn't make a perfect canal, and a number of projects since have changed the canal significantly. For example, in 1933, 16 fixed spillways were approved for construction to reduce shoaling. In 1937, the canal was deepened to 6 feet so that ships could regularly reach Lake

Okeechobee. However, that wasn't enough, and in 1949 more dredging and work made the canal 8 feet deep. A unique part of the canal's design is that water flows both east to the St. Lucie Estuary and west to Lake Okeechobee "on about an equal basis," according to the Florida Department of Environmental Protection. The direction of water flow depends upon evaporation of the lake, recent rains, and storm conditions.

West of the bridge about a mile is the Port Mayaca Lock and Dam, a navigable lock designed to pass ships in and out of Lake Okeechobee. The lock itself is 56 feet wide, 400 feet long, and 14 feet deep. The lift is normally ½ to 2 feet, but there are times that the water levels in the lake and canal are equal, and the lock can just remain open. The dam was built to help raise the water levels in the lake to provide water for agricultural use, city water supply, and for navigation. Additionally, it is designed to reduce flooding caused by hurricanes. Just to the west of the bridge, the L-65 Canal enters the St. Lucie Canal from the north. The railroad closely follows this canal north for a number of miles.

K38.2 **BESSEMER** – In the 1950s, the Florida East Coast Railway had a telegraph station and a 68-car capacity siding at Bessemer, shown as Bessimor in some SCFE documents. The 3100-foot siding is still on the east side of the mainline. The name Bessemer comes from the Bessemer Properties company that developed nearby Port Mayaca.

Bessemer Properties traces its history back to Henry Phipps, who grew up with Andrew Carnegie, and was later Carnegie's business partner in the Carnegie Steel Company. In 1907, Phipps created the Bessemer Trust Company to manage his assets. Part of these assets included a substantial part of Florida, including one-third of the town of Palm Beach, 28 miles of oceanfront between Palm Beach and Fort Lauderdale, prime bayfront property in downtown Miami, and 75 square miles of land in Martin County. The property that became Phipps Park in Palm Beach was donated by the family. The trust still controls land and holdings across the United States, not just for the Phipps family, but also for a small group of other wealthy families.

**Barley Barber Swamp**

Not far north of the Bessemer Siding is Barley Barber Swamp, the remains of a large bald cypress forest and waterway that was part of the Everglades watershed. Today, this area is a 450-acre park owned by Florida Power & Light as a part of their Martin County power plant property.

The park includes a 16-foot-tall sand mound with ramp extensions that dates back as much as 900 years. Anthropologists believe that the mound was a trade center for area tribes. One of the oldest bald cypress trees in the southeast also stands here. It is believed to be more than 1000 years old and measures 88 feet tall and 33 feet around. The park also features Florida strangler figs, swamp maples, and pond apples, as well as nesting bald eagles, American alligators, river otters, bobcats, and white-tailed deer. In addition, a number of birds and plant species unique to the area are protected here.

The swamp and waterway was named after Barley Barber, a man who lived in the area about 1900.

Little is known about him as he fled the area, as legend states, due to "trouble with the law." Development in the area changed the water flow through the swamp, and today the Barley Barber waterway is diverted through the L-65 Canal south to the St. Lucie Canal. The swamp was acquired in 1972 as part of the construction of the Martin County power plant and cooling pond, located to the east of the tracks. A two-mile boardwalk has been built through the swamp and guided tours are available on a limited basis October through May.

**K34.2 FP&L MARTIN POWER PLANT LEAD** – To the east is a several mile line into the Florida Power & Light Company (FP&L) Martin Power Plant. Construction on the plant began in 1972, and today the plant is a mix of traditional natural gas-fired units and a large solar plant. Units 1 and 2 are 800 megawatt (MW, or one million watts) units that use natural gas and low-sulfur residual oil. Units 3 and 4 are 500 MW natural gas-fired units. What is known as Unit 8 is a 1150 MW natural gas-fired unit with light oil backup. It actually consists of several units, including four 170 MW gas turbines and one 470 MW steam turbine. Unit 8 went into service in 2005 and is integrated with the solar plant.

Florida Power & Light Company is the third-largest electric utility in the United States, and the largest in Florida. Its sister company, NextEra Energy Resources, is the world's largest generator of renewable energy from the wind and sun.

The Port Mayaca Polo Club is to the west, across the L-65 Canal. The club was established in 2006, designed and built by Stephen Orthwein, former Chairman of the United States Polo Association and a member of the Executive Committee of the International Polo Federation. The Port Mayaca Polo Club has five championship-quality fields and club barns with paddocks to stable over 200 horses. The Polo Club is designed to handle world-level competition as well as rider development.

This sign marks the entrance to the Port Mayaca Polo Club, located to the west of the railroad.

Heading north, the railroad passes through a mix of citrus groves and open ranch land, still following the C-65 Canal.

**K29.2 MANTOLA** – In 1957, the railroad had a 75-car capacity siding. In that year, this was the location where trains No. 131 (southbound) and No. 132 (northbound) met on a daily basis. These second-class freight trains served the "branch between Fort Pierce Junction and Lake Harbor." Today, there is a short piece of this siding at Milepost K29. The wider grade to the south clearly shows where the siding once was located.

Mantola is where the new Fort Pierce Cut-off joined with the old Lake Harbor Branch (then the Kissimmee Valley Line), which once came south from Edgewater, near New Smyrna Beach, Florida. The change took place at Milepost K29.32. When this change occurred, Milepost K153.1 of the Kissimmee Valley Line became Milepost K30.0 using the new Fort Pierce Cut-off distance. Soon, the original line north of here was either abandoned or sold off. This explains the curve as trains heading to Fort Pierce turn from heading northwest to heading northeast, as the original line once continued straight to Okeechobee and then further north.

**K28.5 MARCY** – Marcy is the crossing between CSX and the South Central Florida Express, but no connection between the two railroads exists here. This is the same line that the South Central Florida Express connects with at Sebring. The CSX line is the former Florida Western & Northern Railroad, built in the 1920s and opened in January 1925. It was controlled by the Seaboard Air Line Railroad. The line started at Coleman and headed south-southeast through Auburndale, Sebring, and West Palm Beach as a part of a plan by Seaboard president S. Davies Warfield to enter the South Florida market and end the monopoly of the Florida East Coast Railway. The line was extended a few years later when the Seaboard-All Florida Railway built on to Miami, Homestead and Florida City.

Under the Seaboard Coast Line, this was the Miami Subdivision of the Jacksonville Division. Today, it is the Auburndale Subdivision of CSX. This was the route of several well-known passenger trains, such as the *Orange Blossom Special*, *Silver Meteor*, and *Silver Star*. Amtrak still uses it for their modern versions of the *Silver Meteor* and *Silver Star*.

In 2018, the crossing frogs (diamonds) were replaced with new OWLS-design frogs. An OWLS (One-Way Low-Speed) frog is a unique type of frog where one line has no flangeway gap to cross, while the other line uses a slower flange-bearing design. At Marcy, the CSX line is the primary route and has no flangeway gap, while the South Central Florida Express route uses the slower flange-bearing side of the frog.

In January 2018, the new OWLS (One-Way Low-Speed) frog was awaiting installation at Marcy.

The South Central Florida Express has a siding (825 feet long) just south of the diamond, and the mainline continues to the northeast as it heads towards Fort Pierce. For the next ten miles, the line is mainly through open lands used for cattle ranching, as well as some citrus and vegetable production.

Northeast of here, the railroad crests over the Rim of the Okeechobee Basin, the high point between the lake and the Atlantic Ocean. Near Milepost K24.5, the rail line peaks at 41 feet above sea level.

**K26.5 PLANTBAMBOO** – Located at the Florida Highway 714 grade crossing, this location has nothing to do with the railroad, but it is a fascinating local attraction. Located to the west of the tracks, Plantbamboo is 600 acres of open agri-tourism land where visitors can see a farm, camp, and ride ATVs. Events such as mud bogging, truck pulls, and almost anything involving dirt and mud is popular here, and Plantbamboo is advertised as "The Best Mud on Earth."

**K22.7 BLUEFIELD** – In 1957, the Florida East Coast had a 4-car track here. This spur track is still in place to the east, and the South Central Florida Express lists it as being 650 feet long. This spur track was named for the adjacent Bluefield Ranch. Until the 1930s, this was a traditional cattle ranch, but that changed when the Iglehart family bought 36 square miles of ranch land to create a hunting retreat for the family and their friends. Today, 3285 acres of this ranch makes up the Bluefield Ranch Preserve. The Preserve includes the largest stand of scrub in St. Lucie County, more than 20 miles of hiking, mountain bike and horse trails, an elevated wildlife observation deck, wildlife blind, primitive hike-in camping and primitive horseback camping.

For railroad enthusiasts, the ranch once featured a 3-foot gauge railroad. This happened in the 1920s and 1930s when much of the property was logged.

The railroad was used to haul the logs, described as being "between 6 and 8 feet in diameter, and 50 feet in height," to a sawmill on the Seaboard Air Line in Sherman, about seven miles west of here. The sawmill was the Sherman-Spann Lumber Company during the 1910s, and then the W. C Sherman Lumber Company by the 1930s. Because of the size of the mill, Sherman was for several years larger than nearby Okeechobee.

**K22.2 COUNTY LINE** – The county line runs east-west and is located just south of the bridge over the County Line Canal. To the south is **Martin County** while **St. Lucie County** is to the north.

**Martin County**, like Palm Beach County, stretches from the beaches of the Atlantic Ocean to Lake Okeechobee. However, unlike Palm Beach County, Martin County doesn't include any of the major cities on the Atlantic coast. Also unlike Palm Beach County, Martin County is rather small, covering only 543 square miles (54th largest in Florida). The county's population is about 150,000, ten percent of what Palm Beach County has. Its county seat is Stuart, the only incorporated city in the county. Martin County was created in 1925, using parts of St. Lucie and Palm Beach Counties. It was named for John W. Martin, the Governor of Florida at the time. The creation of Martin County also included a change in the county lines of several other counties. At the time, Palm Beach County included all of Lake Okeechobee, giving it a larger share of state and federal road tax revenues. This was changed so that the lake was divided among the counties that it bordered.

St. Lucie County was created in 1905 from the southern part of Brevard County, giving the county 572 square miles of territory (Florida's 49th largest county of 67 in total). It should be noted that this was the second St. Lucie County in Florida, as Brevard County had been named St. Lucie County from 1844 until 1855. The area was originally controlled by the Ais tribe, who successfully fought off early Spanish explorers as they explored the eastern Florida coast. Because of this, the Spanish named the area Rio de Ays (later becoming the Indian River), and then Santa Lucia for a nearby late-1500s Spanish fort. Just off the coast is where the 1715 Spanish treasure fleet sank, giving the area the name of the Treasure Coast. The county seat of St. Lucie County is Fort Pierce. The county's population is approximately 300,000.

This area is part of the Allapatah Flats, a large area of wet woodlands named for the Seminole Indian word for alligator. Much of the land was drained to create open pasture for cattle grazing, but efforts are underway to close some of the canals to return the land to its original condition. This was a large area that once extended from the upper St. Johns River basin to the upper reaches of the St. Lucie River.

K22.1 **COUNTY LINE CANAL BRIDGE** – This bridge is a five-span concrete ballast deck bridge, 130 feet long and installed in 1960. It crosses County Line Canal (C-23 Canal), which serves as the border between St. Lucie and Martin Counties. According to the Florida Fish and Wildlife Conservation Commission, the "canal flows south six miles from flood control structure (G-78) and then makes a

90 degree turn to the east and continues to flow 15 more miles to the salinity structure (S-97) located at the southeast end of the canal adjacent to the boat ramp." The canal was built in the mid-1900s as part of a large flood control project. Today, it is a popular fishing location for largemouth bass, bluegill, redear, and black crappie.

**K15.5 BLOCK LIMITS** – This is the north end of the SCFE's **Fort Pierce Block**. North of here, crews must receive permission from the Florida East Coast to proceed.

South of this location, the South Central Florida Express has full local trackage rights with the ability to switch local customers. The SCFE also is responsible for track maintenance on these tracks. North of here toward Fort Pierce, the SCFE simply has overhead trackage rights to reach Fort Pierce for interchange purposes. This agreement means that the large shippers on the north end of the line are still handled by Florida East Coast train crews.

**K14.0 CANA** – In 1957, the Cana siding was described as having a capacity of 75 cars. Today, the siding still is on the west side of the mainline. Cana is the beginning of the industrial zone that stretches all the way into Fort Pierce. Between these rail shippers are a number of vegetable farms, citrus groves, and housing subdivisions. The Florida East Coast still serves the customers along the 15 miles of track east of the Cana area.

In this area are two spur tracks. The one at Milepost 14.7 heads east to serve the Dairy Feeds, Inc., feed mill. The FEC delivers a number of cars of grain and other commodities to this operation. Just north of the siding at Milepost 13.8 is a spur to the east to serve Allied Universal Corporation. Founded in 1954, this company is involved in the water treatment chemical and swimming pool industry. This plant was built in 2010 as a salt-to-bleach plant, the newest and largest of its kind in North America. The railroad moves tank cars full of the bleaches, primarily sodium hypochlorite and sodium hydroxide.

K11.1 **C-24 CANAL BRIDGE** – According to the Florida Fish and Wildlife Conservation Commission, the Diversion Canal C-24 was built between 1959 and 1961 by the U.S. Army Corps of Engineers as part of a large flood control project. Local signs call the canal Rim Ditch and state that it is managed by the South Florida Water Management District.

The bridge is a seven-span concrete ballast deck structure. There is a short spur track (Rim Ditch – three 50-foot car lengths in 1967) just south of the bridge and an equipment detector just north of the bridge. Equipment detectors like this automatically inspect the wheels and brakes of the train as it passes, making sure that the wheels and axles are not overheating. They also inspect to see that all of the wheels are riding properly on the rails. Some detectors can also inspect the wheels for flat spots that could damage the rail, or for shifted loads that could hit a nearby structure. These are all examples of how technology is used by the railroad industry to make things safer.

K9.1 **CARLTON** – This area was named for the Carlton Ranch, a cattle ranch that dates back to the late 1800s. At one time it managed more than 50,000 acres in this area, plus more acreage closer to Lake Okeechobee.

The Florida East Coast considered this short spur track able to hold 4 cars. To the east are several golf course developments, including the PGA Golf Club at PGA Village. For those who want to play, there are 54 holes here. The facility is rated among the 75 Best Golf Resorts by *Golf Digest*, and is actually located in Port St. Lucie, Florida.

K7.7    **INTERSTATE 95** – The railroad passes under this Interstate Highway, described as the longest north-south Interstate, 1910 miles from Miami to Northern Maine. I-95 passes through more states, fifteen, than any other Interstate Highway. It was one of the first to see construction, in 1957, but was not completed until September 2018 when the last few miles were opened in central New Jersey.

K5.4    **FLORIDA TURNPIKE** – The railroad passes under this toll road, part of a 483-mile network in south and central Florida. According to the toll authority, 1.8 million motorists use Florida's Turnpike each day. This route is part of the original core of the system. In 1957, the original 110-mile stretch of roadway from Miami to Fort Pierce – the Sunshine State Parkway – opened. The second section from Fort Pierce to Wildwood was completed in 1964.

In this area are a number of large rail shippers, plus a siding. To the east is a Cemex cement plant, while to the west is the huge Tropicana Products plant. Tropicana was founded in Bradenton, Florida, in 1947 by Anthony T. Rossi, who developed flash pasteurization and pioneered orange juice rail transportation in 1970, moving juice from Florida to the New York market. Tropicana saved $40 million in fuel costs alone during the first ten years of operation of what became known as the Juice Train. This newer plant also ships juice by rail, some of ten or more shipments a week between Florida and New Jersey. Watch for the railcars and the hundreds of truckloads of oranges.

The Fort Pierce area has long been a citrus packing and processing community. This 1937 photo from the Farm Security Administration shows a local merchant loading up grapefruit at a Fort Pierce packing plant. A little-known fact is that most of the best fruit is shipped away to market, and many local merchants sell the fruit that is considered to be unfit for packing. United States Resettlement Administration, Rothstein, Arthur, photographer. *Loading grapefruit unfit for packing to sell to local merchants, Fort Pierce, Florida.* Fort Pierce, Florida, Jan. 1937. Photograph. https://www.loc.gov/item/2017721884/.

Just north of the Turnpike is a track into a sand and gravel distribution center. Further north near Milepost 4 are several more rail customers moving sand and gravel. To the west is Supermix Concrete, while to the east is Titan America, a supplier of aggregate, ready-mix, and concrete blocks.

**K3.6 PETERSON ASPHALT CORPORATION** – In 1957, the Florida East Coast showed that there was a 27-car track at this location. In 1955, the Peterson Asphalt Corporation opened to manufacture "Plant Mix", an asphaltic-concrete which provides an ideal and long-wearing surface for roads, parking lots, driveways, patios, walks and special areas. This area is now Dickerson Aggregate, while the large plant facility to the east is gone. To the west is Helena Chemical.

**K3.2 TENMILE CREEK BRIDGE** – Tenmile Creek merges with Fivemile Creek just south of here to form the North Fork of the St. Lucie River. This timber trestle is approximately 300 feet long. In this area, the railroad reaches its lowest elevation at about 16 feet above sea level.

**K2.6 FIVEMILE CREEK BRIDGE** – Fivemile Creek is half of what it takes to create the North Fork of the St. Lucie River. It merges with Tenmile Creek less than a mile south of here. This bridge is a concrete ballast deck bridge. North of this bridge, the railroad enters the urban area of Fort Pierce.

In 1957, the Yard Limits for Fort Pierce started just east of this bridge, protecting trains while they switched the industrial parks in the Fort Pierce area. Most of the rail customers were on several long leads to the east.

*Sebring and Fort Pierce Subdivisions Route Guide*

**K0.0  FORT PIERCE JUNCTION** – The rail line curves to due north as it junctions with the mainline of the Florida East Coast at the south end of their Fort Pierce yard complex. This is the interchange location between the South Central Florida Express and the Florida East Coast. The FEC yard has about a dozen tracks, a wye, and an intermodal ramp facility. The railroad describes the facilities as a "rock and mixed freight yard, a newly revitalized intermodal ramp, and a terminal for Tropicana juice refrigerated boxcars." Fort Pierce was historically the junction between the Third and Fourth Districts of the Florida East Coast. The Third District went north to New Smyrna while the Fourth District went south to Miami. Don't bother looking for the original Fort Pierce train station; it was torn down in 1967.

USSC #506 sits at Fort Pierce on January 3, 2018, after delivering the Fort Pierce Turn to the Florida East Coast yard. Soon, it will head back south to Clewiston with fertilizer cars and empty tank cars for loading.

One of the common sights around Fort Pierce are the white refrigerator cars of Tropicana. This cut of Tropicana cars is sitting at the Fort Pierce yard waiting to head north to market.

Fort Pierce is the county seat of St. Lucie County and has a population of about 50,000. The name comes from the original Fort Pierce, a fort and supply post built in 1838 during the Second Seminole War. The fort was named for its first commander, Benjamin Pierce, brother of President Franklin Pierce. The fort was abandoned in 1842 and soon burned.

The modern Fort Pierce began as a general store and a few houses. The Florida East Coast Railway reached Fort Pierce in 1894, encouraging more local development. On February 2, 1901, the residents voted to incorporate the community, leading to today's City of Fort Pierce. It became the county seat of St. Lucie County when the county was created on July 1, 1905. Another boom occurred in the 1910s when the Florida East Coast and Henry M. Flagler heavily promoted Florida and the cities on its line, making Fort Pierce a terminal and a tourist destination. The land boom of the 1920s led to the development of Fort Pierce as a "Mediterranean" community, with a number of the buildings now listed on the National Register of Historic Places.

Along with the tourists came agricultural development, including citrus, and beef and dairy cattle. During World War II, a Navy base was located here to train Underwater Demolition Teams, a program that later expanded into the SEAL teams of today.

This Farm Security Administration photo from 1937 shows the Indian River Refrigeration Terminal Company facility at Fort Pierce. This area was part of the famous "Indian River" fruit district, and many such facilities stood in the area. During the 1930s, about one-third of Florida's citrus production was in the Fort Pierce area. United States Resettlement Administration, Rothstein, Arthur, photographer. *Refrigeration terminal at Fort Pierce, Florida.* Fort Pierce, Florida, Jan. 1937. Photograph. https://www.loc.gov/item/2017721886/.

Like many cities, the 1970s and 1980s were not kind to Fort Pierce and many of the historic structures showed decay. During the 1990s, a restoration effort began that led to Fort Pierce being awarded the 2005 City of Excellence Award by the Florida League of Cities, and the 2011 Great American Main Street Award from the National Trust for Historic Preservation. With the recent population growth, the agricultural business has moved west, but Tropicana is still a very important company for the area. Today, Fort Pierce is known as the Sunrise City and benefits from a mix of tourism and national industries.

**Fort Pierce and Brightline Trains**

Fort Pierce has been a base of engineering work on the Brightline passenger train route from West Palm Beach to Orlando. Concrete ties for the project are made by Rocla Concrete Tie at Fort Pierce, with almost one-half million needed for the project. During construction of the line, stacks of concrete ties were staged throughout the Fort Pierce area. Brightline will construct their own tracks next to those of the Florida East Coast freight tracks through the Fort Pierce area.

During late 2019, Virgin Trains USA (then a partner with Brightline) was looking for station locations in the Treasure Coast region, and Fort Pierce was one of the potential sites. However, on November 12, 2019, Fort Pierce rejected Virgin Trains USA's downtown development proposal. Instead, the Fort Piece City Commission selected a mixed-use project for the land alongside the railroad, preventing the railroad from developing transit-oriented real estate around a railroad station.

## SCFE Okeelanta Lead
### Keela (FL) to Okeelanta (FL)

This route cuts through miles of sugarcane, broken at regular intervals by drainage canals and field access roads. The original construction on this line took place after World War II, connecting the Okeelanta Co-op Sugar Mill with the Atlantic Coast Line (ACL) route between Lake Harbor and Clewiston. The August 20, 1948, issue of *The Everglades News* provided details about the construction, saying that a Burro crane was being used to throw up a muck roadbed. Then track would be laid and a work train would follow, dumping sand on the track. The track was then jacked up on the sand ballast. After the muck dried, more sand was used to again level the track. The paper also reported that "practically all muck fill is in, five miles of track laid, and four miles of track surfaced on sand fill."

A report in the September 19, 1948, issue of *The Palm Beach Post-Times* stated that two contractor crews were working on this ACL branch, one working from near Clewiston and one from the Okeelanta end. The report also stated that the railroad would serve as "a dike to prevent flood waters from the open glades from backing up on developed land to the north of the railroad."

The Okeelanta Subdivision of the Atlantic Coast Line opened in 1949, allowing the Okeelanta Co-op Sugar Mill to move their shipments by rail, eliminating the many local truck moves. By 1965, the line was simply shown as being the Okeelanta Branch. The line was extended beyond the sugar mill that year with the hopes of serving another sugar mill and several vegetable farms. However, this business never materialized and the line was cut back in 1979 to Cane, and it was again the Okeelanta Subdivision of CSX by the late 1980s. Today, the South Central Florida Express operates the line as their Okeelanta Lead, also known as the Cane Block. The railroad essentially rebuilt this line in 2016 to mainline standards. There are no sugarcane loading facilities on this line, and the only real customer is the Okeelanta Sugar Mill. The SCFE Local generally serves the line on Tuesdays and Fridays.

# SCFE Okeelanta Lead Route Guide
## Keela (FL) to Okeelanta (FL)

**0.0**   **KEELA** – This line starts at a wye at Keela, sometimes known as Wye Junction. The Clewiston-Fort Pierce mainline curves to the east while the Okeelanta Lead heads off to the southeast before curving due south.

The Atlantic Coast Line had Keela as Milepost 953.7, and continued the mileposts to the end of the line. Today, the mileposts start here with 0.0. Both sets of mileposts will be provided.

The Okeelanta Branch is protected by the **Cane Block** from Milepost 0.0 at Keela to Milepost 15.5. This line has no cane loaders or other U.S. Sugar facilities, so only the Clewiston Local operates regularly over the line.

Signs for the speed limit, milepost, and Cane Block stand side-by-side at the Keela Switch for the Okeelanta Lead.

The Okeelanta Lead passes through miles of sugarcane fields, and crosses dozens of drainage and irrigation canals. Because of this, alligators are often seen along the line, such as this one sunning itself at Milepost 1.2 on a nice spring day in 2021.

**1.8** **U.S. SUGAR LINE DIAMOND** – The former ACL route crosses the Clewiston Mainline Division sugarcane line of U.S. Sugar at what was ACL Milepost 955.5. The Clewiston Mainline connects with the former ACL line near the Clewiston Sugar Mill and heads generally east before connecting with the former Florida East Coast line at South Bay, and then further north at Bryant. There are a number of cane loaders on this sugar line.

In 1983, the Seaboard System Railroad's *Tampa Division Timetable No. 1* stated that the diamond was protected by "stop" boards (stop signs according to CSX in 1987). In SCFE Timetable No. 8, it states that the "automatic interlocking diamond at the mile post 1.8 on the Cane Block mainline is a signal system that works on a first arrive, first right of movement basis. A distant signal is placed 1 mile in advance to the crossing in either direction." These distant signals show green when a train can cross the diamond at normal speeds, while a yellow instructs the crew to be prepared to stop at the diamond. Additional signals at the crossing provide further information.

Distant signals are used as part of the signaling system for the U.S. Sugar Line Diamond. These distant signals show green when a train can cross the diamond at normal speeds, while a yellow instructs the crew to be prepared to stop at the diamond.

This view looks southward at the U.S. Sugar Line Diamond.

Steam locomotive #148 passes a recently cut sugarcane field near the U.S. Sugar Line Diamond on the Okeelanta Line.

2.8   **ROGERS ROAD** – This is a main east-west road through the cane fields. It connects Evercane Road to the west with Miami Canal Road to the east. Coming from the north, the SCFE crosses a canal using a small I-beam bridge before crossing Rogers Road at grade. The canal is a popular area for observing alligators.

This small bridge on the Okeelanta Lead is located just north of Rogers Road.

This sign warns about the presence of alligators. Just about any waterway along the railroads of U.S. Sugar will be full of them.

4.3 **VAUGHN** – The location of Vaughn is easy to find by the large area to the east used to store fertilizers and other products for local sugarcane farming. The station was located at ACL Milepost 957.9.

The name Vaughn has a great deal of meaning in the Clewiston area. Harry Thomas Vaughn, Sr., served as President of the U.S. Sugar Corporation during the early 1960s. His son, Harry T. Vaughn, Jr., was born in Clewiston on July 12, 1932, and later served as Executive Vice President of U.S. Sugar. The Clewiston Public Library uses the name Harry T. Vaughn Library due to the donations by the sugar company and friends of the family.

5.8 **BOLLES CANAL BRIDGE** – The Bolles Canal (Canal L-16) is a major east-west canal that stretches 6.6 miles and connects the Miami, North New River, and Hillsboro canals. It was completed in 1931 and was designed to balance the water flows between the various canals south of Lake Okeechobee. The canal received a great deal of work in 2016, opening it up and removing sediment to allow better water flow. The ACL milepost was 959.4.

The Bolles Canal takes its name from Richard J. Bolles, who developed and promoted the community of Ritta Shore. He also built a hotel on the site in 1911.

8.4 **CURVE** – The railroad, which has been heading south when traveling away from Keela, starts to turn to the east.

10.3 **MIAMI CANAL BRIDGE** – The Miami Canal is a major connection between Lake Okeechobee and the Atlantic Ocean at Miami. Also known as C-6

Canal, it was built during the early 1900s as a part of the effort to drain and irrigate the Everglades Agricultural Area. The Miami Canal connects with Lake Okeechobee at Lake Harbor and heads south more than 75 miles to the Miami River, which flows five more miles to the ocean. Steamboats once operated on the canal and the remains of a lock are still visible at Lake Harbor. Next to the Canal is Miami Canal Road, a popular route into the area for fishermen.

The bridge includes a central I-beam span, with short timber trestle spans off each end. A pumping station for a local drainage canal is located just to the southeast of the bridge.

15.5  **BLOCK LIMITS** – This is the south end of the **Cane Block**. From here to Milepost 17.1, the railroad is operated using yard limits.

This sign marks the south end of Cane Block on the Okeelanta Lead.

**16.0 OKEELANTA** – The townsite of Okeelanta is located about two miles to the north, centered approximately four miles south of South Bay at the U.S. Highway 27 – County Road 827 crossroads. There is nothing there today but sugarcane and the junction of the North New River and Bolles Canals. The Bolles Canal is a major east-west canal, stretching east from the Miami Canal to the Hillsboro Canal. The canal received a great deal of work in 2016, opening it up and removing sediment to allow better water flow.

Okeelanta, a combination of Okeechobee and Atlantic, was created by Thomas E. Will, editor for the American Forestry Association. It started in 1910 when Will and others created the Florida Everglades Homebuilders Association to develop homesites in the area. However, they were unable to buy solid blocks of land in the South Bay area, and a second plan created a "new" Okeelanta and the Okeelanta Corporation in 1913.

Thomas Will and his son, Lawrence E. Will, moved into a small shack in December 1914 and began to promote the farming community. Soon small farms were growing Irish potatoes, corn, beans, tomatoes, and eggplant, and by 1917, the community had 110 families, a hotel, town hall, lumberyard, blacksmith, and barber. By 1920, the community had added a school. An issue with farming did develop as the soils at Okeelanta were different from areas previously settled, and Thomas Will spent years researching the muck left over after draining the swamps, inventing farming equipment and testing various crops to see which would grow.

The end for Okeelanta began with a flood in 1922, forcing even the Wills to leave the community. Reportedly, a visitor in 1925 described Okeelanta as soggy and deserted. The last of the residents left after the town was destroyed by flooding and winds during the Hurricane of 1928. The Okeelanta Corporation soon declared bankruptcy and the effort to develop Okeelanta was over. A few farms and businesses are scattered along Highway 27 north of here, a road that carries the name "Thomas E. Will Memorial Highway" from South Bay to Miami.

**Okeelanta Sugar Mill**

While Okeelanta was at Milepost 969.7, the end of track is now just east of the wye at Milepost 15.5, but the mill is 16.6 miles from Keela. There were once several tracks curving to the north, with the one to the east going to the current Florida Crystals bagging and distribution center. These tracks are now unused. The tracks that head north at the wye serve the Okeelanta Sugar Mill. This mill was opened in 1947 and is now part of the Florida Crystals organization. Construction on the mill began during World War II from parts of the Vieques mill that was moved from Puerto Rico. The project was designed to guarantee access to sugar without the need for ocean shipping. Reportedly, much of the construction of the mill and the surrounding roads and ditches was performed by German and Italian prisoners of war. The mill has been modernized significantly and includes a generating plant which produces both electricity and steam using biomass as fuel. The railroad handles bulk sugar, molasses, and other products for the mill, but no raw sugarcane is moved as trucks handle that for the company.

On a hot day at the end of the sugarcane season, the Okeelanta Sugar Mill is shown across an uncut field.

Florida Crystals has an international story, dating back more than five generations. It started in Cuba in the mid-1800s when Andres Gomez-Mena arrived and began investing in the sugar business. By the time of his death in 1910, he owned four sugar mills and was a major property owner in Havana. His son, Jose 'Pepe' Gomez-Mena, reorganized the holdings as the New Gomez-Mena Sugar Company. His position in the business world led him to the role of Cuba's Secretary of Agriculture in the 1930s, and also as president of the National Association of Sugar Mill Owners and the Cuban Institute for Sugar Stabilization.

Meanwhile, the Czarnikow Rionda Company in New York and the Cuban Trading Company were founded by Manuel Rionda, who operated six sugar mills in Cuba. Eventually these companies were controlled by Alfonso Fanjul, Sr., a great nephew. In 1936, Alfonso married Lillian Gomez-Mena, combining the two empires which totaled ten sugar mills, three distilleries, the Czarnikow-Rionda Company, and a large amount of real estate across Cuba.

This ended when Fidel Castro seized power and nationalized all private business holdings in 1959. The family fled to Florida and worked to get back into the sugar business. They purchased 4000 acres of land and bought the parts of three closed mills in Louisiana and used them to build the Osceola Sugar Mill. The company continued to buy and lease land, and by the mid-1980s, it was earning $240 million a year with tens of thousands of acres. During the 1990s, the company became Florida Crystals and was the state's largest sugar company.

In 1998, Florida Crystals and the Sugar Cane Growers Cooperative of Florida partnered to create the American Sugar Refining Group (ASR), now owned by Florida Crystals. ASR Group is now the world's largest cane sugar refining company and it owns and operates sugar refineries in Louisiana, California, New York, Maryland, Canada, Mexico, England, Italy and Portugal. Its products are sold through the Domino, C&H, Florida Crystals, Redpath, Jack Frost, and Tate & Lyle brands.

Today, the Florida Crystals Corporation, headquartered in West Palm Beach, Florida, is a fully integrated cane sugar company, farming 190,000 acres of land in Palm Beach County, operating two sugar mills, a sugar refinery, a packaging and distribution center, a rice mill and the largest renewable power plant in North America. The company states that it "is the only producer of certified organic sugar grown and harvested in the United States."

**Duda Rail Line**

As previously stated, the line east of the Okeelanta Sugar Mill is now abandoned. The line east of here had an interesting history, well documented in Interstate Commerce Commission and various legal documents. In the legal case of *Florida East Coast Railway Company v. United States* (May 19, 1965), the Florida East Coast attempted to halt construction by the Atlantic Coast Line Railroad Company of "an extension of an existing rail line, now terminating at the Okeelanta sugar mill, a distance of 6.5 miles east, and from this point it was proposed that one branch would run north 2.5 miles to the site of a packing house and precooling plant which A. Duda & Sons (Duda) proposed to build, and another branch would run south to the mill of the South Florida Sugar Company." The Florida East Coast (FEC) proposed to build their own line to the same customers, an "extension of an existing rail line from a sugar mill near Belle Glade, Florida, south and southeast, for a distance of about ten miles, through the property of Duda and others to the mill of the South Florida Sugar Company."

An important piece of information from the court hearing was that the FEC "reported to the court that it was informed that the owners of the South Florida Sugar Mill had sold its properties and that the mill would cease operations and be dismantled." Both the Interstate Commerce Commission and the courts approved the construction of the line by the Atlantic Coast Line. However, that may not have been good for the ACL as the line was abandoned in 1979.

18.2 **CANE** – This milepost was where the tracks crossed U.S. Highway 27 and the North New River Canal. The North New River Canal was built as part of an effort to drain parts of the Everglades. The canal was also a transportation route for steamboats between Fort Lauderdale and Lake Okeechobee, and then on to Fort Myers via the Caloosahatchee River. Locks were built on the canal, and Lock No. 1 at the south end of the canal was the first to be built in South Florida, and is now listed on the National Register of Historic Places. Regular service on the canal ended in 1926 and the locks were deactivated.

In 1977, the Seaboard Coast Line showed that there was a 21-car siding at Cane, Milepost 971.9. The town of Okeelanta was located two miles north of here.

24.2 **DUDA** – The end of this line was once at the Duda Belle Glade Farm, about five miles south-southeast of Belle Glade, Florida, at ACL Milepost 977.9. Duda was created by the family of Andrew Duda, who emigrated from Slovakia to America in 1909. They joined with others to found the small Slovak community of Slavia in Central Florida. The Duda family harvested their first successful cash crop – celery – in 1926, creating A. Duda & Sons. Over the past few decades, the company has expanded across Florida and into Texas and California. Some of their major crops are cattle, sugarcane, citrus, and sod. They have also begun developing planned communities on some of their properties.

Seaboard Coast Line Employee Time Table No. 8, dated October 30, 1977, showed that there was a rail yard at Duda.

This sign, located near Belle Glade, points the way towards the facilities of A. Duda & Sons.

# Route Guide for the U.S. Sugar Corporation Railroad (USSC)

One of the largest changes on the railroads of U.S. Sugar are the new lines being built to reach into the sugar cane fields of the company. In particular, the track sometimes known as the Bryant Connector has impacted almost the entire sugar cane railroad system. This line has connected the former Eastern Division at Bryant, and the Western Division at Clewiston. A history of each of these two divisions is provided here.

Another significant action taken with the completion of the Bryant Connector was a renumbering of the mileposts on the sugar cane railroad system. As the earlier lines were built, most started with Milepost 0.0. This created a number of conflicting mileposts, often at locations near each other. As an additional safety step, the company has created a mainline which starts with Milepost 0.0, and a series of branch lines that each have their own unique milepost series.

Another recent change was the creation of several new blocks, and the adjustment of others. These blocks allow trains to be assigned to specific locations on the railroad, providing safer operations than using yard limits or similar systems.

A final comment must be made about the track and trains. When many people hear about private tracks used to serve the sugar cane industry, they probably think about bad track weaving and wandering through farmland. However, that is far from the truth for U.S. Sugar. These tracks are built and maintained to the same standards as the tracks of the South Central Florida Express. Heavy welded rail, new ties, stone ballast, crossing gates and signals, regular inspections, and dispatching all are part of the system. Trains run fast, as much as 40 miles per hour hauling long trains of empty and loaded sugar cane cars.

The locomotives come from the same pool of equipment used by the South Central Florida Express, In fact, if you don't know what track they are on, you generally can't tell which operation you are seeing. The same can be said for the cane car fleet, which can operate almost anywhere on the two systems.

**Former Eastern Division**

The Eastern Division of the U.S. Sugar Corporation's railroad consisted of the rail lines that once supported the Bryant Sugar Mill, and earlier Southern Sugar. These lines are based at Bryant Yard and head north and south from the east end of the yard, using a wye to connect all of the tracks. During the sugarcane harvest season, cane trains served the cane loaders on the former Bryant-Prewitt South Line (BP Line), former Bryant-Martinez Line (BM Line), and the former Bryant-Boy North Line (BB Line).

The **Bryant-Prewitt South Line** headed south from the Bryant Wye and served cane fields all the way to the east side of Belle Glade. While just a bit more than a dozen miles long, the line served nine cane loading facilities. Various maps and documents indicate that this was the first rail line built in the area by Southern Sugar.

Almost all of this line became part of the new Clewiston Mainline Division when the Bryant Connector was built between the former Western Division and the former Eastern Division. The last 1.5 miles became the Prewitt Lead when the lines were redesignated.

To the north was the **Bryant-Boy North Line**. This line supported the sugarcane harvests northeast of U.S. Highway 98 and southwest of the DuPuis Management Area and the J. W. Corbett Wildlife Management Area. Lake Okeechobee is to the west. There were eight sugarcane loading facilities on this 19.7-mile line. Much of this land is shared with the Osceola Farms complex, which the railroad almost encircles.

The USSC Boy North Line forms a large backwards question mark, surrounding the Florida Crystals Osceola Mill. This sign along Florida Highway 700 marks the entrance to the mill.

According to the South Florida Water Management District, the DuPuis Management Area "is a 21,875-acre multi-use natural area located in northwestern Palm Beach and southwestern Martin counties." The property is a mix of Everglades marsh, wet prairies, and a combination of cypress and pine. For visitors, there are campgrounds, hiking and horseback trails, fishing, and seasonal hunting. The site was earlier a ranch for Dutch white-belted cattle, sheep and goats, but 6500 acres of wetlands were restored by 2001.

To the east is the J. W. Corbett Wildlife Management Area (WMA) of the Florida Fish and Wildlife Conservation Commission. The WMA includes signs of thousands of years of activity by native people. According to the WMA's website, they "reshaped the local environment by building mounds and digging canals through the sawgrass marsh between villages. Significant archeological sites include Big Mound City and Big Gopher. Big Mound City covers 143 acres and consists of at least 23 mounds, some with radiating causeways and crescent-shaped ponds. Big Gopher is one of the best-preserved earthwork sites in the Lake Okeechobee basin and consists of linear ridges, crescents, mounds and middens." This area was one of the last refuges of the Seminole Indians, who were forced out only by starvation, giving the area the name Hungryland.

The land eventually became the property of the Southern States Land and Timber Company, which logged it and used it for cattle grazing. In 1947, 52,000 acres of the property were bought by the Florida Game and Fish Commission, predecessor of the Fish and Wildlife Conservation Commission. The area was named after James Wiley Corbett, a former commissioner. In 1932, the WMA was enlarged by 2331 acres as part of an effort to protect the water flows through the marsh.

The Wildlife Management Area features hiking, bicycling and horseback riding, camping, wildlife viewing, fishing, and one of the only public hunting areas along the highly populated Gold Coast. Deer, turkey and feral hogs are the most hunted wildlife in the WMA.

This line became part of the new Clewiston Mainline Division when the Bryant Connector was built between the former Western Division and the former Eastern Division.

The **Bryant-Martinez Line** used the Bryant-Prewitt South Line to Martinez Junction, and then curved to the east and followed the south side of a canal for its entire length. The rail line ended not far west of the Old Conners Road. There is only one cane loading facility on this route, which is 3½ miles long. The entire line is now known as the Martinez Lead.

The tracks west of Bryant Yard to the South Central Florida Express are actually considered to be SCFE tracks. Historically, during the harvest, cane trains delivered loads to Bryant Yard, where they are picked up and put together for the run to the Clewiston sugar mill, using trains known as Bryant Turns over the Florida East Coast line. These mainline SCFE trains have historically operated 24 hours a day to support the mill. In a typical year, more than 60,000 cars hauling almost 2.5 million tons of sugarcane were moved this way through Bryant.

With the construction of the Bryant Connector, a second option exists to move the sugar cane from Bryant to the mill at Clewiston. This new route allows cane to move the entire distance over U.S. Sugar private routes, but with the potential of additional conflicts as the new Clewiston Mainline passes more than a dozen cane elevators.

Bryant Yard has more than ten miles of track with seven primary tracks plus several additional tracks used by customers of the railroad, as well as U.S. Sugar. On the north side of the yard is the former GBW Railcar Services facility. The operation has repaired railcars owned by various companies, and has also remanufactured cars for U.S. Sugar.

Also to the north of Bryant Yard are two 4.2-million-gallon tanks owned by the Florida Sugar & Molasses Exchange. This facility opened in 2015 to distribute blackstrap molasses worldwide. The product is sent out by rail or truck to more than 25 states and numerous foreign countries, with blackstrap molasses being the largest bulk export from the Port of Palm Beach to foreign ports. The molasses is a thick, dark syrup that remains after sugar has been crystallized from sugarcane juice. Because it isn't for human consumption, it's primary use is as a part of beef and dairy cattle feed. The Florida sugar industry's molasses production is valued at more than $70 million a year. U.S. Sugar also has a yard office in this area.

## Former Western Division

The Western Division of U.S. Sugar Corporation's railroad (USSC) consisted of the two lines that radiate out of the Clewiston Sugar Mill, serving the fields as far east as South Bay and as far west as the west side of the Airglades Airport. The **Wetherald Line** served the sugarcane fields to the southeast of Clewiston, with trains heading towards Wetherald and South Bay considered to be heading south. The rail line generally followed the former Atlantic Coast Line and Florida East Coast lines now operated by the South Central Florida Express, but was several miles to the south of these lines. The entire route passes through sugarcane fields and crosses a number of small drainage canals, using fills instead of bridges. Cane access roads cross the tracks about every mile. Today, this line is the first part of the USSC Clewiston Mainline Division, which connects the Clewiston Sugar Mill with the sugar cane around Bryant Yard.

The second line headed west from Flaghole Junction on the Wetherald Line. Known as the **Flaghole Line**, this route turned west towards Flaghole Road. There, the line continued west to the Southern Gardens Citrus processing plant on Sam Jones Trail, also known as Hendry County Road 833. The tracks west of Flaghole Road are new, built in 2012-2013, and part of it is technically the Citrus Subdivision of the South Central Florida Express. USSC has an exclusive trackage rights agreement to use the new part of the line. This Flaghole Line was approximately eighteen miles long and served five cane loading facilities. This line is now part of the USSC Flaghole Mainline Division.

The **Southern Gardens Citrus Line** is another part of the construction that took place in 2012-2013. This line had one purpose - to serve the Southern Gardens Citrus processing facility on County Road 833. The plant is located not far south of Florida Highway 80, which connects Clewiston and LaBelle, both in Hendry County. The line is now known as the Citrus Lead.

The Western Division was the true heart of U.S. Sugar Corporation. It featured the Clewiston Sugar Mill and the large rail yard that supports it. Approximately 70,000 carloads of sugarcane move off these lines to the mill each year. However, the sugarcane from every single source eventually passes through the Clewiston Terminal (Sugar Yard), the large yard on the east side of the Clewiston Sugar Mill of U.S. Sugar.

*The Railroads of U.S. Sugar: History Through the Miles*

# USSC Clewiston Mainline Division Route Guide
## Clewiston Yard to End of Track

This 60.6-mile-long-line includes the majority of the U.S. Sugar private sugar cane lines. It consists of parts of the former Wetherald, Prewitt South, and Boy North lines, as well as much of the new Bryant Connector construction project. All other U.S. Sugar mainlines and lead tracks branch off of the Clewiston Mainline Division.

Trains heading from Clewiston toward the Bryant tracks are considered to be heading east. However, this cane line curves in almost every direction imaginable. Because of this, the directions will often be given based upon the compass.

**0.0** **CLEWISTON YARD** – This is a ten-track yard, plus several tracks in a material yard, that serves the Clewiston Sugar Mill. Known by many as Sugar Yard, there are almost 17 miles of tracks in the entire complex. Both inbound cane loads, and outbound empty cane cars and loads of product are held here. At the west end of the yard are two sheds used for sugarcane unloading. The cane is then moved by conveyor into the large cane processing facility to the north. Farther west is a three-bay locomotive shop, known as South Shop, used by the trains hauling sugarcane, plus a track for freight car repairs. Plans are to move most of the locomotive maintenance and repairs to this facility.

Milepost 0.0 is at the east end of the yard, just south of the yard office, labeled as "USSC Railroad

– Clewiston Depot." There are two parts of the yard. The north part is known as the Long Yard and is generally used by the SCFE to pick up and drop off freight cars. The southern part of the yard is known as the Short Yard. This yard is used primarily by the cane trains. Working the yard, crews often use remote control locomotives, aided by remote control switches. At night, it is a very colorful scene as the remote control switches have lights that show the positions of their switch points.

North of the yard are two huge warehouses used to store the processed sugar. Alongside the buildings are long tracks for sugar loading. Also on the north side of the mill are tracks for the loading of other products such as molasses, the cleaning of railcars, and many other purposes. To the west are a series of mill buildings that are designed to make sugar from sugarcane. These include **Milling**, the process of crushing the cane to extract the juice; the **Boiling House** where the juice is concentrated, often called evaporation; the **Refinery** where the sugar is crystalized and dried; **Packaging** where the sugar is prepared for the customer; and the **Power Plant** which uses bagasse to produce steam and electricity for the facility.

It must be noted that the entire Clewiston Mill is a secure facility and is off limits to uninvited guests. Views of the rail and manufacturing operations are almost impossible, with only a few glimpses possible along Sonora Avenue. However, tours are sometimes offered. Check with the Clewiston Chamber of Commerce for information on their Sugarland Tours, which often feature views of the sugarcane harvest and manufacturing.

## USSC Clewiston Mainline Division

Milepost 0.0 is at the east end of the Clewiston Mill Yard, far from the eyes of Clewiston visitors.

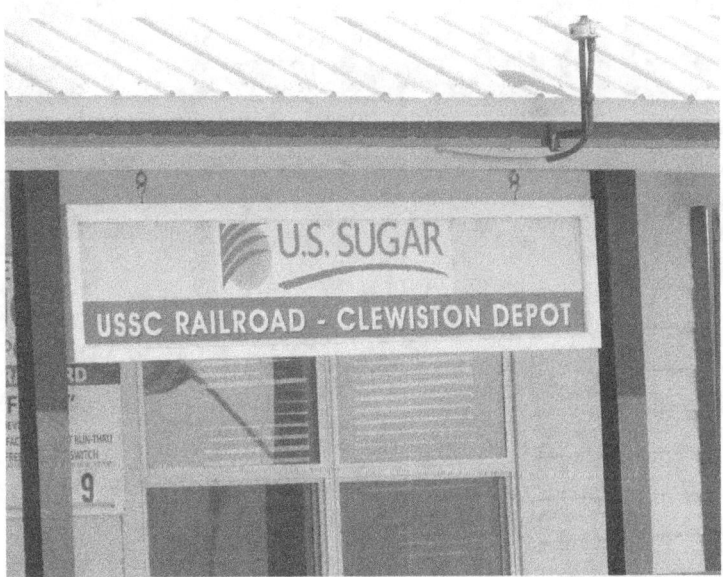

Located near Milepost 0.0 is the "USSC Railroad – Clewiston Depot."

This early morning view at Clewiston Mill Yard shows some of the lights used on the turnouts throughout the yard.

Clewiston Yard can be a very busy and dangerous place, and U.S. Sugar has installed a number of signs reminding its employees of these dangers and to be safe at work.

0.3 **WEST MILL WYE SWITCH** – There is a wye here to allow trains from both west and east of Clewiston to enter the mill from the South Central Florida Express mainline. To the south of the wye are two tracks that connect to the USSC sugarcane lines. These two tracks eventually join to form one track which heads to the south before splitting again to serve the sugarcane loading facilities east and west of the mill.

0.5 **MAINLINE CROSSOVER** – This new switch and crossover to the South Central Florida Express mainline allows freight trains to enter the USSC Clewiston Mainline Division and head west to reach the Southern Gardens Citrus facility at the west end of the new line to the west of Flaghole Road. Just south of here, the South Central Florida Express mainline curves away to the southeast.

1.1 **TOWNSITE #1** – This sugarcane loader, featuring an elevator with a ramp, is the closest one to the Clewiston Sugar Mill. While sugarcane fields line the south side of the sugar house, the cane is still hauled here for loading in railcars. This is because the mill is designed to accept cane by rail, in the specific quantities that the railcars deliver. The siding for the cane loader can handle about 30 cars on either side of the loader, which is located on the west side of the line.

The name Townsite comes from the original name used for the worker housing near the sugar mill. Workers from this community were assigned to handle the work in the area of this cane loader.

## The Railroads of U.S. Sugar: History Through the Miles

Cane loading facilities have been greatly improved over the years. This photo from 1939 shows the early process to load sugarcane into awaiting rail cars. The cane was bundled by hand and then lifted into the cars using a small crane. Today, ramps and conveyors do the work much faster. Wolcott, Marion Post, photographer. *Loading sugarcane for USSC United States Sugar Corporation near Clewiston, Florida.* Clewiston, Hendry County, Florida, Feb. 1939. Photograph. https://www.loc.gov/item/2017800321/.

**1.4 FLAGHOLE JUNCTION** – The U.S. Sugar Corporation's private sugarcane lines split here, with the USSC Clewiston Mainline Division continuing south, while the recently extended USSC Flaghole Mainline Division to the Southern Gardens Citrus plant curves to the west. Information on the Flaghole line can be found on page 393.

Heading south, trains on the Clewiston Mainline Division enter the **Town Block** and pass through miles of sugarcane fields. To control train operations and improve safety, the railroad authorizes train movements by giving the train crews permission to operate in each specific block along

*USSC Clewiston Mainline Division*

the various rail lines. Town Block is named for the Townsite cane loaders. North of here and into the Clewiston Yard at the mill the tracks are protected by yard limits. The Clewiston Yardmaster controls movements arriving and departing the yard.

The switch at this location is an automatic switch. Signals govern the movements of the trains over the turnout, and push buttons are used to operate the switch points.

**4.1** **TOWNSITE #2** – This cane loader is to the west of the main track and features a large modern ramp with an elevator used for loading cane into railcars. It is designed to handle approximately 30 empty cane cars. The Townsite cane loaders were all close enough to Clewiston for workers to come from the sugar company townsite during the early years of the company.

**4.8** **CURVE** – The railroad makes a ninety degree turn to the east just south of Townsite #2.

**5.7** **EVERCANE ROAD** – Evercane Road, also known as County Road 835, heads south from the Clewiston area into the sugarcane fields to the south. It, along with County Road 846, forms a route south and west to Immokalee, Florida. While there are no crossing gates, there are lots of lights to warn the highway traffic about any approaching trains.

This sign can be found on the signal box where the Clewiston Mainline crosses Evercane Road, County Road 835.

USSC #311 crosses Evercane Road with a loaded cane train during January 2015.

*USSC Clewiston Mainline Division*

Three years later (2018), USSC #405 crosses Evercane Road heading east on the Clewiston Mainline with an empty cane train.

**6.7    COUNTY LINE** – The county line is located just east of the west switch of the Townsite #3 siding. Look for the canal which runs along the county line. To the west is **Hendry County,** and to the east is **Palm Beach County.**

**Hendry County** has a population of 40,000, most of them in Clewiston, even though the county seat is LaBelle. The county was created in 1923 and named for Captain Francis Ashbury Hendry, a captain of Confederate calvary troops during the Civil War and one of the first area settlers. Hendry had been involved with the creation of Polk and Lee Counties, as well as the town of LaBelle. Because of his ranching experience, he was known as the "Cattle King of South Florida".

**Palm Beach County** was established in 1909 from part of Dade County. It was named for one of the oldest and largest communities in the area – Palm Beach. The county has had its borders changed several times, the latest in 1963, but it is still the second-largest county in Florida with 1969 square miles of territory. The county has a population of about 1,400,000 people, making it the third-most populous county in Florida. It is also Florida's wealthiest. Palm Beach County also leads the State of Florida in agricultural productivity, the second largest industry in the county. The largest is real estate.

**6.9** **TOWNSITE #3** – This cane loader is to the south and has an elevator and a ramp to transfer sugarcane from trailers and wagons into railcars. The siding is shown to have the capacity of 40 empty cane cars.

During recent years, sugarcane from the southwest that is located along Evercane Road has been brought to this loader by trucks. As new acreage is placed into production, studies are being conducted to build new rail lines so that loaders can be built closer to these new fields.

**7.8** **SCFE/USSC INTERLOCKING** – This line is the former Atlantic Coast Line Okeelanta Subdivision, now the Okeelanta Lead of the South Central Florida Express. The line connects the Okeelanta Co-op Sugar Mill with the Atlantic Coast Line (ACL) route at Keela, located between Lake Harbor and Clewiston. Information on this line can be found on page 319.

This can be a busy diamond, and signals to protect trains crossing the line have recently been installed to allow heavy trains to maintain their speed. Approach signals to the diamond can be seen along Rogers Road.

The railroad states that this automatic interlocking diamond is "a signal system that works on a first arrive, first right of movement basis. A distance signal is placed 1 mile in advance to the crossing in either direction and will either show a green signal which means that movement may be made though the diamond at normal speed, or a yellow signal, which means that movement must be made at a speed that allows stopping" at the signal near the diamond.

8.2 **CURVE** – Just east of the SCFE Diamond the Wetherald Line curves to the south. At the south end of the curve is a switch for another sugarcane loader.

8.8 **VAUGHN #1** – Located to the east, this loader is on a relatively short siding that can handle 30 empty cane cars. All of the cane loaders on this line feature an elevator with a ramp.

About a mile to the west was a company employee base named Vaughn. The name Vaughn has a great deal of meaning in the Clewiston area. Harry Thomas Vaughn, Sr., served as President of the U.S. Sugar Corporation during the early 1960s. His son, Harry T. Vaughn, Jr., was born in Clewiston on July 12, 1932, and later served as Executive Vice President of U.S. Sugar. The Clewiston Public Library uses the name Harry T. Vaughn Library due to the donations by the sugar company and friends of the family.

This view of the Vaughn #1 cane loader includes a few cane cars, the elevator used to move the cane into the railcars, and the distant signal for the SCFE diamond.

The east switch of the Vaughn #1 siding is at Milepost 9.0, located a short distance from Rogers Road.

*USSC Clewiston Mainline Division*

**9.4** **ROGERS ROAD** – Rogers Road is a major road used by trucks as a shortcut around the Clewiston area. They take the Miami Canal Road south to Rogers Road, and then head west to Highway 835, Evercane Road. Rogers Road is also unique in that it is one of the few paved roads that reaches into the sugarcane fields in the Everglades, although it can be bumpy in many places.

In January 2015, USSC #407 crosses Rogers Road and a small canal hauling cane to Clewiston late in the afternoon.

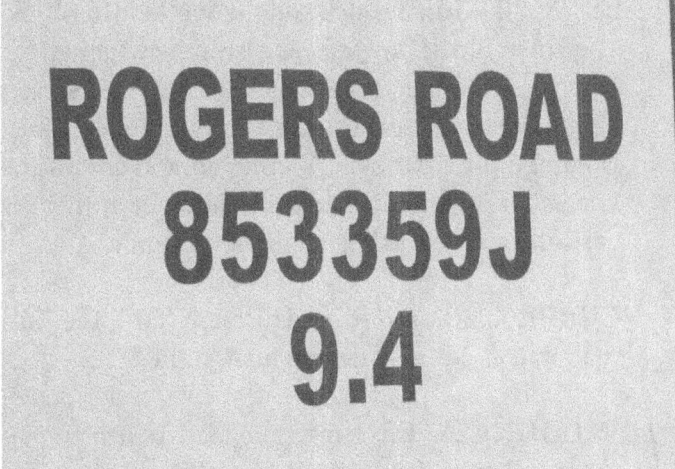

These markings on the Rogers Road grade crossing signal box clearly state that this is Rogers Road at Milepost 9.4.

353

USSC #405 hauls a cut of empty cane cars across the canal alongside Rogers Road during January 2018.

Just north of Rogers Road, the tracks cross a canal on a three-span I-beam bridge. Alligators are commonly seen in this canal, so watch your step.

**10.0**    **BLOCK LIMITS** – This location is the boundary between the **Town Block** and the **Wetherald Block**. The Town Block (toward Clewiston) was named for Townsite, the original name used for the worker housing near the sugar mill. The Weatherald Block is named for Charles E. Wetherald and covers the line as far as Milepost 19.9. Heading east, there is basically a cane loading facility every mile.

**10.1**    **CURVE** – Heading towards Bryant Yard, the railroad makes a ninety degree turn to the east.

**10.9**    **VAUGHN #2** – This sugarcane loader with an elevator and ramp is to the south of the mainline. The siding that serves the cane loader can hold about 40 cane cars each side of the loader. Cane from fields to the southwest is often brought to here by tractor-hauled wagons.

**11.9** **GARDENA** – Gardena, also spelled Gardenia or Gardinia, was a small farming community on the banks of the Miami Canal. It was one of many such small communities created in the early 1900s on lands recently drained south of Lake Okeechobee. Also like many of these communities, it was destroyed in the late 1920s by a series of hurricanes.

Located on the west side of the Miami Canal is the Miami Canal Road, a popular route into the area for fishermen and access to sugarcane fields across the region. It is also a shortcut often used by trucks to get around the south side of Clewiston. Here, the road actually crosses over to the east side of the canal for travel further south. The bridge handles both rail and highway traffic. This part of the Miami Canal Road can be gated at times due to the volume of cane traffic moving through the area, and to protect the many structures associated with the Miami Canal.

**12.0** **MIAMI CANAL BRIDGE** – The Miami Canal is a major connection between Lake Okeechobee and the Atlantic Ocean at Miami. Also known as the C-6 Canal, it was built during the early 1900s as a part of the effort to drain and irrigate the Everglades Agricultural Area. The Miami Canal connects with Lake Okeechobee at Lake Harbor and heads south more than 75 miles to the Miami River, which flows five more miles to the ocean. Steamboats once operated on the canal and the remains of a lock are still visible at Lake Harbor.

The bridge once served as the dividing line between the Vaughn Block (no longer in existance) to the west and the Weather Block to the east (now Wetherald Block). While the spelling Weather was sometimes used, this block is named for Charles E. Wetherald, president of U.S. Sugar from December 1947 through 1958.

USSC #407 is shown heading west across the Miami Canal on the former Wetherald Line. To the east are a series of cane loaders, and #407 is moving recently cut sugarcane to the Clewiston mill for processing.

This sign, once located just east of the Miami Canal, marked the start of the Weather Block on the Wetherald Line. Today, this is part of the Wetherald Block of the Clewiston Mainline Division. Things seem to constantly change on the railroads of U.S. Sugar.

USSC Clewiston Mainline Division

**12.9** **WETHERALD #1** – This loader is to the north and it was built with an elevator and a ramp. This allows sugarcane in both non-self-dumping truck trailers and self-dumping tractor-hauled cane wagons to be unloaded and then lifted into railcars.

The name Wetherald comes from Charles E. Wetherald. Wetherald was born in 1884 and joined Buick in 1904. He rose from foreman to superintendent of inspection before becoming involved with the creation of Mason Motors, which later became part of Chevrolet. He retired in 1945 from the position of general manufacturing manager of Chevrolet. By June 30, 1946, he had the title of Executive Vice-President of the United States Sugar Corporation. He later served as president of U.S. Sugar from December 1947 through 1958.

**13.9** **WETHERALD #2** – This elevator and ramp cane loader is also to the north. This loader and Wetherald #1 can hold as many as 40 empty cane cars since both sidings are about 3520 feet long.

**14.9** **WETHERALD #3** – This loader is to the north and also features an elevator and a ramp. This cane loader has a shorter siding then some, and can hold only 30 empty cane cars.

**15.9** **WETHERALD #4** – This loader is to the north. Like Wetherald #3, this cane loader handles about 30 empty cane cars and consists of an elevator with a ramp for unloading cane wagons from the fields. Both sidings are about 2650 feet long.

**16.9** **WETHERALD #5** – This elevator and ramp loader is to the north and can handle 40 empty cane cars. Wetherald #5 was the eastern-most sugarcane loader on the old Wetherald Line, but the route continued on to eventually connect with the SCFE at South Bay.

These loading facilities are scattered about a mile apart and operate only when cane is being harvested nearby. Having loaders about a mile apart reduces the time it takes to get the sugarcane to the railroad, and saves on fuel and wear for the harvesting machinery. Different loaders will be used in different years, depending upon which sugar cane is being harvested.

**17.2** **CURVE** – Just east of Wetherald #5, the rail line turns north towards South Bay. The east switch (railroad-south) of the loader is actually in the middle of the curve at Milepost 17.3.

**18.0** **WETHERALD YARD JUNCTION** – This location marks where the new line – sometimes known as the Bryant Connector – breaks off from the former Wetherald Line and turns east. The old route northward from here to the SCFE mainline at South Bay is considered to be Other Than Main Tracks (OTM).

In late 2021, the new Bryant Connector track, also known as the Southeast Extension Project, was opened between the Wetherald Line and the Prewitt South Line. This new line connected the cane tracks around Bryant with those around Clewiston, allowing cane trains to operate directly between the two systems without the need for the Florida East

Coast mainline. A number of new cane loaders will also be built on this line.

Operating details on this line are still being developed, but the primary construction was completed by June 2021. More work will certainly take place as cane loaders and other features are added. Planning on this 16-mile line was well underway by 2018, and meetings with Palm Beach County were started by December of that year. Notes from the meetings provided justification for the project, as well as the county's support in approving several new railroad-highway grade crossings. The Florida Department of Transportation also played a major role in designing the track around the grade crossings.

> The southeast extension project eliminates the need for sugar cane operations to utilize public roads to deliver cane to the nearest elevator for transport on rail. Both train traffic and heavy truck traffic will shift from the center of South Bay to the south city limits away from populated areas.

New grade crossings were required at U.S. Highway 27, and Palm Beach County Roads 827A and 880. The roads were redesigned at all three locations. At least for the county roads, the railroad performed all of the work associated with the construction of the new railroad-highway grade crossings, and "SCFE shall, at its expense, maintain and replace in perpetuity the crossing and automatic railroad crossing warning devices."

Multiple companies were involved in building the Southeast Extension Project. These included

Crouch Railway Consulting, The Ryan Companies, Danella Rail Services, and Star Quarries. The project consisted of 22 miles of new grade and track, the installation of approximately half a million cubic yards of material, 120 culverts, several bridges, and numerous public and private grade crossings.

The new line breaks off from the former Wetherald Line just south of the G2 Canal (about MP 18.1). Using a Number 20 turnout, the new line curves to the east and crosses to the north side of the G2 Canal. It then heads east alongside the waterway. To provide some reference, the G2 Canal is in line with Rogers Road, located to the west of the Miami Canal. The canal connects the Miami Canal to the west, with the New River and Hillsboro canals to the east.

The original Wetherald line still continues a short distance to the north, reaching a small rail yard known as Wetherald Yard on the former Florida East Coast line.

19.8 **U.S. HIGHWAY 27** – The new tracks cross U.S. Highway 27 at-grade just south of the South Bay Correctional Facility. U.S. Highway 27 connects Miami, Florida, with Fort Wayne, Indiana. The four-lane highway follows the South Central Florida Express from South Bay to Sebring.

This crossing is part of a number of improvements along the highway in this area. The crossing features cantilevered flashers as well as gates.

USSC Clewiston Mainline Division

These gates and cantilevered flashers are located on U.S. Highway 27 and are designed to protect the new Bryant Connector tracks.

**19.9 NEW RIVER CANAL BRIDGE** – Located just east of U.S. Highway 27 is the New River Canal, often known as the North New River Canal or Canal L-18. Like most canals in the area, it was built as part of an effort to drain parts of the Everglades. The canal was also a transportation route for steamboats between Fort Lauderdale and Lake Okeechobee, and then on to Fort Myers via the Caloosahatchee River. Locks were built on the canal, and Lock No. 1 at the south end of the canal was the first to be built in South Florida. It is now listed on the National Register of Historic Places. Regular service on the canal ended in 1926 and the locks were deactivated.

A five-span concrete ballast deck bridge has been built to cross the canal. This bridge design is used throughout the new line and is popular all across the United States for new railroad bridge construction.

This modern concrete ballast deck bridge carries the new Bryant Connector across the New River Canal.

This sign marks the block limits between the Wetherald and Prewitt Blocks on the Clewiston Mainline.

**19.9** **BLOCK LIMITS** – Located at the east end of the New River Canal Bridge, this is the boundary between the **Wetherald Block** and the **Prewitt Block**. The Wetherald Block (toward Clewiston) is named for Charles E. Wetherald. The **Prewitt Block** is an older block that has been extended to here from the former Prewitt South Line. The name Prewitt comes from William C. Prewitt, for many years Vice President, Agriculture, for U.S. Sugar. A 1956 report from the Committee on Government Operations, U.S. House of Representatives, stated that:

> *William C. Prewitt, vice president in charge of agriculture of the United States Sugar Corp. at Clewiston, Fla., has for many years had the responsibility of directing the planting, cultivation and harvest of the firm's 25,000 acres of sugarcane in the Florida Everglades. He has had broad experience in the growing of sugarcane and has a wide knowledge of the industry from the standpoint of varieties, culture, and harvest. He is a college graduate, interested in public affairs, and a leader in his community.*

**21.4** **SPOONER ROAD** – At Spooner Road, the new line curves to the south. At this location, Spooner Road is little more than a field road, but north of Florida Highway 80, it is Florida Highway 715 and serves as a bypass around the west side of Belle Glade.

**22.0** **G2 CANAL BRIDGE** – The new line crosses the G2 Canal again about 0.7 miles west of County Road 827A.

**22.8 CURVE** – The railroad again changes direction, this time to the east to follow along the south side of a small drainage canal.

**23.1 BRIDGE** – The Bryant Connector crosses a small field canal and heads east alongside its south side.

**23.5 COUNTY ROAD 827A** – The railroad crosses Palm Beach County Road 827A, a busy bypass road that loops around the east side of South Bay. It connects Florida Highway 80 on the south side of Belle Glade, with County Road 827, which is located on the north side of the Bolles Canal. County Road 827 connects with U.S. Highway 27 at Okeelanta, completing the bypass route.

The new railroad grade to the west of County Road 827A uses part of a former field access road, and the new grade is designed to accommodate the railroad and the farm road. The area is also wide enough that a cane loader could be built here.

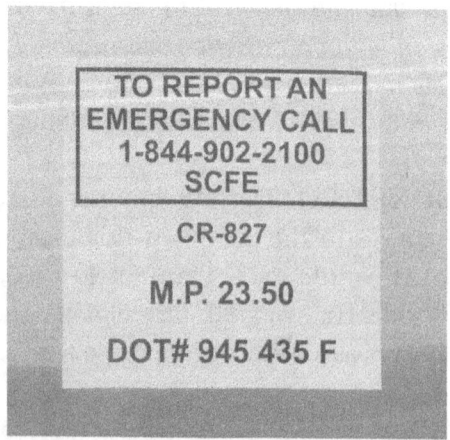

With the construction of the Bryant Connector, which completed the Clewiston Mainline, the new grade crossing at County Road 827 (shown as 827A on most maps) was assigned Milepost 23.5. This sign on the signal box marks the location.

**25.5** **DUDA ROAD** – While this road is generally gated, this is a significant landmark on the new line. Duda Road reaches far into the properties of the A. Duda & Sons firm. The company currently has more than 45,000 acres owned and leased across the country. The firm has four basic divisions. The first is Duda Farm Fresh Foods, producers and suppliers of citrus, celery, other vegetables. The second is Duda Ranches, which operates facilities that produce sod, sugarcane, citrus and cattle. The third part is the Viera Company, a community developer and real estate management firm. The final part is Viera Builders, a residential home builder.

In this area, sugarcane rules, with vegetables and grass sod grown on fields when sugarcane is not being produced. A sign of this is the new Prewitt #4 sugarcane loading facility that has been built just east of Duda Road. A number of the sugar cane loading facilities across the railroads of U.S. Sugar have been built so that farmers can sell their sugarcane to U.S. Sugar. By having dedicated loaders, the exact amount of cane, and eventually the amount of processed sugar created, can be tracked directly to each farmer.

**25.6** **WEST PREWITT #4 SWITCH** – This is a new siding to the south to serve a new cane elevator, which has been named Prewitt 4. This siding is slightly more than a mile long and can handle 40 cars for sugar cane loading.

**26.2** **BOLLES JUNCTION WEST WYE SWITCH** – At this location is a wye, designed to turn the mainline northward toward the Bryant sugarcane lines, yet provide a route to the south to reach additional sugarcane fields on the Bolles Lead. The switches are planned to be automatic Number 20 turnouts to allow increased train speeds and to improve safety.

The line to the south is designed to reach into the fields acquired a few years ago from Triple S Holdings, Gladeview Holdings, and others. A description of this branch is included on page 385.

26.5 **BOLLES NORTH WYE SWITCH** – This switch consists of a Number 20 turnout. The primary route heads north from here.

26.6 **EAST PREWITT #4 SWITCH** – This is the east end of the new siding built for the Prewitt #4 cane loading facility.

27.5 **G2 CANAL BRIDGE** – Heading north, the line makes a short S-Curve to the east and then crosses the G2 Canal for the third time.

28.4 **COUNTY ROAD 880** – The railroad crosses County Road 880 about 1.1 miles east of Duda Road. Palm Beach County Road 880 is almost 19 miles long and connects Twenty Mile Bend with Belle Glade. Here, it is on the southwest shore of the Hillsboro Canal.

USSC Clewiston Mainline Division

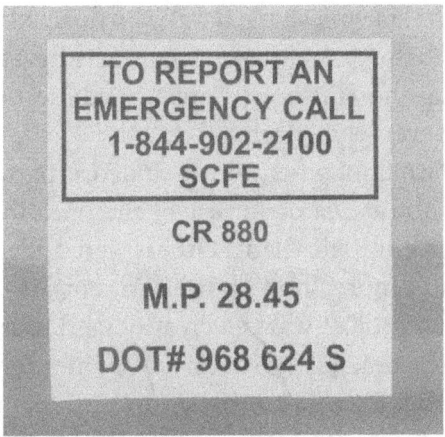

With the construction of the Bryant Connector, which completed the Clewiston Mainline, the new grade crossing at County Road 880 was assigned Milepost 28.4. This sign on the signal box marks the location.

28.5   HILLSBORO CANAL BRIDGE – A new three-span concrete ballast deck bridge has been built to cross this stream. The Hillsboro (or Hillsborough during the early 1900s) Canal (Canal G-08) stretches from Lake Okeechobee to the southeast to the Atlantic Ocean at Deerfield Beach. The canal actually replaced a river that could range from a few puddles to a roaring stream throwing alligators into the Atlantic Ocean. Early maps called the river by many different names, including the Sharkstail River, Rio Seco, Rio Nuevo, and the Potomac River. In 1820, it took the name of the Hillsboro River, named for the Earl of Hillsborough, the British Secretary of State for the U.S. colonies in the 1770s.

In the early 1900s, efforts were made to drain this part of Florida and the Hillsboro River was dredged over a ten-year period. The canal is credited with making much of Palm Beach County liveable, including the land west of Boca Raton and Pompano Beach, which would be under water. Construction of the 55-mile-long canal was finished by the early 1920s, and narrow canal boats began operating along the Hillsboro Canal, handling mail, freight, and even passengers.

Two floodgates were included as part of the project, one at Deerfield Beach, and one other just west of here at Belle Glade. Others were added in 1949 as part of more flood prevention projects. A final part of the project was the creation and preservation of the Loxahatchee National Wildlife Refuge, where the marshy characteristics of the original Hillsboro River were maintained.

Immediately north of the canal, the railroad makes a broad S-Curve to the east to align the tracks with those of the former Prewitt South Line.

Another concrete ballast deck bridge is used to cross the Hillsboro Canal, southeast of Belle Glades.

**29.8 CANAL BRIDGE** – The rail line bridges over the canal that it has been following to reach the former Prewitt South Line.

*USSC Clewiston Mainline Division*

**30.0** **PREWITT JUNCTION** – The new Bryant Connector connects straight to the former Prewitt South Line. The track to Prewitt #3, now known as the Prewitt Lead, still curves off to the southwest, but uses a newly installed Number 10 turnout to do so. A description of the Prewitt Lead can be found on page 389.

**30.4** **PREWITT #2 EAST SWITCH** – Prewitt #2 has its east switch on the Clewiston Mainline, while its west switch is on the Prewitt Lead, certainly a unique situation. The sugarcane loader at Prewitt #2 is shown as being on the Prewitt Lead.

**30.9** **AIRPORT ROAD** – The Belle Glade State Municipal Airport is to the west on the northeast side of Belle Glade. The road also has several different names in that direction, including Ice Plant Road and NW Avenue L. The Prewitt Village housing subdivision is to the east. This neighborhood started as housing for workers on area farms.

**32.0** **BLOCK LIMITS** – The signs for this change in blocks can be seen just north of Airport Road. To the north is the **Pelican Block**, while to the south is the **Prewitt Block**.

The name Pelican Block honors the former worker community that was once located at the Muck City Road grade crossing, seven miles north of here. Pelican Lake Village was once the home of many of the workers who planted and harvested the sugar cane along this part of the railroad.

**32.2** **PREWITT #1** – To the west is a large sugarcane loader, with a siding that can handle more than 40 rail cars on either side of the loader. This loader has both a ramp and an elevator. This allows the use of self-dumping cane wagons as well as non-self-dumping truck trailers. This design lets trucks operate on the nearby highways and still bring sugarcane to the railroad at this location.

During the early days of the company, this loader was assigned to nearby Prewitt Village. William C. Prewitt was an engineer who served as a vice-president of U.S. Sugar during the 1940s. Several generations of the family have worked for U.S. Sugar over the years. In 1946, Prewitt obtained a patent on a weed burner that could be used on a cultivated field.

**33.0** **HIGHWAY 80** – This four-lane road has seen a number of improvements over the past decade, providing a short cut between Belle Glade and West Palm Beach as opposed to the old U.S. Highway 98 route via Canal Point. While the railroad knows this as the historical Florida Highway 80 name, today it is better known as U.S. Highway 441. U.S. Highway 441 stretches from Miami, Florida, to Rocky Top (formerly Lake City), Tennessee, a total of 939 miles. Many older records show that this road was the State Road 80 Extension North.

*USSC Clewiston Mainline Division*

With the recent changes on the Clewiston Mainline, the grade crossing of Florida Highway 80 is now at Milepost 33.0.

**34.2    EAST SHORE #3** – Located to the west of the main tracks, this is one of the modern concrete ramp loaders that are replacing the older dirt ramps. Cane loading facilities are normally grouped by their design. For example, there are a number of ramp loaders near here so the tractor-hauled self-dumping cane wagons can be used in any of the fields in this area.

**34.4    OLD VANDERGRIFT ROAD** – The road heads west to the Paul Rardin Park on Lake Okeechobee, and east deeper into the sugarcane fields. Immediately to the south is a canal and then another dirt road that provides access to nearby sugarcane fields.

**35.2** **EAST SHORE #1** – The siding and ramp cane loader are to the west. The siding is about 3000 feet long. This cane loader can only handle 30 empty cars while most others in the area can handle 40 cars.

**36.4** **PELICAN #2** – This ramp cane loader is also to the west and has a long siding for cane loading. Just south of the south switch is a short S-curve that takes the railroad east a short distance. This curve is at 26 degrees 46 minutes north latitude. All north-south survey lines move to the east just south of this location.

**37.4** **PELICAN #1** – This is another cane loader to the west with a long siding capable of handling almost 40 railcars. This facility uses a ramp that allows self-dumping cane wagons to unload directly into railcars.

The name Pelican comes from the worker community that once supported the facility – Pelican Lake. Heading south, there is a cane loader about every mile.

**38.6** **MARTINEZ JUNCTION** – A 3.5-mile-long track heads east to reach into the sugarcane fields in that area. Information on this Martinez Lead can be found on page 391.

**39.0** **PELICAN LAKE** – Look for the grade crossing with Highway 717, also known as Muck City Road. While the Florida East Coast once had a station two miles west of here on their mainline named Pelican Lake, this is the real community with that name. While today shown to be an unincorporated community, Pelican Lake, also known as Pelican Lake Village, was a worker community for U.S. Sugar. For a number of years, the company had a commissary here, as well as a welcome sign that read "Pelican Lake Village – a housing community for agricultural employees of United States Sugar Corporation." Pelican Lake had a post office from 1939 to 1964, when it was replaced by the Pelican Lake Rural Station that finally closed in 1992.

To the west of the tracks are offices and shops for Integrity Farms.

This is the old commissary and office building at Pelican Lake.

With the recent changes on the Clewiston Mainline, the grade crossing of Muck City Road is now at Milepost 39.0.

40.4 **BRYANT #1** – To the west is a large sugarcane loader. Known as BRY1 or Bryant #1, the loader can hold only 24 empty cars, the fewest of any loader in the Bryant system. It also has the shortest siding at 2286 feet. The loader features an elevator with a ramp, so it can handle the transfer between both non-self-dumping truck trailers and self-dumping cane wagons and the railroad sugarcane cars.

40.5 **BLOCK LIMITS** – This location marks the east end of the **Pelican Block**. From here until Milepost 41.3, the railroad uses yard limits on the mainline. This is because of the wye that connects the mainline with Bryant Yard, located a short distance to the west.

**40.8** **WEST BRYANT YARD SWITCH** – The Bryant Wye connects the line west to the South Central Florida Express mainline, and the U.S. Sugar lines that head north and south from Bryant. These lines supplied the large Bryant Sugar House mill, once located at the west end of the wye. Today, several cane trains cover the Bryant lines, while several Bryant Turns work the Bryant Yard, hauling the cane on to the mill at Clewiston.

**41.0** **EAST BRYANT YARD SWITCH** – This is the connection with the east leg of the wye. The east leg of the wye is 0.3 miles long. Just west of here on the north leg of the wye is the grade crossing with Mill Road, which serves as a sugarcane field access road. It follows the Pelican Block closely for several miles, providing road access to the various cane elevators.

Heading north from here, now railroad-east, the track was once the Bryant-Boy North Line. Now, it is part of the Clewiston Mainline Division.

**41.3** **BLOCK LIMITS** – Located just south of Florida Highway 700, this is the west end of the **Bourne Block**, once the longest cane line block on the system at 13.4 miles. Today, it has been shortened to 9.7 miles and it protects the four Bourne cane loaders on this part of the line. The Bourne Block is named for the series of cane elevators named for Benjamin Bourne.

**41.5** **FLORIDA HIGHWAY 700** – Heading north, the railroad crosses Florida Highway 700, and then the West Palm Beach Canal. Highway 700 is also known as the Old Conners Road, as much of it uses the grade of the original Conners Toll Highway, built in the 1920s and opened on July 4, 1924. William J. "Fingey" Conners built the toll road, the first to connect roads across the State of Florida, as a part of his real estate development efforts. Conners had bought a farm and a great deal of property east of Canal Point, but access was limited. A road was his solution, so he spent $1.8 million to build it himself. His road was built from Twenty Mile Bend, where a road out of West Palm Beach already existed, all the way to Okeechobee on the north side of the lake, more than 50 miles of paved road. Conners used dredges to drag up the dirt and then a narrow-gauge railroad to distribute it. When opened, the road made $1000 to $2000 a day in tolls. Conners died in 1929 and the State of Florida bought the road and removed the tolls.

This area was once the site of the Bryant Sugar Mill, and it is still a base of operations for U.S. Sugar. This building at Bryant is still labeled for the Agriculture Department of the company.

**41.5 WEST PALM BEACH CANAL** – Just north of Highway 700, the railroad bridges over the West Palm Beach Canal using a five-span cast concrete and steel bridge, with the deck built to allow both trains and highway vehicles to cross it. The West Palm Beach Canal, also known as the C-51 Canal, was built in the early 1900s to lower Lake Okeechobee and drain a part of the Everglades in order to farm the land, today part of the Everglades Agricultural Area. The canal starts at Canal Point on Lake Okeechobee, and flows southeast to Twenty Mile Bend, immediately adjacent to Florida Highway 700. In this area the canal flows through acres of sugarcane, providing drainage for the farms. At Twenty Mile Bend the canal flows into the West Palm Beach Canal, and the waters then flow southeast as the northern boundary of the Loxahatchee National Wildlife Refuge. It flows south of the Palm Beach International Airport and then into the Lake Worth Lagoon, a part of the Intracoastal Waterway at Palm Beach.

This bridge allows railroad and highway vehicles to cross the West Palm Beach Canal near Bryant.

On the north side of the canal, the railroad immediately enters miles of sugarcane fields, generally inaccessible from any public roads.

42.5   CURVE – The railroad has been heading northeast, but here it curves to due north.

43.1   BOURNE #2 – To the west is a sugarcane loader, served by a 3/4-mile-long siding. All of the Bourne cane loaders are rated for 40 empty cane cars and this one features an elevator but without a large ramp. This limits this loader to self-dumping wagons.

Benjamin Bourne was a plant pathologist from Barbados who had worked on sugarcane production at the U.S. Department of Agriculture's Canal Point research facility. He later worked at the Southern Sugar Company, where Dahlberg had hired him to work on cane-breeding. After Southern Sugar failed, he obtained a Ph.D. from Cornell University. He then returned to the Clewiston area and began research on sugarcane production. His work greatly increased cane production and he introduced varieties of sugarcane that were not impacted by freezing weather and other crop issues.

45.3   CURVE – After heading north for about three miles, the railroad curves to the east to head to the L-8 Canal. The railroad serves two cane loaders before it reaches the canal.

45.8   BOURNE #3 – This cane loader, located to the north of the mainline, is served by a relatively short siding, but it is still listed as having a 40-car capacity based upon empty cane cars. Pretty much any cane hauling equipment can be used in the fields as this cane loader includes both an elevator and a ramp.

**46.7** **BOURNE #4** – This is another cane loader to the north, also with a relatively short siding and just an elevator. Several miles to the south is a sugar mill. This is the Osceola Farms Company Pahokee Mill. The facility started with 4000 acres of sugarcane farm, bought by Alfonso Fanjul Sr. and Czarnikow-Rionda in 1960. Both had owned mills in Cuba and fled after Fidel Castro took over the country. They bought the parts from three Louisiana mills and built this mill starting in 1961. They were part of the group that was also associated with the Sugar Cane Growers Cooperative of Florida and the Okeelanta Sugar Mill. Today, the Okeelanta and Osceola mills operate in partnership.

By 1913, Cuba was the largest exporter of sugar in the world. The Rionda and Czarnikow families combined their operations to dominate much of this business. The firm brokered about 60% of the Cuban sugar sales in the United States. Additionally, the company owned a number of sugar mills in Cuba, including Central San Vicente, Central Elia, Central Cespedes, Central Tuinucu, and Central San Jose (which was reorganized as the Washington Sugar Company). All of these activities provided the organization the connections needed to enter the United States market.

This old sugarcane crusher is on display at the Florida Crystals Osceola Mill near the former Boy North Line.

**48.1** **CURVE** – At the L-8 Canal, the railroad curves to the southeast to follow the canal's south shoreline for the next five miles. The L-8 Canal flows from Lake Okeechobee at Sand Cut and heads southeast to the West Palm Beach Canal at Twenty Mile Bend. The canal first passes through citrus groves, sugarcane, and corn, and then flows between the sugarcane fields of U.S. Sugar and the J. W. Corbett Wildlife Management Area.

**50.3** **BOURNE #5** – To the southwest is another cane loader that consists of a ramp and an elevator. The siding is about ½-mile long and has a capacity of 40 empty cane cars, typical for this line.

**51.0** **BLOCK LIMITS** – This is the limit between the **Bourne Block** and the **Boy Block**. The Boy Block is

9.6 miles long and covers the line to the end of the tracks.

**51.9** **BOURNE #6** – To the southwest is another Bourne cane loader with a long siding. This one has had most of its equipment removed and is not listed as an active cane loading location. The two sugarcane loaders on this part of the line were designed to serve the very northeast fields of U.S. Sugar.

**53.6** **CURVE** – The railroad curves to the south, leaving the L-8 Canal and the J. W. Corbett Wildlife Management Area. The railroad begins to follow the Big Mound Canal, a part of the Big Mound Drainage District, which connects the L-8 Canal with the West Palm Beach Canal. This canal was in place by the early 1920s. It was dug by the Megathlin & Clark dredging firm, owned by Jesse L. Megathlin. Megathlin had earlier supervised the Everglades drainage work consisting of the North New River Canal, Hillsboro Canal, Miami Canal, and South New River Canal.

**55.7** **BOY #1** – This ramp and elevator loader is to the west of the main tracks, towards the majority of the fields in this area. This loader and two more are named after John B. Boy, former CEO and president of the U.S. Sugar Corporation. Mr. Boy had a degree in mechanical engineering from the Georgia Institute of Technology and captained three different U.S. Navy ships during World War II. After the war, he moved to Clewiston to become an assistant superintendent of the U.S. Sugar's sweet potato starch plant. He later became an engineer in the company's agricultural equipment shops and is responsible for many changes in equipment design. Two of these include a redesign of the sugarcane loading machines and the move away from track-mounted tractors to rubber tires. He also headed up the project to build the Bryant Sugar House, the acquisition of the South Bay Growers vegetable and sugarcane operations, and the production of orange juice from company-owned trees. John B. Boy spent 41 years with the company, including as president from 1970 until his retirement in 1987. He died in 2013.

57.2 **WORK BASE** – To the west is a small worker base for equipment operations. Facilities like this are scattered throughout the fields to reduce the distance that the slow-moving farming equipment has to travel, and the distance that workers have to travel to get parts, supplies, and fuel.

58.2 **CURVE** – The railroad and the Big Mound Canal both curve to the southwest. This area is a major field road junction with a route across the Big Mound Canal, and a number of roads into nearby fields. Several canals join here also.

58.2 **BOY #2** – This is another ramp and elevator cane loader to the west of the main tracks. USSC states that it has a capacity of 40 empty cane cars. The Big Mound Canal is immediately to the east.

59.8 **BOY #3** – Located to the west of the main tracks, this is the last cane loader on the line. Like the other Boy cane loading facilities, company documents show that it features an elevator and a ramp and has a capacity of 40 empty sugarcane cars.

**60.6** **END OF TRACK** – The line ends not far north of the West Palm Beach Canal and Florida Highway 700.

*The Railroads of U.S. Sugar: History Through the Miles*

## USSC Bolles Lead Route Guide
## Bolles Junction to End of Track

There are three sugarcane leads off of the Clewiston Mainline – Bolles Lead, Prewitt Lead, and Martinez Lead. This new Bolles Lead is only 3.9 miles long and serves a new cane loader built to handle fields acquired a few years ago from Triple S Holdings, Gladeview Holdings, and others. The Bolles Lead branches off of the Clewiston Mainline at Milepost 26.2.

To reduce any confusion about duplicate mileposts across the system, the Bolles Lead is also known as the 300 Line. The Lead covers the tracks from the north end at Milepost 300.0 (Bolles Junction), to Milepost 303.9 at the south end of the track. No part of this line can be viewed from public roads.

**300.0**    **BOLLES JUNCTION** – This switch is the west end of the wye that turns trains northwards towards the cane loaders around Bryant. Trains heading to the Bolles loader turn south at this location.

**301.3**    **BOLLES CANAL** – The railroad bridges the canal and then makes a short S-curve to the east. The Bolles Canal (Canal L-16) is a major east-west canal that stretches 6.6 miles and connects the Miami, North New River, and Hillsboro canals. It was completed in 1931 and was designed to balance the water flows between the various canals south of Lake Okeechobee. The canal received a great deal of work in 2016, opening it up and removing sediment to allow better water flow.

**302.5 NORTH BOLLES SWITCH** – Loaded sugarcane cars are pushed north in the Bolles siding, and this switch is used by sugarcane trains to reach into the loader and collect these cars for movement to the sugar mill at Clewiston.

**303.0 BOLLES** – This new sugar cane loader has a siding that is 4400 feet and that can handle 40 empty cane cars. It is located on the west side of the Bolles Lead. The area uses the Bolles name from the nearby canal.

The canal, and a number of features in this area were named for Richard "Dicky" J. Bolles. Bolles was born in New York City in 1843 and had acquired a seat on the New York Stock Exchange by 1886. He used his connections to acquire various businesses across the country, including a mine in Colorado and farm lands in Oregon. His reputation for developing businesses led Florida government officials to get him involved in developing southern Florida. Basically, he was to develop and sell swamp land that was owned by Florida, helping to get the state out of debt. On December 26, 1908, the trustees of the Florida Internal Improvement Fund signed over about 500,000 acres of overflowed state lands for two dollars an acre, with half of the money to be used to drain the property.

One of Bolles' creations was the Florida Fruit Lands Company, which held 180,000 acres in Dade and Palm Beach Counties. The land was broken up into about 12,000 farms, and those who were interested could buy into a scheduled auction. One of the problems was that Florida had yet to drain the land, and a series of lawsuits were filed claiming that Bolles was selling swampland as prime farmland.

The court eventually halted the land sales until the land was proper for farming, but let Bolles keep the money he had already been paid. A big reason the court made this decision was the many reports produced by federal and state officials. These reports stated the high potential of the Everglades, and Bolles claimed that he had simply relied upon their expertise. When Bolles died in 1917, little had actually been accomplished. Few of the buyers ever got their property, the planned communities weren't built, and most of the property reverted to the state for nonpayment. Basically, this was a case of selling swampland in Florida.

303.4 **SOUTH BOLLES SWITCH** – This switch is located just far enough north of the end of track to allow a locomotive with 40 empty cane cars to switch the Bolles cane elevator.

303.9 **END OF TRACK** – The tracks end on the north side of a small canal. Less than a mile to the west is a large agricultural complex. This complex was once the end of the Atlantic Coast Line's (ACL) Okeelanta Subdivision, located at the Duda Belle Glade Farm. The ACL finished their line to here in 1949, but the business never materialized and the line was cut back in 1979.

*The Railroads of U.S. Sugar: History Through the Miles*

# USSC Prewitt Lead Route Guide
# Prewitt Junction to End of Track

This the second sugarcane lead that breaks off of the Clewiston Mainline. This is actually the end of the former Prewitt South Line, made a short stub track when the new Clewiston Mainline Division was created. The Prewitt Lead branches off of the Clewiston Mainline at Milepost 30.0.

To reduce any confusion about duplicate mileposts across the system, the Prewitt Lead is also known as the 400 Line. The Lead covers the tracks from the east end at Milepost 400.0 (Prewitt Junction), to Milepost 401,5 at the west end of the track. This line can sometimes be viewed from across the fields from County Road 880.

**400.0  PREWITT JUNCTION** – This junction is located at Milepost 30.0 of the Clewiston Mainline Division. It is actually located between the switches of the Prewitt #2 cane loader. The switch is opposite of the Prewitt #2 sugarcane loader. This ramp cane loader is to the west of the main tracks.

**400.1  WEST PREWITT #2 SWITCH** – Prewitt #2 has its east switch on the Clewiston Mainline, while its west switch is on the Prewitt Lead, certainly a unique situation. The sugarcane loader at Prewitt #2 is shown as being on the Prewitt Lead.

**400.2  EAST PREWITT #3 SWITCH** – The switches of the sidings serving Prewitt #2 and #3 are very close to each other. This is because the two cane loaders are located on opposite sides of a large canal, making it difficult to move the cut cane from one field to another. Therefore, Prewitt #2 serves the fields to the north, while Prewitt #3 serves the fields to the south.

**400.6** **PREWITT #3** – This is a big loader that includes an elevator and a ramp, and the siding can handle about 45 cane cars on each end of the loader. It is located to the north of the Prewitt Lead.

**401.1** **WEST PREWITT #3 SWITCH** – This station is listed as it is the last switch on the line.

**401.5** **END OF TRACK** – The end of this sugarcane line is just east of Duda Road. It leaves a line west of the Prewitt #3 long enough to switch the sugarcane loader.

## USSC Martinez Lead Route Guide
## Martinez Junction to End of Track

This the third and final sugarcane lead that breaks off of the Clewiston Mainline. This is the former Martinez Line, a route that curves to the east from Clewiston Mainline Milepost 38.6 and follows the south side of a canal for its entire length. The rail line ends not far west of the Old Conners Road. There is only one cane loading facility on this route, which is 3½ miles long. The entire line is now known as the Martinez Lead.

To reduce any confusion about duplicate mileposts across the system, the Martinez Lead is also known as the 500 Line. The Lead covers the tracks from the west end at Milepost 500.0 (Martinez Junction), to Milepost 503.5 at the south end of the track. Like most of the sugarcane lines, this route cannot be viewed from public roads.

**500.0 MARTINEZ JUNCTION** – This junction is located at Milepost 38.6 of the Clewiston Mainline Division. This switch takes trains coming off of the Martinez Lead north so they can reach Bryant Yard. For trains heading onto the branch, the line makes a ninety degree turn to the east. Just east of the curve is a large cleared space to the south. While there is no siding here, the area is graded so that a cane loader and siding could be installed where the old Martinez #1 loader once stood. The location is also used by field forces to store and maintain their equipment.

**502.8 MARTINEZ #2** – This cane loader and long siding is to the south. It has the capacity of 40 empty cane cars and uses an elevator with a ramp. The west switch for the siding is at Milepost 502.4 while the east switch is at Milepost 503.1.

**503.5 END OF TRACK** – The end of the track is in the middle of a series of sugarcane fields, just west of Florida Highway 700 and the West Palm Beach Canal. The track is just long enough so that trains can switch the Martinez #2 facility.

# USSC Flaghole Mainline Division Route Guide
## Flaghole Junction to End of Track

Once known as the Flaghole Line, this 14.1-mile-long line serves the sugar cane loaders that are located south and east of the Clewiston sugar mill. Starting at Flaghole Junction (Clewiston Mainline Milepost 1.4), the line heads west to serve five cane loading facilities.

For years, the line only went as far west as Flaghole Road. In 2012-2013, new construction extended the line to the Southern Gardens Citrus processing plant on Sam Jones Trail, also known as Hendry County Road 833. This route can only be viewed from the two major roads – Flaghole Road and Hendry County Road 833.

To reduce any confusion about duplicate mileposts across the system, the Flaghole Mainline Division is also known as the 100 Line. The Lead covers the tracks from the east end at Milepost 100.0 (Flaghole Junction), to Milepost 114.1 at the west end of the track.

**100.0** **FLAGHOLE JUNCTION** – The U.S. Sugar Corporation's sugarcane lines split here, with the Clewiston Mainline toward Bryant continuing south, while the recently extended Flaghole Mainline curves to the west. **Flag Block** begins at Flaghole Junction, and heads west ten miles to near Flaghole Road. To control train operations on the line, the railroad authorizes train movements by giving the train crews permission to operate in each specific block. North of here and into the Clewiston Yard at the mill trains are protected by yard limits. The

Clewiston Yardmaster controls movements arriving and departing the yard.

The switch at this location is an automatic switch. Signals govern the movements of the trains over the turnout, and push buttons are used to operate the switch points.

Much of this line is surrounded by drainage canals. A number of equipment maintenance facilities are also located near the tracks.

**102.7** **FLAGHOLE #1** – To the north and across the canal is a cane loader, shown as capable of holding 40 empty cane cars. The loader features a ramp that allows both non-self-dumping truck trailers and self-dumping tractor-hauled cane wagons to unload their cane into a bin where an elevator then raises the cane and drops it into railcars.

In this area, the railroad is on a grade between two canals, so any loader sidings involve fills or bridges to cross them. At the east switch of this cane loader, Milepost 102.3, there are several U.S. Sugar facilities to the south. The large barns were once part of the company's cattle business, but are now used for equipment storage.

**105.5** **FLAGHOLE #2** – This cane loader is across the canal to the south, and is shown to have a capacity of 39 empty cane cars, and features a ramp with an elevator. These two cane loaders, Flaghole #1 and #2, are located close to each other on opposite sides of the canal to place them closer to the cane fields. They are so close that the west switch of Flaghole #1, and the east switch of Flaghole #2, are located immediately across a field road from each other at

Milepost 4.5. Heading west, the line passes through miles of sugarcane fields.

**106.5 FLAGHOLE #3** – Near Milepost 6.0, the canal to the south of the tracks flows under the railroad to merge with the canal to the north. This allows cane loaders to the south to be easily reached by both the railroad and by trucks and tractors delivering sugarcane from the fields. Flaghole #3 was built to take advantage of this design, and is immediately south of the mainline.

This cane loader consists of an elevator with a ramp. It is not owned by U.S. Sugar and is used by independent sugarcane growers. This is another facility that can handle 40 empty cane cars at a time.

**108.3 FLAGHOLE #4** – This loader is also to the south and can handle 40 empty cane cars. Like Flaghole #3, this loader is not owned by U.S. Sugar and is instead used by independent growers who sell their sugarcane to the sugar company at Clewiston.

The elevator and ramp loader is at the southwest end of a series of sugarcane fields and the beginning of a series of large citrus groves. Several miles directly north of here is the Airglades Airport.

The new Airglades Airport was once Riddle Field, a World War II British Flying Training School (BFTS). Officially BFTS #5, this facility was designed to provide extensive training in formation flying, acrobatic maneuvers, armaments and instrument navigation for British pilots. BFTS #5 operated between September 1941 and September 1945, training more than 2000 Royal Air Force and 100 American pilots. There is a small museum at the airport to preserve the history of Riddle Field.

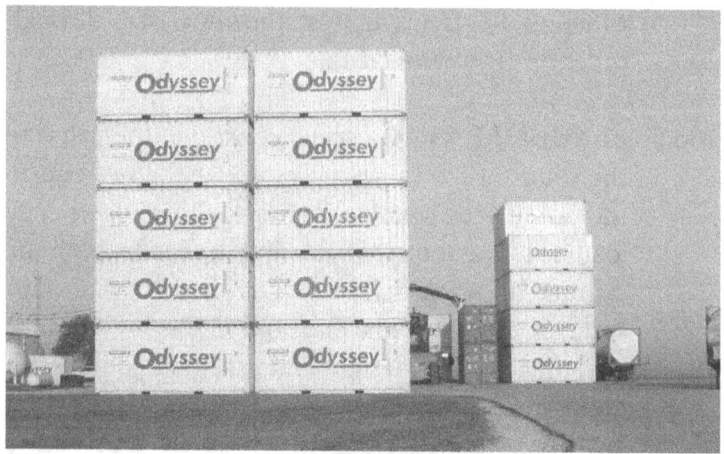

The area north of the Airglades Airport is slowly developing into an industrial area. This photo shows a stack of Odyssey containers.

**109.4  FLAGHOLE ROAD** – Until recently, this line ended just east of the Flaghole Road crossing. The railroad was extended in 2012-2013 to serve the Southern Gardens Citrus plant west of here, as well as a new cane loading facility.

The name Flaghole comes from a housing development in this area, sometimes spelled Flag Hole. The area started as a small community founded by Drayton Redin Kilpatrick, but it is now basically a rural community. There are actually a number of such developments near here, some successful and some not. The name Flaghole is also used for other features in the area, including a large cypress swamp and a drainage district. Just west of Flaghole Road, the tracks curve to the south for about a mile. The line passes through the middle of citrus groves.

## FLAGHOLE ROAD 945426G

This painted sign on the signal box identifies the location of Flaghole Road.

To the south is the farm of Hilliard Brothers of Florida. This farm was started during the 1930s by brothers Joe A. and Marlin Hilliard. Initially the brothers were in the cattle business, but the farm now produces sugarcane, citrus, fruit, sod, vegetables and timber on its more than 60,000 acres in Hendry and Glades Counties, plus two other states. Some records state that the farm began producing sugarcane in 1974, about the time the original Flaghole Line was built. Hilliard Brothers of Florida is still a family operation with the grandchildren of Joe A. Hilliard involved in the operations.

**New Flaghole Line Construction**

Just east of Flaghole Road is where the new construction began in 2012. The line was mentioned in the *2010 The Florida Rail System Plan: Investment Element* of the State of Florida, when the South Central Florida Express asked for State assistance to "Build 5.8 miles of new rail line along with 2.4 miles of yard to service Southern Gardens as a new customer. Along with a cane elevator to transport cane from western side of Clewiston to U.S. Sugar Mill."

When approved, Crouch Engineering of Nashville, Tennessee, was selected to design and supervise the line's construction, with support from Johnson Engineering. A major part of the construction was the permitting process and dealing with water drainage districts. Crouch's website described the project as a "state-funded 10-mile-long main line track, a passing siding, a storage yard, material loading tracks, 15 grade crossings, over 20 drainage structures, etc., for the Citrus Rail Project for the South Central Florida Express." Unique for such a project, the bids for the work came in under budget, allowing the installation of an additional nine track miles of 136 RE Continuous Welded Rail (CWR) for the replacement of 85-pound rail "on the main line segment connecting with the new main line near Clewiston, FL." Surveying for the new line began during the fall of 2011, with construction starting in late 2012, and ending in 2013.

**110.0 BLOCK LIMITS** – Located in the orange groves west of Flaghole Road is the boundary between **Flag Block** and **Dover Block**. Flag Block is named for the Flaghole area

**110.4 CURVE** – Heading towards the Southern Gardens Citrus facility, the railroad curves back to the west. Across the canal to the south and in the wooded area is Camp Nocatee, a camp operated by the Girl Scouts of Southeast Florida. Camp Nocatee occupies 640 acres with a 13-acre lake, swimming pool and campsite units. Reports from the camp ranger indicate that the wildlife there includes Florida panthers, black bear, alligator, coyote, and many other native animals.

Heading west, the railroad stays north of a small canal and passes through orange groves and sugarcane fields.

This sign marks the location of Camp Nocatee, a camp operated by the Girl Scouts of Southeast Florida. It is just south of the tracks at the Milepost 201.1 curve.

**112.8 CITRUS JUNCTION** – This is a junction between a route serving a sugarcane loader and a citrus plant. The line to Southern Gardens Citrus heads north from here while to the west is a cane loading facility known as Dover Spike.

**113.3 DOVER SPIKE** – This new cane loader, located on a siding to the south of the new line, was built as part of the 2012-2013 project to serve Southern Gardens Citrus. The name Dover Spike comes from the land owner whose land was used for much of the new construction. The track at Dover Spike is shown to have a capacity of 40 empty cane cars and the cane loader uses a ramp and an elevator, allowing both tractor-hauled self-dumping cane wagons and non-self-dumping truck trailers to use the facility.

**114.1 END OF TRACK** – The line curves to the north and follows County Road 833 to the end of the track. This ensures that there is enough room to pull a 40-car train west of the Dover Spike siding, so they can be shoved into the facility for loading. This is the west end of the **Dover Block**.

## USSC Citrus Lead Route Guide
## Citrus Junction to End of Track

What is known by many as the Southern Gardens Citrus Line is another part of the construction that took place in 2012-2013. This line had one purpose – to serve the Southern Gardens Citrus processing facility on County Road 833. The plant is located not far south of Florida Highway 80, which connects Clewiston and LaBelle, both in Hendry County. The line is now known as the Citrus Lead.

The Citrus Lead breaks off of the Flaghole Mainline at Milepost 112.8, and then heads north to the end of track at the citrus processing facility. To reduce any confusion about duplicate mileposts across the system, the Citrus Lead is also known as the 200 Line. The Lead covers the tracks from the south end at Milepost 200.0 (Citrus Junction), to Milepost 203.4 at the south end of the track. Like most of the sugarcane lines, this route cannot be viewed from public roads.

**200.0 CITRUS JUNCTION** – This is a junction between the new line from Flaghole Road and a citrus plant to the north. The line to Southern Gardens Citrus heads north from here while to the west is the Dover Spike cane loading facility. Heading north, the rail line passes through citrus groves and sugarcane fields.

**202.4 CITRUS YARD** – North of here, there are three tracks, with two used to hold railcars needed for Southern Gardens Citrus. Much of the product shipped out is by-product of the juice production, such as oils and supplements for animal feeds.

**203.3** **NORTH CIT STORAGE** – In the middle of the yard, the railroad makes a ninety degree turn to the west. At the north end of the yard, the tracks curve to the northwest and cross a main road into the groves and fields in the area.

**203.4** **END OF TRACK** – Just north of the road, the track splits, forming two stub tracks to the west and three stubs tracks to the north.

**Southern Gardens Citrus**

Southern Gardens Citrus grows and processes its own oranges, from 1.8 million trees on more than 12,500 acres of orange groves, as well as oranges from independent growers. The company, one of the largest suppliers of pure not-from-concentrate Florida orange juice, produces up to 90 million gallons annually.

A subsidiary of U.S. Sugar Corporation, the company grows its own trees from seed, one of a few companies that controls every step of orange juice production. Besides making juice, the peels are made into cattle feed pellets and shipped across the country, the oils are used in fragrances and natural cleaning products, and the cleaning water is treated and used to irrigate the orange groves. U.S. Sugar got involved in the business heavily in 1985 when the company sold its cattle operation and converted much of the land into orange groves. A new citrus processing plant was also built as a part of the operation, the first new such plant in Florida in approximately 50 years.

In late 2019, processing at the Clewiston Plant was halted, with the fruit being processed at other area facilities. Three things have been blamed: diseases like citrus greening and citrus canker, a series of hurricanes that have damaged thousands of acres of trees, and the importing of lower cost orange juice from Brazil and Mexico. Nevertheless, while processing is currently taking place at other plants, juice is still stored and distributed from the Clewiston facility.

Citrus greening, an incurable bacterial disease which can be found around the world, broke out in Florida citrus groves in 2005 and spread quickly. Production declined from 240 million boxes a year, each weighing 90 pounds, to about 70 million boxes. Another issue hitting the citrus market is a change in drinking habits as about 95 percent of Florida's orange crop is processed into juice. Foreign imports and the acquisition of citrus groves for residential and commercial development have also caused a reduction in Florida citrus production.

There have been several proposals to develop the area into an industrial park, especially along the highways to the north. However, no actual construction has taken place.

These tank cars are at the loading facility of Southern Gardens Citrus.

For years, trucks full of oranges could be seen at Southern Gardens Citrus.

# Changes at U.S. Sugar

Anyone who has ever written a book knows that it is never over as something new can always come up. This is especially true when writing about the United States Sugar Corporation, a company that is always trying to stay several steps ahead of the market. As the final draft of this book was being prepared, numerous news items and changes were noted. These included new tracks being built, a crisis in the orange industry, additional land purchases, the growth of the grass sod business, new plans for steam locomotive #148, and the planned acquisition of Imperial Sugar. It is very likely that other changes will occur between the final edit of this book and the time that it gets into your hands.

## U.S. Sugar and its Tourist Trains

One of these changes will certainly be noticed by the general public. Efforts to use steam locomotive #148 for special events, and possibly even public excursions, will attract national attention. The acquisition of a fleet of passenger cars is planned, and more news about being able to ride behind steam through the Everglades Agricultural Area will certainly come out. The first public trip occurred in December 2021, a roundtrip from Clewiston to Lake Placid.

In July 2021, U.S. Sugar and FMW Solutions announced that the former Wabash Railroad turntable at St. Louis had been acquired and will be moved to Clewiston, Florida. The turntable was once a part of the Wabash shops on the northwest side of St. Louis, but wound up on the property of the St. Louis MetroLink light rail system when it was built.

The turntable is 90 feet long and weighs 62 tons, and it once was used at the Vanteveter Avenue roundhouse of the Wabash Railroad. It was built in 1917 by the American Bridge Company, and became the property of Bi-State Development (MetroLink) in 1989. For several decades, the light rail system has looked for a way to preserve the turntable, but to get it off of their property. U.S. Sugar will use the turntable as a part of their "Sugar Express" operations out of Clewiston, Florida.

## The Expansion of U.S. Sugar

The expansion of U.S. Sugar, along with the increased production of sugarcane across the region, has created more transportation challenges. As shown with the new Bryant Connector, new rail lines are possible and likely. U.S. Sugar takes great pride in its practices to produce sugar with the lowest environmental impacts and public safety, and the use of trains instead of trucks is a part of this effort.

Another area of change deals with the other agricultural products produced by U.S. Sugar. For years, the company has also grown vegetables. It is currently the largest producer of sweet corn in the state, and other vegetables are commonly grown on fields that are being set aside after several years of sugarcane production. A significant growth area is in the production of sod. Hundreds, if not thousands of acres of St. Augustine sod are produced in the area. So much is grown that it is hard to travel without seeing a truckload of sod heading to market.

One negative agricultural change is a reduction in activity at Southern Gardens Citrus. While the company has 1.8 million trees scattered over 12,500 acres, processing at the Clewiston Plant is currently stopped. Three things have

## Changes at U.S. Sugar

been blamed: diseases like citrus greening and citrus canker, a series of hurricanes that have damaged thousands of acres of trees, and the importing of lower cost orange juice from Brazil and Mexico. Nevertheless, while processing is currently taking place at other plants, juice is still stored and distributed from the Clewiston facility.

Finally, in March 2021, U.S. Sugar announced that it was acquiring Imperial Sugar. With the increased production at Clewiston, the company needed to expand to process the supply of raw sugar. Imperial owns a refinery at Port Wentworth in Savannah, Georgia, and a sugar transfer and liquification facility in Ludlow, Kentucky. U.S. Sugar had long sold its raw sugar to the refinery at Port Wentworth before building its own Clewiston refinery in 1998. However, with increased cane production, additional capacity was desired. Additionally, this purchase will allow USSC to have its own line of consumer brand sugar – Imperial.

Imperial Sugar is one of the oldest processors and marketers of refined sugar in the United States. It was formed in 1905 from the Imperial Mill in Sugar Land, Texas. The company sells to retail grocers, food manufacturers, and food service distributors. It was acquired by the Louis Dreyfus Company in 2012 and primarily processed international sugar for Louis Dreyfus. With the ownership change, the facility at Port Wentworth will go back to handling domestically grown sugar.

More changes will certainly take place, and later editions of this book will attempt to include them.

*The Railroads of U.S. Sugar: History Through the Miles*

## About the Author

Barton Jennings has written more than a dozen books about railroads and other transportation modes. This includes the textbook *The Basics of Transportation: Policies, Practices and Pricing – An Applied Perspective*. He has also written a number of articles about various railroads for rail hobby magazines, including one on the railroads of U.S. Sugar. His house has several rooms full of books, timetables and other documents about this and other railroads – important research items from a time long before today's internet. This book on the railroads of U.S. Sugar is part of his effort to preserve railroad history.

Bart's interest in the U.S. Sugar railroads began when a number of employees began attending his workshops on the Federal Railroad Administration's Track Safety Standards. Multiple visits to the railroad have led to a love for the unique operations – a mix of traditional sugarcane railroading and modern rail operations. The company also has a fascinating history that touches people from around the world, and heavily influences the business world around Lake Okeechobee in South Florida.

Bart Jennings worked for Union Pacific and several shortline railroads, and now is a professor emeritus of supply chain management and teaches transportation operations. He also still teaches workshops for the railroad industry, a way to stay in touch with the industry he loves. For almost three decades, Barton Jennings has been organizing charter passenger trains and writing the route descriptions, both for planning purposes and for the enjoyment of the passengers. These trips have been from coast to coast, often covering operations that haven't seen a passenger train in decades. This work has led to a series of route guides for railroads across the country, some of which have been expanded into books.

This route description was begun about 2010 as the author started to explore the railroad's history and routes. Much of the information comes from internal railroad records, government and public records, and conversations with old and new friends. The value of the information obtained from various railroad managers and employees cannot be overstated – they all get my thanks. It is hoped that you enjoy your adventure with the railroads of the U.S. Sugar Corporation. Hopefully this book will be of assistance in some ways – *The Railroads of U.S. Sugar: History Through the Miles.*

Bart Jennings stands in front of Cane #5 at Childs on a beautiful spring day. Photo by Sarah Jennings.

www.ingramcontent.com/pod-product-compliance
Lightning Source LLC
Chambersburg PA
CBHW071948070526
44583CB00015B/1114